MICHELLE COLLINS

THIS IS ME

MICHELLE COLLINS

THIS IS ME

Michael O'Mara Books Limited

For Maia

I love you with all my heart.

First published in Great Britain in 2014 by
Michael O'Mara Books Limited
9 Lion Yard
Tremadoc Road
London SW4 7NQ

A CIP catalogue record for this book is available from the British Library.

Papers used by Michael O'Mara Books Limited are natural, recyclable products made from wood grown in sustainable forests. The manufacturing processes conform to the environmental regulations of the country of origin.

ISBN: 978-1-78243-232-6 in hardback print format
ISBN: 978-1-78243-233-3 in trade paperback print format
ISBN: 978-1-78243-265-4 in ebook format

1 2 3 4 5 6 7 8 9 10

www.mombooks.com

Designed and typeset by Design 23

Printed and bound in UK by CPI Group (UK) Ltd, Croydon, CR0 4YY

CONTENTS

ACKNOWLEDGEMENTS

To the wonderful Terry Ronald who sat and shared my thoughts with me for over twenty hours, thank you. We laughed a lot, I cried a few times along the way, but with your fantastic humour and warmth I think you have captured my voice really well. I promise I'll learn to type with two hands.

Huge thanks to all the Michael O'Mara team: Lesley, Mike, Emily, Jess and Alison and my editor, Allie, who had to put up with my madness, particularly in the last week when we had such a tight deadline. A big thank you to Jonathan Shalit from the Roar Group and all the lovely people at Cole Kitchenn for looking after me: Stuart, Ollie, Dominique, Alex and gorgeous Ashley who came to the first meeting at Michael O'Mara Books with me. Also thanks to Lucy at Persuasion PR, and the wonderful Simon Frost – what would I do without you? Scott Beswick – thank you for doing my hair and make-up on the cover and thanks Jason for the styling, not forgetting Cat Bradley who took the fab photograph.

To my amazing mum, Mary, and to Sid, Vicki, Charlotte, Jack, and my beautiful daughter, Maia – I don't know what I'd do without you all in my life. Also, thank you to Melissa and Julian for sharing childhood memories, Sharon and Tim for being such loyal friends, Phil Collinson for believing in me, Caroline Stirling and David Thomas for changing the course of my life in that winter of '95/'96, to Peter Polycarpou for helping me out in Cyprus, and to Michael Cashman and Paul Cottingham for making me politically aware.

Andrew and Russell, thanks for letting me stay in your gorgeous house in Manchester, and thank you to Mal Young and Mari Wilson for your beautiful house in La La Land. Many thanks to Leona, Izzy and Charlie for your friendship, and to Channing School for the support through good and bad times. Beverly, I miss you in Oz. Bunmi and Debbie, miss you both too. Dr Mark and Andrew, Sheila, Rebecca and Gavin, Ruth and Tony, Tony and Bennie, Richard and Anthony, Sancha and William, Paul and Stacey – I love you all so much.

Uncle Daniel and Auntie Jenny, Fabrizio, Matthew, Damian Bilton, Ian Brown, Martyn Hesford and Keith, Susan Oudot, Marie Barrat, Maurice, Josie, Jessica and Lulu, Ollie Picton-Jones, Ian Hunter-Meek, Ray Burmiston, Jill Roberts – thank you.

And finally, huge thanks to the two gorgeous men in my life: Michael and Humphrey.

CHAPTER 1:

MY GIRLS

From as far back as I can remember there were only ever three of us: my mum, my sister Vicki, and me. I never questioned it, or at least I don't remember doing so when I was little. It was only when I reached junior school that I began to realize that we weren't the same as a lot of other families, and even then it never really bothered me. As far as I'm concerned, you don't really miss what you've never had. On the rare occasions when someone at school asked me where my dad was, I told them he was dead. I don't know why; perhaps it just sounded exciting. With hindsight I realize how tough it must have been for Mum, bringing up two young kids on her own, but even though I now know the extent to which she went without, my sister and I never once felt hard done by or in any way deprived as kids. We never wanted for anything, and Mum made sure we were being entertained by something or someone every day of our young lives. 'My girls', as she called us, were always her priority, and we were a tight-knit trio to be reckoned with.

It wasn't surprising that Mum was so big on the importance of family. One of five siblings in a Welsh family, my mum, Mary Josephine Horton, was orphaned at a young age and brought up by her maternal grandparents, who lived in Hayes, Middlesex, and could scarcely cope with five young children. Two of them, Daniel and Jenny, were sent off to the Pestalozzi orphanage in Switzerland, but Mum was deemed too old to go so the children were split up.

Her other sister was Yvonne, and she had a brother called Raymond (who sadly died at the age of nineteen) and they grew up at their grandparents' house, all missing their younger brother and sister terribly. It must have been very hard for them, especially after losing their parents. Despite this, Mum was a clever girl who did well in school, but in those days it was virtually unheard of for working class girls to go on to some kind of further education, so she had to leave school as soon as she was old enough and go out to work. She doesn't really like talking about her childhood, and I have to respect that, but it's clear that she didn't have it easy growing up. I think that's the reason she was always determined for us to have all the things and the opportunities that she didn't, and when we were children she made sure that Vicki and I always understood and respected the importance of education.

Daniel and Jenny eventually came back to the UK when they were around sixteen, and these days Uncle Daniel (who I inherited my middle name, Danielle, from because we have the same birthday) lives in Wales, while Aunt Jenny lives in south-east London. Mum has always been very close to Jenny, and as a child we spent a lot of time with her and her husband, my Uncle Lenny, and their five children – four sons and a daughter. It was great for Vicki and me to have boys around to play with, despite the fact that they were right little tearaways at times, and when I was little I adored running around their flat with its huge sitting room (which I thought very posh because it had a serving hatch through into the kitchen). I have a particularly vivid childhood memory of us all standing on their balcony toasting the New Year at midnight; we had wonderful times there.

Tragically, my dear Uncle Lenny was killed when his lorry crashed in the Blackwall Tunnel while I was away on holiday with some friends aged eighteen. Nobody could get hold of me to let me know, and when I eventually called home and told Mum that I wanted to stay out in Greece for a little while longer, she didn't have the heart to tell me what had happened because she didn't want to ruin my holiday. It was devastating for all of us, and I don't think my aunt

Jenny has ever fully recovered. I've always stayed close to the family across the years, particularly my cousin, Matthew.

It's often been reported that I grew up in Hackney, but that isn't the case. I was born in Hackney South East hospital – which became Homerton Hospital – on 28 May 1962, but we actually lived in Highbury. Mum tells me I was such a good and quiet baby that she was constantly prodding me to make sure I was still breathing. From what I can gather I slept through most of my infancy, which was the exact opposite of my sister, Vicki, who I don't think was particularly happy with my arrival. There were only fourteen months between us and I think she'd set her sights on being an only child. Younger children tend to snatch the attention away from older siblings from the start, and I was certainly no different. Mum told me that when I was a baby she left me in my big Silver Cross pram outside the butcher's while she was inside making her order. Suddenly a man came in from outside and said to her: 'Is that your little boy out there? Because he's eating raw sausages and throwing eggs out of the pram ... '

'That's not a boy, she's a little girl,' Mum snapped, angrily.

The truth of the matter was I didn't have much hair and I did look a bit like Winston Churchill until I was two. Meanwhile, Vicki would often get hold of Mum's make-up bag and paint my face completely black. Perhaps it was the only outlet she had for that sibling rivalry.

I was painfully shy around other people, and unlike my older and more extrovert sister, I could often be found hiding behind my mum's skirt when I was a kid. It's funny, because I sometimes think that my desire to act came out of my shyness. I saw performing as a way of coming out of my shell without giving anything of myself away. I was hiding behind someone else in the character I was portraying, and that's the way I've always liked it. It seems to me that the people with the loudest and most outrageous personalities in real life don't always make the best actors, though often people imagine that they might. There's a big difference between acting and showing off, and I was never a show-off, especially as a child.

3

I wouldn't say boo to a goose back then. Even on my first day at nursery, my mum dropped me off and I screamed the place down. It was in a church hall in Islington, and I have this memory of sitting on the stage and swinging my legs, desperate for my mum to come and rescue me from this terrible place.

At the Gillespie Infants School in Highbury I had a lovely teacher called Miss Adler, who I thought was beautiful and who organized the Christmas nativity play. This was my first ever acting role, but pretty low-key, performance-wise. I can't say for sure what my part in this extravaganza was, but I think I was just a sheep or some other farmyard animal. I certainly wasn't Mary and I certainly wasn't anyone with any clout as far as the ins and outs of the story went. In fact, for quite some years I landed boring roles in all the school productions. It's a wonder I ever considered a career in acting, to be honest. I mean, how good is it ever going to get when you're cast as a sheep at four? At one point I told Mum that I wanted to be a traffic warden or a policewoman when I grew up, swayed, perhaps, by the idea of hiding behind a uniform. It was Mum's words that kept me going as the years went on.

'It doesn't matter how many lines you have, darling, or who you are playing. You're always good.'

I guess she had a point. After all, Dame Judi Dench got an Oscar for *Shakespeare In Love* and she was only in it for fifteen minutes. Mind you, it didn't help that although Mum wasn't too bad with a needle and thread, she wasn't exactly speedy when it came to making costumes, or, indeed, anything that involved knitting. I remember she started knitting a jumper when I was four, which I finally got to wear when I was about ten and my arms had grown about two feet, so it's no wonder I never received any of the more coveted roles in those early years. Anyway, the day after my woolly debut the classroom burned down because somebody forgot to blow out the candles. I remember being devastated that the nativity scene had been wrecked, not to mention Miss Adler's classroom. It was terribly sad, and the first in a long line of fiery episodes for me.

Apart from not having a man around, our family seemed different

4

in other ways as far as I was concerned. My life at home was a lot more exciting that most of the other kids at school. It was a bit like a London, working-class version of that movie, *Hideous Kinky*, where the bohemian mother, played by Kate Winslet, whisks her kids off to Marrakech. Of course, we were only ever whisked off to Blackpool or Cornwall in a Morris Minor, but as far as we were concerned it was an adventure. Sometimes Mum would drive us all to Selsey Bill, West Sussex, and we'd stay in a great big caravan with Aunt Jenny and all her kids. It was on those trips that we had the best fun: tearing around on the beach all day, free as a bird, and then going to the caravan park clubhouse at night for a bit of a disco. It was there, in fact, that I got my first taste of fame. I didn't enter the beauty pageant, but I did end up winning the coveted 'knobbly knees' contest one summer when I was about seven.

Mum was always slightly unconventional. Everyone used to call her 'Big Mary' because she was unusually tall, standing at a statuesque 5ft 10. She was impeccably dressed, well spoken and quite striking, with jet-black hair coupled with eyes of bright blue. Years later we discovered that although she'd been born and raised in Wales, her father had been adopted and had originally hailed from Belgium, which I guess went some way to explaining her unusual and captivating looks. As well as being beautiful, she was always on trend, with her maxi coats and hot pants – quite outrageous and cool for a mum. The problem is, when you're seven years old the last thing you want is an outrageous mother outside the school gates waiting to collect you, and at that age no one thinks their mother is cool, do they? At the time, I just wanted my mum to fit in with all the other mums, but that was never going to happen, and I remember noticing a lot of the other women staring at her whenever she came up to the school for any reason. Mum was always the forthright one who asked all the questions at any sort of school meeting, too, which, at the time, mortified me. She wanted to be on top of everything because she knew the importance of education, and she was determined that Vicki and I weren't going to get left behind. A few years later, in fact, Mum went back to education herself, doing a degree in Law and Politics in her late thirties.

She was assertive and outspoken, but it was always well intended. She never let anyone get the better of her, and I admired her for that, despite the fact that it sometimes got us all into hot water. I remember an occasion on the 171 bus on the way to my Aunt Jenny's when Mum had a bit of a set-to with the bus driver, who she felt was being rude to her.

'I'm not having this!' she snapped. 'No! I'm not having anyone speaking to me and my girls like that!'

We were all turfed off at the next stop, watching the warm bus full of people disappear up the high street while we waited for the next to come along in the freezing cold.

We lived in the basement flat of a massive, rambling house in Highbury Hill, Islington – right opposite the Arsenal stadium. It had a huge and wonderfully overgrown garden that we could run wild in, just like an adventure playground, and it was perfect for the occasional big bonfire. These days, a house like that might cost four of five million, but in those days the area was far less affluent: quite bohemian in its way, but rough and ready in parts. Vicki and I shared a bedroom with Mum and had bunk beds across the room from her double bed. There were all sorts of weird and wonderful people living under that roof, and there always seemed to be lots of interesting comings and goings, with music coming out of every room. Most of Mum's friends and acquaintances were colourful characters, too, and they were usually quite hip and forward-thinking. Mum's good friend Eileen, for instance, was engaged to a black actor back in the 1960s when mixed-race relationships were still very thin on the ground. I remember seeing them all go off to the register office wedding when I was about eight, with all the women wearing fur coats. The bride was kitted out in a short fur coat and high boots, and I remember thinking it was all tremendously stylish. It was so unusual to see a mixed-race wedding back then, but to my mum and her friends it was just a happy occasion to be celebrated, and I feel quite proud that we had such a cool mother. It was embarrassing at times, but mostly I loved the fact that we were different from the other kids I went to school with.

On the top floor of our house lived a woman who made hats, and my sister and I would sometimes go up to her place if we came home from school before Mum was back from work. She was forever attaching feathers and other bits and pieces to her fancy hats with something that smelled like paraffin. Chances are it wasn't actually paraffin, but whatever it was she used, it was flammable, as we discovered one day to our cost. My sister and I often played with this woman's little boy, and a few days after Vicki's birthday, she took all her cards up to proudly show him. At some point during the afternoon, Vicki and the boy got into a scrap and he decided it might be a good idea to set fire to her birthday cards with a match. As you can imagine, the whole place went up fairly quickly, what with the cards, the fabric for the hats, and whatever flammable substance this woman, whose name I don't remember, was using to attach all her trimmings. The whole top floor was suddenly ablaze: it must have been terrifying for two little girls, but I don't remember too much about what happened next. What I do know is that my sister took me to hide behind a sideboard until a fireman came into the room and picked me up, taking me down a ladder to safety. Meanwhile Vicki ran and hid under a table and nobody knew where she was. In the end, an old man who lived in one of the other flats bravely went back into the burning building with a wet towel over his head and rescued her. Luckily nobody was hurt badly in the fire, but Vicki still has the scars on her hands where they were burned. It wasn't the first time fire had touched my life, and it wouldn't be the last, either.

CHAPTER 2:

'I'LL LET YOU RIDE MY CHOPPER FOR FIFTY PENCE!'

When I was seven, we moved to the top floor flat of a house with a big yellow door, 7 Fairmead Road, which was just off Holloway Road. This was another huge place with lots of flats within one building, owned by a friend of Mum's, so Mum got the job of looking after the place – a sort of live-in caretaker. It had a communal phone box in the downstairs hall, and whenever I talked to my school friends on the phone I'd shove as many coins as I could into the slot so the pips never went. I'd have been so embarrassed to admit that we couldn't afford our own phone, especially further down the line when I was chatting to a boy that I had a crush on. It was the same with our gas and electric meters, which you had to feed to keep the power running. I'd have been horrified if one of my friends had been round at ours watching television when the electricity went off. Not that it was particularly unusual in the 1970s anyway; it was the decade of strikes and power shortages. In the early- to mid-seventies the Conservative government introduced the three-day week to save electricity, and by the end of the decade uncollected rubbish was piled high on the streets during the 'winter of discontent'. Then there were the seemingly endless power cuts, which Vicki and I didn't mind so much, because if there was no light when we got home from school it meant that we couldn't do our homework. Mum told us that she used to read by candlelight as a child, simply to save on electricity, and that's the reason her eyesight got so bad while she was still young.

During the power cuts, Mum would take us down to Pete's Café on the Holloway Road, which always seemed to stay open, lit by candles. For a special treat she'd take us to the Italian restaurant at the top of Highbury Hill, where she'd order two plates of spaghetti Bolognese and split them between the three of us.

'Two dinners and three plates,' she'd always say.

It was her way of being economical yet still taking us out for a posh meal. I thought it was terribly glamorous going out for dinner at a proper Italian restaurant, with its freshly laundered tablecloths and those squat bottles of Chianti encased in straw, all lined up on the shelf behind the bar. The mid-1970s were difficult times, but they could be strangely exciting for us kids.

Holloway Road was a very working-class area with a big Irish community, and there seemed to be an Irish pub on every corner: the Cock Tavern, the Half Moon, and at the top of the Holloway Road was the Gresham Ballroom, which was a well-known dancehall and a big meeting place for the Irish people in the area. Many of my happiest childhood memories come from growing up around there. Memories of the sound of the ice cream van and the bell of the rag-and-bone man ringing along the street, of roller-skating up and down Fairmead Road and playing with all the other neighbourhood kids, who came from a rich, cosmopolitan mix of cultures and backgrounds. There was an Italian family living across the road, a Polish family one side of us and a Jamaican family on the other. We would quite often go for dinner with the Jamaican family because Vicki and I were friends with their twin girls, Erthia and Donna. The food they had was delicious: spicy jerk chicken and rice. It was very different from the stuff we ate at home, although Mum loved to cook, too, and she wasn't afraid to try something different or 'modern'. I remember thinking us very cosmopolitan when we had our first spaghetti Bolognese with garlic bread. We even had curry – even though it was out of a tin from Marks and Spencer.

When you were a kid in those days, 'playing out' was what

you did. There were no Xboxes or internet. You went out into the street with your scooters or roller skates, and there was someone to play with right outside your front door. At weekends and during the school holidays we'd be out there all day, until a stream of synchronized cries cleared the streets.

'Your tea's ready!' 'Time to come in!'

Bikes were a very big deal, with who had what bike and which was the best bike being a big topic of banter on our street. Daniel Painter was a very good-looking boy who proudly cruised up and down Fairmead Road on what was considered to be the ultimate bike of the early 1970s.

'I'll let you ride my Chopper for fifty pence,' he'd tell many a young girl, and they'd all fall for his charms, as well as his cool wheels.

I was as taken with him as the next girl, but I wasn't going to give the cocky little sod any of my hard-won pocket money for a go on his Chopper – no way! My sister Vicki, on the other hand, was a bit more of a pushover. Like most of the boys, Daniel fancied her because she had the gift of the gab and was much more confident than I was. She accepted a ride and ended up falling off and cutting her leg quite badly. After the accident, Daniel turned up with a toy ring and 'proposed' to Vicki by way of an apology. She kept that ring for years.

Tuesday was always my favourite day of the week because that was when *Jackie* magazine came out, and I'd tear across the road to the newsagent to get my copy without fail. All the girls loved *Jackie* with its pop star posters, fashion and beauty tips and true-life stories, but for me the best bit was the 'Dear Cathy & Claire' problem page. Years later, I worked with children's author Jacqueline Wilson on a film adaptation of her book *The Illustrated Mum*. Jacqueline had worked on *Jackie* when she was very young and just starting out, and it's been said that the magazine was actually named after her. She told me that on a quiet week the writers had to sit around the office making up a few of the problems that went on the 'Dear Cathy & Claire' page, which made me chuckle.

Growing up in the sixties and seventies there were some things you just took for granted. Like your parents going into the pub and leaving you outside in the street with a bag of salt and vinegar crisps and a glass of lemonade, or the fact that there were no seatbelts or children's car seats in the backs of cars. On Saturdays we always went to Saturday morning pictures at the Odeon on Holloway Road, but my mum never went with us. It's hard to imagine today's mums and dads dropping their seven- or eight-year-old kids at the cinema on Saturday and leaving them there, unsupervised, but that was the way it was back then.

The show would start at about 9.30am, and we'd watch cartoons, then a serial (usually some black-and-white classic like *Flash Gordon* or *Tarzan*) and then there'd be a movie. If you were lucky you'd get a Cliff Richard or a Frank Ifield film, which I loved. Then afterwards there might be a little disco or a dancing competition, with kids jumping on the stage and throwing themselves around to the latest pop hits. It was utter mayhem but all very innocent, and everyone was there to have fun. When the show was over we'd get a bag of chips for five pence down the Holloway Road and wander home. Then on Saturday afternoons we'd usually go swimming at the Hornsey Road baths. Things seem so different now. I would never have considered letting my daughter Maia go out and about without an adult at that age, but back then it was just the done thing. We were always doing something under our own steam.

I had a thing for markets, and Mum would often take us to Chapel Market in the Angel, Islington, where almost everyone seemed to know her.

'All right, Mary, how are ya?'

'Hello Mary! Hi Vicki, Michelle!'

People would shout at us from all the stalls. At the end of the market there was a toy shop, which Mum would take us to every Sunday if we'd both been good girls. There we were allowed to pick out new outfits for our dolls: Vicki's Barbie and my beloved Sindy doll. I adored the commotion and the noise of the market and the constant flurry of different people all going about their daily lives.

My mum still uses it now, and whenever I go down there with her I'm overcome by an incredible nostalgia. I think there's something magical about those good old working-class markets, especially growing up in London in the sixties and seventies when they seemed to be everywhere, before the supermarket chains took hold. Years later I even worked on one, selling earrings on Portobello Road, and nowadays I always try to seek out the local markets wherever I travel.

We were very self-sufficient as kids, and we had to help with the household chores. We took our clothes to the launderette on Sundays and we helped to keep things clean and tidy at home. It wasn't that we were neglected, but Mum was always doing lots of little part-time jobs so that she could make ends meet as well as taking care of Vicki and me. We had to help out, and in those days it wasn't unusual for kids to look after themselves from time to time. We weren't mollycoddled or cocooned, but that's just the way it was. There were a few times when we'd get home from school and Mum would still be out working, but it wasn't a big deal. We'd just make ourselves a snack and then sit down and watch *Scooby-Doo* or *Magpie* on the telly until Mum got home and cooked our tea. Vicki was very good at keeping an eye on me, as well as helping around the house, and she was quite the domestic goddess from a young age. It's no surprise that I grew up being so untidy, because back then Vicki did everything for me. Despite the fact that she wasn't that much older than I was, she was very nurturing and capable and in fact she ended up going into childcare as an adult. She has worked in child protection and fostering for thirty years.

I was quite taken with a friend of Mum's called Jackie who sometimes stayed with us. She was a go-go dancer and probably the first professional entertainer that I ever knew. I was fascinated by the fact that her job was to get up on stage each night and entertain people, and I thought it might be something I would enjoy, too. Vicki and I loved it when Jackie stayed home to look after us while Mum was out. She'd let us try on her fabulous outfits – her shoes and her hot pants – and Vicki would put eyeliner all around my eyes, so I looked like a mini Dusty Springfield. Then I'd dance around in Jackie's tiny little shorts to Freda Payne's 'Band Of Gold' on the record player while Jackie showed us all her signature moves so that I could pretend to be a go-go dancer. To be honest I really had my heart set on being Freda Payne: I adored music. That was something I definitely inherited from Mum, because in the early seventies she had all the latest records. She loved anything from Rod Stewart and The Faces to Tony Bennett and Frank Sinatra. On the occasions when she had her friends around for a bit of a party I loved hearing Mum and her friends all chatting and laughing together. I'd listen through my bedroom wall while she played her favourite Timi Yuro and Aretha Franklin records on her old mono record player, and eventually I was allowed to buy my very first record when I was about nine – Michael Jackson's 'Rockin' Robin'.

As well as my love of music, I was mesmerized by my favourite shows on the television. Mum rented a colour TV and Vicki and I used to invite our friends over after school to come and watch it. In those days everyone seemed to rent their TV sets from Rediffusion or Radio Rentals; in fact, I still remember the very annoying TV commercials for the latter. Like most kids back then, Thursday night's *Top of the Pops* was the major TV event of the week for me, but I also loved *The Val Doonican Show* on a Saturday evening. I adored the Irish crooner with his endless collection of terrible jumpers and his rocking chair, and I used to kiss the screen whenever he came on. On a Sunday night, if Vicki and I were good girls, Mum would make us cheese and cucumber sandwiches and we were allowed to stay up to watch *The Forsyte Saga* as a treat. I also loved old black-and-white movies, especially those starring Bette Davies, like *Whatever Happened to Baby Jane?* I was a bit of an idle dreamer, and the drama of those fabulous old films was like an escape from reality for me. I wanted to be just like the glamorous, dramatic actresses in the movies. I was fascinated by the stage and screen from a very young age, obsessed in fact.

However, my first experience of meeting a real live famous person was disappointing to say the least. Mum had taken us to see

Tommy Steele in pantomime at the London Palladium. I remember being transfixed by the whole spectacle and I was thrilled at the idea that it was live theatre happening right before my eyes. After the show, which I think might have been *Babes in the Wood*, we waited excitedly at the stage door for an autograph. When Tommy came out of the theatre he refused to come over and sign my photo and Mum could see how disappointed I was.

'Please come and sign her autograph,' Mum implored. 'She's been so excited to meet you.'

But Tommy was having none of it and I was terribly disheartened. I remember thinking that one day I would be a famous actor, and I'd make sure that I was a lot nicer to my fans than Tommy bloody Steele was. I always sign autographs for people when they ask, remembering how disappointed I was that day.

I guess you could say that I'd got the bug. Whether it was acting, singing or dancing, I knew that I wanted to be an entertainer of some kind but I was too scared to tell anyone. The trouble was, I wasn't the best at sticking with things. I'd got bored with the Brownies as soon as my mum had got me the outfit, and I seemed to be the same with most things. Still, there had to be something I was good at, didn't there?

'I want to do ballet and tap,' I announced to Mum when I was eight.

Mum enrolled us and went all-out to get me the tap shoes and ballet shoes, and both Vicki and I ended up going to lessons above a funeral parlour on the Holloway Road. There were thirty-odd girls there some nights, clattering on the floor with their terrible tap-dancing while the recently departed were peacefully laid out to rest downstairs – talk about waking the dead. We went for about a year but I was certainly no Ginger Rogers, and typically I got bored with it and threw in the towel, which made Vicki leave as well. In the last few years a couple of people have asked me if I've ever fancied the idea of competing on *Strictly Come Dancing*. I only have to cast my mind back to those evenings thundering around above a funeral parlour to know that the elegant art of ballroom dancing probably wouldn't be my forte.

So how was I ever going to shine if it wasn't through dancing, then? How was I going to make my mark? I knew I loved music, and I knew I loved TV, movies and the stage – but what was I actually good at? Surely something would turn up ... eventually?

CHAPTER 3:

MUSIC AND BOYS

At Yerbury Primary School we were all expected to play some musical instrument or another, but I've no idea why I decided to take up the cello. If I remember rightly it was simply because they'd run out of violins and I got what I was given. Still, I devotedly sacrificed hanging out with my friends at lunchtime to practise every day, and unlike the ballet and tap dancing I stuck with it, but being in the string section wasn't exactly the coolest thing in the world back then. This was in the days before The Corrs and Vanessa-Mae, and there didn't seem to be any beautiful cellists or cool violinists knocking around. Apart from that, the cello isn't the easiest thing in the world to be lugging around when you're ten years old. Hauling that bloody great thing on the top deck of the 43 bus was a nightmare, especially when I got a bit older and there was a boy I had a crush on sitting up there with his mates. I spent five years going back and forward to school on the 43 bus fancying that boy, who always sat in the same seat on the top deck. After five years I finally plucked up courage to talk to him, and he was the campest boy I'd ever met. I really don't think he was interested in me at all.

Both Vicki and I went to Yerbury Primary, which was, and still is, a very good school. It was about a fifteen-minute walk from our house; kids always seemed to go to the most local school back

17

then because there weren't the choices that there are now, and I think there's something to be said for that. There was more of a community feel, and all your friends lived near you. It was here that I met two of my best friends, Jill Roberts and Melissa Haddon. Jill lived around the corner from me in a huge house, and had two sisters and two brothers. She was a Libran: always calm, well-balanced, and the perfect antidote to my Jekyll-and-Hyde Gemini personality. Melissa, meanwhile, was a confident, forthright redhead and the three of us became fast friends. Melissa's family lived just down the road from us. Her father was a postman and her mother had trained as a teacher, and to me they seemed like the perfect family. Apart from Melissa having her own bedroom, which was nothing but a distant dream to me, the other major difference between us was that she watched *Blue Peter* and I watched *Magpie*, which was ITV's more commercial and slightly cooler version of the format. I always felt happy and contented when I spent time at Melissa's house, and I got on very well with her dad, Harry. I remember him teasing me because I was a clumsy kid and I'd somehow always manage to get jam or whatever I was eating over the pages of his newspaper at teatime.

Over the coming years, Melissa and I shared plenty of adventures and I'm not sure who was leading who astray, but there was always some sort of mischief afoot when the two of us were together. One afternoon, along with Jill, we bought a red bus rover, which was a single bus ticket that allowed you to get on and off any London bus for the entire day. We ended up in far-away Kensington High Street where we discovered the legendary fashion store, Biba. When the three of us walked through the doors of that place we were overwhelmed. It was just so glamorous and elaborate, and we were completely enchanted by the interior design, with each room laid out more beautifully than the last. Of course we couldn't afford anything that the store was selling, so we decided to steal the most opulent and decadent thing that we could manage without getting caught. In the end we plumped for an ostrich feather – God knows why. We didn't really want to steal but we were desperate for some small memento of that fabulous place. Then we got back on the 38 bus and went home again. Melissa and I told all our secrets to each other and she was the first person I ever got drunk with – making ourselves ill on cider, aged fifteen. We thought it might be a good idea to see how much we could drink and how far we could walk whilst doing it, and the answer turned out to be not very much and not very far.

In 1994, Melissa's dear dad Harry died of a heart attack while he was out in his Robin Reliant car. The whole tragic event was made worse because Melissa happened to be going past on a bus at the time, and saw his car stopped at the side of the road. That was how she discovered her father's death. We were both in our early thirties by then but still the best of friends, so when she called and told me the news I dashed straight over. I stayed with her at the house she'd been brought up in for three straight days along with another friend of hers, Morgan, all sleeping on the sofas. I had so many memories of that house and of Harry, and the three of us ate, drank, laughed and cried together the whole time. We're still great friends today and I'm godmother to her son, Owen.

One morning Melissa and I both had to play in the school assembly with the rest of the orchestra and I was petrified. Melissa, who played the violin, always did everything perfectly, never putting a foot wrong whatever the occasion. I was very much the clumsy friend whom disaster seemed to follow and this performance was to be no different. I remember sitting down and trying to find a nook or a hole in the floor where I could rest the endpin of my cello, but unfortunately the hall floor had been freshly polished so there weren't any holes to be found. As the teachers hushed the assembled school, ready to start, I still hadn't sorted my music or a resting place for my cello and I got into a real flap. Then, as the orchestra struck the first note, I put my cello down in what I thought was a suitable spot, placed the bow across the strings and readied myself. Suddenly, and quite unexpectedly, my cello shot away from under me and smashed unceremoniously on the floor. Everything stopped and everyone in the room turned to look at me. I was absolutely mortified, and worse still the entire school burst into fits of hysterical laughter. I sat there in shock, wanting to cry, and to make matters worse our terrifying headmaster, Mr Terell, shouted at me in full view of everyone.

'Well that was a very stupid thing to do, wasn't it?'

I was so upset; it took me weeks to get over the shock of it. It was the first time I'd ever felt public humiliation and it had a big effect on me over the coming years. Even now I hate putting myself in a position where I might publicly fail at something, or mess something up in front of an audience. If ever I have to make a speech or present an award, for instance, I rehearse to the point of obsession to make sure I know exactly what I'm doing. I find that kind of thing difficult and always have. That fear of having a roomful of people laughing at my expense has stayed with me. I kept the cello up for some time before throwing in the towel – I think I was about fourteen – and I wasn't bad in the end. I wish I'd kept it up now; it might have been another string to my bow, so to speak. I also had a go at piano lessons, which didn't last long, and I had a trumpet for a while, but I left that on the bus. My only other musical foray back then was when Melissa and I joined a guitar club, aged ten. For our big show we stole a couple of my mother's fur coats and dressed up as The Wombles. Mum wasn't too thrilled about that one.

At Yerbury I started to get the measure of the opposite sex, especially as we got to the fourth and fifth year juniors. Some of the boys in my class were a handful to say the least. Cecil Brown, Brian Young and Keith Harvey were the cool boys, the naughty boys, and they never missed a trick. We had a teacher called Miss Price, who endlessly sipped cappuccinos in which she dunked biscuits, giving her an almost permanent frothy moustache. I thought Miss Price was dead sophisticated, with her Italian coffees and digestives, but the boys were all convinced that she seldom, if ever, wore any knickers. They were forever dropping things in class in an attempt to make her bend over so somebody could nip around the back and look up her skirt to make sure.

'She's not wearing any!' you'd hear one of them giggling.

They were only about ten years old at the time, but already pretty cheeky. I remember some of them being quite taken with a beautiful Asian girl in our class called Nassima, who was fairly well developed – a source of fascination for most of the boys in my class. They all called her 'Titsalina' and chased her round the playground at lunchtimes. Some of the kids were equally horrid to an unfortunate girl called Margaret O'Keef. She came from a poor family of about ten siblings and some of the kids at Yerbury used to say that they'd eaten their dog. Margaret had alopecia and sported a rather obvious wig, and the boys would think it was hilarious to chase her into the toilets and rip it off her head. Children don't realize how cruel they can be, but my mum insisted that we invite Margaret to any birthday parties that we had at home. She didn't like the idea of a child being left out just because of her background.

'Oh Mum, please don't make me invite her. Nobody likes her, it'll be awful!' I can still hear myself saying.

'She's coming and that's that!' Mum said.

I was secretly quite pleased when Mum made me invite her along to my birthday party because deep down I felt so sorry for her. Mum even made sure we turned a blind eye while Margaret shovelled sandwiches and cakes into her coat pocket to take home.

'Just let her have them,' she'd say. 'She's not as lucky to have all the things you girls have.'

It wasn't until a couple of years later that I actually kissed a boy properly – and it wasn't one of the boys at school, it was the son of the local vicar. Mr and Mrs Westbrook, who were a sweet old couple living next door to us, would sometimes take Vicki and me to the Baptist church, and we also attended the Sunday School there. In those days our local church was very involved in helping families in the community. To be honest, I think the Westbrooks only took us so my mum could have a bit of a break on a Sunday afternoon, but I enjoyed church with all the music and the hymns. These days I still appreciate anything ecclesiastical, even though I'm not religious, and I love visiting churches, particularly at Christmas time. I did once become Buddhist for a while, but that was mainly because I fancied a guy who I knew would be at the Buddhist centre. How terrible is that? Sunday School was different from church, though: very freethinking and non-judgemental. We played games, read stories and sang hymns (my favourite was always 'Jerusalem', which, years later, I had to learn to play on the piano when I toured in *Calendar Girls*).

We even went on camping trips with our Sunday School, which is where the vicar's son came in. I don't remember an awful lot about it, not even the boy's name, but I was thirteen and we were standing in the long grass together one sunny afternoon when he bravely kissed me on the mouth – a proper Frenchie as we used to call them – with tongues! A young girl's first kiss is an important event in her life, and I remember it being a very exciting, but short-lived thrill.

A couple of years later I went on a school journey to Italy, when I was fourteen. It was an expensive trip but my mum was determined I was going to go and so we paid the money in weekly instalments. Nobody at my school was particularly wealthy, but I remember feeling so happy when Mum said I could go on the trip because I knew how hard it was for her to find the money. I'd never been abroad before, and although I was anxious I was also very excited because I got my very first passport. We took the train there, and I was spellbound as we went through the Pyrenees: I remember waking up at about 6am and looking through the windows and seeing them thick with snow. It was a stunning view and I was completely taken aback. It was all so new and beautiful.

On that trip we had two teachers accompanying us, Mrs Butcher the headmistress and Miss Charlesworth, her deputy. I think Mrs Butcher had visions of it being a bit like *The Prime Of Miss Jean Brodie*, with her girls being the *crème de la crème*, when in fact it was more like *St Trinian's* at times with the two of them guarding us like Rottweilers. It was then that I fully realized just how persistent boys can be, and also how girls reacted to them. We were constantly hassled by young Italian guys – mostly soldiers – everywhere we went in Pisa and Florence. Of course, Mrs Butcher and Miss Charlesworth were quite vigilant, especially about things like that, so many of the girls on the trip pretended to be Catholic so they were allowed to go to Mass. Then they could slip away from the watchful eyes of the teachers and run off to meet the town's eager boys. I remember thinking that Italian men were such flirts, and very attractive with it, but at the time I had no idea what a big part all that would play in my adult life. It was only a taste of things to come.

CHAPTER 4:

A MOVE TO THE COUNTRY

From when I was about ten or eleven, Mum had a serious boyfriend called Mickey, who Vicki and I really liked. He was one of the funniest, cleverest men I'd ever met: always joking around. I'm certain he could have been a comedian with his wonderfully dry wit, and he and Mum really complemented one another. Mickey was a Londoner, and a good friend of the actor Bob Hoskins. He was a charmer who always had a wad of cash and he was always suited and booted, with people often declaring him to be the best-dressed man in Holloway. However, despite the fact that he was a bit of a lad, Mickey could recite Shakespeare and was fascinated by history. Whenever he and my mum took us on holiday, Mum would love to take us on long walks, while Mickey would show us wonderful old buildings and churches, which he seemed to know the history of inside out. He was part of our lives for a good few years, but after he and Mum broke up I didn't see him again for a long time. Years later, in 2009, I was touring in a play called *Deceptions* with Rupert Hill, and Mickey had flowers sent to my dressing room while we were playing in Richmond. Mum told me that he'd wanted to see the play, but tragically he'd got throat cancer. Surgeons had to take a skin graft from his arm to put into his throat, but the hair on the original skin had continued to grow. It was constantly irritating the inside of Mickey's throat so he couldn't stop coughing, and consequently he wasn't able to sit through a theatre show. After that we all stayed in contact, and Mickey later told me that he'd followed my career ever since I'd started acting, and watched everything I'd done on television.

'All these years I've been watching you, and I'm so proud of you,' he said.

We remained friends right up until his death in 2010.

Back in 1973 my mum and Mickey embarked on a business venture that was to turn my whole world upside down, and I was far from happy about it. My great-grandparents, Evan and Jane, lived in Hayes in Middlesex in a funny little horseshoe road called Snowdon Crescent. There were a few little shops nearby: a Martin's newsagent, a Co-Op, and a launderette that needed new management. Mum decided that it might be the perfect business opportunity for her and Mickey. She could run the launderette and keep a regular eye on her grandparents, and perhaps we could all find a nice place to live out there. Vicki had already been at senior school for a year, but I hadn't yet started, so while Mum and Mickey were trying to finalize the details of taking over the launderette, Mum decided that Vicki and I should move in with our great-grandparents and start the new school term in Hayes. Mum didn't see the point of me starting a brand new school in north London if we were all going to be moving to Hayes in the not-too-distant future. I was very fond of my great-grandparents, but the thought of living with them didn't exactly excite me. Still, Vicki and I would be together, and we decided that it might be a big adventure. Within a few weeks the two of us were living in Middlesex, with Mum travelling back and forth from Fairmead Road every day to run the launderette, but it wasn't as exciting as we'd imagined.

Hayes wasn't all that far from London, but after a few weeks living there, it might as well have been the other side of the world. I was a London girl and as far as I was concerned, Middlesex was the countryside and I found it very hard to adjust. Both Vicki and I were sent to Harlington Secondary School, which we were supposed to get to by bus. We'd often keep our bus fares, however, and walk to school, crossing over the construction of the M4 every morning. I don't remember an awful lot about the school itself, only that I hated it. It was bad enough having to leave my lovely primary school, but being forced into a new school where I didn't know anyone made things seem even tougher. 1973 was the year of Princess Anne's wedding to Captain Mark Phillips in Westminster Abbey, and I remember some of the local girls eyeing me suspiciously in the playground as we talked about it and I mentioned that I had lived in London.

'No you haven't!' one of them barked.

'I have! I'm from London,' I assured them.

'You're not from London, no way!'

'I am,' I protested 'and I'll be going back again soon, you wait and see.'

'No you're not. You're lying.'

I was eleven years old and I felt like a fish out of water. Despite the fact that I saw my mum most days, I missed living with her and I missed my friends and my lovely flat in Fairmead Road.

My great-granddad, Evan Bowen, was from Aberdare in Wales and had a thick Welsh accent. He was a very tall, thin and wiry man, typical of his generation. He'd been through two major wars and he'd had it tough. He'd worked down the mines, broken his back, smoked forty ciggies a day, and still he went on until he was in his nineties. He could be very cantankerous at times, and rather scary, but beneath that exterior there was always a wry smile desperate to shine through. He loved his garden and his tools and I can still picture him bending over and fixing something or other with a non-tipped gold flake cigarette hanging on the tip of his lips. He was always fixing something in his shed. Like a lot of men, I think he saw it as his very own private refuge or inner sanctum. He'd met my great-grandmother, Jane Croft, while he was in London on leave from the army during the First World War. Granny always inferred that she'd married beneath her. Her parents ran a butcher's shop in Holborn and they were quite well to do. She always said that the day Granddad brought her back to Wales once they were married was the worst day of her life.

'It was downhill all the way after that,' she'd laugh, but we knew she was joking and loved him dearly.

They were together for over fifty years all told, and years later I celebrated with them at their golden wedding surprise party.

Granny was rather short and round and she reminded me of Mrs Pepperpot, always tying her very long grey hair up in a little bun on top of her head. Also typical of her generation, Granny did the cooking, the cleaning, and all the fetching and the carrying. In fact she did almost everything. She was a mother, grandmother and great-grandmother, and every birthday without fail, Vicki and I would get a parcel wrapped in brown paper. It would usually contain underwear or socks plus a great big bar of chocolate, and I always looked forward to it. When we visited, she'd bake gooseberry or blackberry pie from the fruit that grew in their garden, and even now I can still smell the 4711 Eau de Toilette she used to wear.

Granddad's views were quite old-fashioned, and when I told him that the girls at Harlington were allowed to wear trousers in the winter months he wasn't at all keen on the idea.

'Girls don't wear trousers,' he said. 'It's not ladylike.'

He also put a stop to me doing cartwheels on the green outside, because people might see my knickers. Don't get me wrong, I loved my granny and granddad, but being my *great*-grandparents they were in their eighties, and living with them was hard because they were both very set in their ways. It was always fish on a Friday, and food on the table at the same time every day. It was almost regimented and so different from what we'd been used to with Mum. We weren't even allowed to watch any television in the evenings, unless it was *The Good Old Days* or the boxing or wrestling. Our treat if we were good was a glass of R White's Cream Soda from the pantry on a Friday night.

The little house on Snowdon Crescent was a three-up, two-down and Vicki and I shared a bedroom, but even things like bedding and toiletries were different from what we'd been used to. At home we'd had lovely modern duvets, but now we were back to heavy grey blankets, hard toilet roll and coal tar soap. Granny and Granddad were always very careful about money, because they had to be, and any luxury items had to be saved up for or bought with Co-Op stamps.

Vicki sometimes helped Granny with the house and with the cooking, but I wasn't so helpful; in fact Granny sometimes called me a little minx! It wasn't that I was badly behaved, but I just didn't want to conform. Vicki had similar feelings, but she was much better at hiding them than I was. I felt like I was a free spirit and I didn't like the confines of the house. I wanted to get out and about. Sometimes my Aunt Yvonne and her fiancé Ivan would come and visit us, and that was always something to look forward to. Aunt Yvonne lived locally, and because Granny and Granddad had brought her up, she was sympathetic to how hard it was for Vicki and me.

Music became my salvation. I had a little portable record player that my mum bought me, and I'd play David Bowie endlessly. I also had a radio cassette on which I'd tape my favourite songs from the Top 40, which was counted down every Sunday night on Radio 1. I always think if you have music you can get through almost anything in life.

Vicki and I were both homesick and living with Granny and Granddad was a strain, but we felt guilty moaning about it because we knew that Mum was simply trying to get her new business off the ground for everybody's sake. I guess it was hard for her, because deep down she could see how it was affecting us. Eventually I saw an advert that somebody had put in the local paper advertising a bicycle to sell. It was only a fiver and very basic, but it was just what I wanted. I'd take off and ride for hours on my own, imagining I was in a different world where I could be anyone I wanted to be. I was like Emily Lloyd in the film *Wish You Were Here*, cycling along with my skirt yanked up, rebelling against the world.

As luck would have it the launderette didn't really work out for Mum and Mickey, and in the end they decided to throw in the towel. Vicki and I were over the moon when Mum announced that she was taking us back to Fairmead Road and that we were going to change schools. She'd decided that I was too clever for the school I was in anyway, and now she wanted me to go to the only grammar school left in Islington, Highbury Hill. At last things were going to get back to normal, and I was going to be a London girl again. I still loved my great-grandparents very much, but I certainly wasn't sad to be going home. We visited them regularly after that, and I always stayed close to them, but one of my biggest regrets in life is that Granddad never got to see me on television. Granny did see me once, when I was in an episode of *Bergerac* playing a teenage tearaway. Vicki tells me that Granny couldn't understand what had happened to me and why I was behaving like that. Apparently it took some convincing to make her understand that I was only acting.

CHAPTER 5:

THE ACTING BUG

Because there wasn't much difference in our ages, Vicki and I were dressed the same and looked the same until we were about ten, almost like twins. In fact, on a couple of occasions I remember Mum wearing the same outfit, too, and then putting her hair in bunches – just like ours – so we were all completely matching. Looking back it must have been quite a sight when we were all striding through the corridors of our primary school. I always wanted feather-cut hair and platform shoes, and Mum wouldn't let me have either, but that's not to say that some of my outfits weren't quite eye-catching. One of my favourites from when I was nine was a T-shirt that had 'ARSENAL DID THE DOUBLE' emblazoned across the chest, referring to our local team's victory in both the league and the FA Cup in 1971. This I teamed with a pair of orange crimplene hot pants with an apple on the front. We all loved The Arsenal: where we came from football was a huge thing in everyone's lives and the footballers were like pop stars. Young players like Charlie George and Frank McLintock were big heroes of mine, and I had pictures of Charlie on my bedroom wall. Years later I got to meet him when he was my football star guide on the Legends Tour of the Arsenal stadium. He was a lovely man and I wasn't disappointed.

Outfits aside, Vicki and I were quite different in our characters and traits. Vicki was a practical child who could look after herself: she cooked, she was level-headed, and she was great with kids. I wasn't particularly adept at any of that stuff, but I was reasonably clever and did well academically. It was for this reason that our mother finally decided to separate us, encouraging us to each follow our own particular paths and sending us to separate schools. Vicki wanted to go to Parliament Hill, which was a decent girls' school, but Mum wanted me to go to a grammar school. By that time Vicki and I were poles apart in every way; in fact we were known as Bette and Joan (after the famous Hollywood rivals, Bette Davis and Joan Crawford) and as we approached our teenage years we started to argue and fight all the time. In fact I don't think we even spoke to each other for about two years unless it was to yell about something; it must have driven poor Mum mad. On one occasion Vicki even tried to push my head through a window during a row. I don't remember the details now, but I probably asked for it. I was as vile to her as she was to me and I gave as good as I got.

Mum had set her heart on me going to Highbury Hill, the girls' grammar school, but because the term had already started there were no places left. The headteacher suggested that if we waited a few months maybe a place would become available and that I should enrol in a different school for the time being. The only place I was offered was at quite a rough comprehensive and Mum was adamant that I wasn't going there. She was certain that I was bright enough for a grammar school education and she wasn't going to settle for anything less, so in the end she kept me away from school altogether until a place became available at Highbury Hill. I'd already spent a couple of terms at school in Middlesex, so by the time there was a place for me I'd missed a whole seven months of their school year. On the day of the interview I'd just started my period, and I was completely traumatized when my mother announced to the headmistress: 'Michelle started the curse today'. It wasn't the best of starts!

Seven months is a long time in terms of school, and because I started late I felt like I didn't quite fit in at Highbury Hill. It wasn't that I was unpopular or disliked – I made a few friends – but I didn't really fall in with any one particular group because a lot of the close friendships were already formed by the time I arrived. My best friends were still Jill and Melissa and they both went to different schools. I also think I missed having boys around and I found the all-female environment quite stifling. When Maia was little I said I'd never send her to a girls' school for that very reason, but in the end I did. The truth of the matter is that girls often thrive in single-sex schools, but I didn't feel like that was the case for me.

Highbury Hill was very strict on rules and especially on uniform. If your shoes, for instance, weren't exactly the right height, they would be taken away and you'd be made to wear hockey boots until you got the correct ones. My mum always made me wear Clarks shoes, which always seemed gigantic to me, much bigger than a normal shoe. I had large feet for my age anyway, so with great big boats stuck on the end of them I looked like a clown. I used to think that people were looking at me and laughing, and at times I suffered from a bit of an inferiority complex. Apart from the strict rules, the other problem was that all the other school kids in the area hated the Highbury Hill girls because they thought we were stuck-up coming from a grammar school. We were always getting hassled and bullied. I'd had such a great time at my primary school that the sudden change in atmosphere and the fact that I was expected to knuckle down was a bit of a shock to the system. Luckily, I was the studious type and I worked quite hard. I was good at History and I loved English. I even won a competition for writing a ghost story when I was twelve – another little glimmer of my creative leanings.

The thing I really enjoyed at that time was my new job at the Manor Gardens Library. It felt grown-up having a job, and whenever I was there I could pretend to be someone else: my own person, away from school and my usual surroundings. I enjoyed spending quiet time at the library and although I wasn't exactly a loner, I was certainly a bit of an outsider and quite content with my own company, away from the other kids at school. Perhaps it came from always having to share a bedroom with my sister and never having my own space, but the occasional slice of solitude was somehow liberating. It's a characteristic that's followed me through life, I suppose. I've never felt at ease in large groups, and always try not to get too embroiled when I'm working in a big company of actors. It's not that I don't like being sociable, and I've made some great friends along the way, but my instinct is to keep a bit of distance between me and any particular clique.

By the time I was fourteen, I wasn't really enjoying my time at Highbury Hill any more than when I'd first started there. Although I had mates, I still hadn't made any really close friends and at the same time I began to wonder if strict academia was really for me. I found myself drawn to creativity rather than study and it was around that time that I started getting interested in drama. Some of us started putting on plays, which included our all-female version of *Oliver!* – rebranded *Olive!* – in which I played Fanny rather than Fagin. Drama was quite thin on the ground, however, so I was intrigued and excited when a visiting lecturer called Ellis Jones arrived at the school. Ellis was a proper bona fide actor and had, a couple of years previously, starred in a popular ITV children's programme called *Pardon My Genie*. I was completely mesmerized by his talks about performing and I decided that I wanted to act. I became more and more enthralled with the thought of it, even though I was still quite shy and I just didn't think it was possible. When I went to see the careers officer at our school I plucked up the courage to tell her about my plans.

'I'd quite like to act, I think,' I said, nervously.

She looked very unimpressed for a moment and then laughed.

'How exactly are you going to do that? It's ridiculous!'

I knew there were places like the Anna Scher Theatre in north London where lots of young people started off in acting, but I'd heard there was a two-year waiting list for that. Apart from that, I really didn't know what else was out there for a budding actress. The other thing was that I was an ordinary working-class girl, despite being educated at grammar school, and everyone on television in the 1970s seemed to be middle class. There didn't seem to be anyone like me in the sitcoms or the dramas I watched.

'Why don't you think about becoming a teacher or a nurse?' my careers officer suggested. 'It's always good to have something to fall back on!'

God, the years I spent having people tell me that I needed 'something to fall back on', and looking back they had a point: acting is a precarious profession at the best of times. As far as I was concerned, though, having something to fall back on was like admitting defeat. It was failure. If I'd had other options at my fingertips I might well have given up when the going got tough, but I'm very glad I didn't.

I joined the Cockpit Youth Theatre on Lisson Grove in Marylebone when I was around fourteen. I was still quite shy, really, but I was so determined to do some proper acting that I went along on my own to audition for the group. This was my first taste of real theatre, although I was given some fairly strange tasks during some of the early classes. I can remember crawling around the floor pretending to be an amoeba or a baby emerging from a mother's womb, or failing that, a tree. It all seemed a bit arty and middle class to me in the beginning. I'd come from Islington: nobody had ever asked me to be a tree before.

'I can't believe I'm doing this,' I'd mutter to myself.

Deep down I really enjoyed it. Although I was quite aware of where I came from and how I spoke, I loved being thrown in amidst all the different types of people in the group. There was no race or class divide; everyone was in there together and nobody judged you or cared where you came from. Most of the time we did sketches, which I really got into. The acting teacher, Ian Brown, would give us a newspaper article and we'd get into groups and come up with a short scene related to what we'd read in the article. I was often quite nervous at first, particularly when I had to show something to the rest of the group, but at the same time I got a real kick out of it. There was a sense of excitement when I was acting that always helped me overcome my nerves. It also helped that Ian was a great teacher, and I had such a crush on him. Of course, I was much too young for him, and even if I hadn't been it wouldn't have made any difference, as Ian was gay. At the time I was completely oblivious to the fact. I'd never met any gay people before, as far as I knew. In fact, I don't think I really understood what being gay even meant. Ian went on to become the artistic director at the West Yorkshire Playhouse and was one of the many people I met at the Cockpit who went onto bigger and better things. People like Julie T. Wallace, who went on to star in the drama series *Lives and Loves of a She-Devil* and Neil Conrich who was in *The Bill* and *Foyle's War*, amongst other shows. There were lots of boys in the group, too, which made a pleasant change from the all-female environment of my school, and it slowly began to dawn on me that I quite enjoyed the company of men.

At the Cockpit we put on plays like *Epsom Downs* and *Bus Stop* and I always landed the character roles. I was always the nurse rather than Juliet, but I didn't mind at all. My mum would always come to watch me in every show that we did, however small the part, and she was always very supportive and encouraging. Each time I got out on that stage I got a buzz like no other – despite my nerves – and I knew then that acting was all I wanted to do. I loved the whole experience and found it liberating. Thursday nights became the highlight of my week because I was sharing my love of performing with other like-minded people of my own age, and it didn't matter that some of them were better spoken than I was. We were all there because we shared a love of acting and that was all that mattered. Before then I'd always been very aware of class, and although I never felt inferior coming from a poorer background, I think I'd got it into my head that acting and the theatre was only for posh people. Suddenly I began to realize that it didn't really matter where somebody came from or what their background was, it was who they were as a person that was important.

The only thing I didn't much enjoy about the Cockpit was the journey home from Marylebone. It was a long way on the tube, and I used to get quite scared coming back late at night on my own. It wasn't surprising, really. Melissa and I had also attended the Mountview Theatre School in Finsbury Park for a while and it was a rare evening when we didn't encounter a flasher on our way home. It wasn't unusual for guys to grope you if they thought they could get away with it. One night I was all on my own at a bus stop – coming home from my Saturday job – when a young guy who was also waiting asked me the time. As I turned around he grabbed my boobs and I was horrified. Luckily an old man nearby started shouting over at him.

'Oi! Leave her alone!'

The kid backed off and I ran down the road to the next stop, but when the bus came along I spotted him looking out of the upstairs window, laughing at me. It's weird but as a young girl in London back then you just got used to blokes behaving like that and I didn't really think of it as that big a deal. We still made the journey the following week; we just prayed that we didn't bump into the same creepy men. And just like everything else, our parents never took us to these classes; we just got on with it by ourselves. I suppose it was that sort of thing that made me streetwise and quite brave, too. Taxis and lifts in cars were a luxury, so I had to learn to be self-sufficient.

I loved my time at the Cockpit. It was the place where I really got the taste for acting, and it was then that I started to convince myself that getting my O-levels might not be as important as I'd once thought. It was an idea that would only get worse as time went on, and further down the line my schoolwork would start to suffer.

CHAPTER 6:

KATE

The Brownies or the Guides had never been my cup of tea because they always seemed a bit too traditional and conformist, but there was another social group that I did really grow to love. A girl who lived next door to us told us about an organization called The Woodcraft Folk, which is an education movement for kids and young people based around the idea of learning and developing skills for living outdoors, close to nature. It's also socially and culturally mixed and not attached to any religion, and it's an alternative to the Scouts or the Brownies – much more left wing and hippy-like. We started there when I was about fourteen, taking the bus to Tetherdown School, Muswell Hill, where the meetings were held. To be honest, we weren't really interested in the whole philosophy and politics behind the organization, we just went because there were boys and it was something to do on a Friday night. The main idea behind Woodcraft Folk seemed to be about supporting and looking after one another, and as well as that, helping and encouraging city kids to get out of London and appreciate the beauty of nature. We did lots of walks and regularly went camping, and I learned a lot from it. We washed our own clothes and cooked all our own food on these trips into the wild. We even went on a trip to Romania for four weeks in the summer of 1977 to meet up with other Woodcraft Folk from around the world. Vicki and I were very excited about it, and I remember leaving Victoria Station, leaning out of the window and waving frantically at my mum. I knew it was hard for her letting us go, because once we were out of sight there wouldn't be any method of regular contact, just an emergency phone number. She knew it was the trip of a lifetime, though, and that my big sister would look out for me. Unfortunately, being rather accident-prone, I was almost decapitated by a rather large sign as the train picked up speed leaving the station. Mum almost had a heart attack right there and then, and I hadn't even left London yet. It was a long, four-day train journey (which is why the entire trip only cost my mum £75) and we took a huge picnic, along with little stoves to cook on. On the Hungary border, armed soldiers boarded the train and started riffling through our luggage. I was petrified, eyes fixed on their guns. Then when we arrived at our destination we discovered that there'd been an earthquake in Bucharest, so everything that we'd planned to do had to be shelved. There was no one to meet us from the station, and the place that we were due to sleep in was uninhabitable.

There were twelve of us in all – nine children and three adults – all dressed in our green Woodcraft Folk shirts, which made us look like a band of little Che Guevaras: a right motley crew. Everybody stared at us wherever we went. Some of us wore brand name jeans, which in a communist country was such a rarity, and I was shocked when a man offered me fifty pounds for mine. There was no way I was parting with my Levis, though. The other big surprise was the heat. Living in Britain we just weren't accustomed to that sort of sun, and with my pale skin I got the worst sunstroke and got terribly sick. In the end, we slept on the floors of a local college and the food we ate certainly wasn't what we'd been used to: dry bread, funny-tasting cheese. Even the chocolate was vile. Under the repressive dictatorship of Nicolae Ceausescu, Romania's population were suffering shortages of food, fuel and medicine, and although we'd had our tough times in Britain, it was nothing compared to what the people there were going through. It wasn't what I'd pictured at all, and the first few days of the trip were a rather huge culture shock for a group of naive teenagers.

After a few days in Bucharest we headed to a lovely place called

Sinaia where the international Woodcraft Folk camp was being held. At the time I thought it must be the Blackpool of Romania, where everyone went for holidays, and that's where things started to look up. It was like one huge camp-out and I met kids from all over the world – it was incredible. Like a lot of the girls I had a little romance with a Romanian boy for the duration of my time there, whose name was Rajvan. I felt very lucky because he was very handsome and had a little 'tache. We couldn't communicate that well, but it was lovely having someone to hold hands with around the campfire or have an innocent little kiss with. Of course, we made devoted promises to write to each other as I tearfully said goodbye at the end of our trip, but I'm not sure we ever did. The day I arrived back in London was the day Elvis died – 16 August 1977 – and not long afterwards *The News of the World* did a ridiculous so-called exposé on The Woodcraft Folk, claiming that it was a sinister Communist organization, set on twisting and corrupting the minds of children. Mum wasn't having any of that nonsense, telling everyone that she thought it was a wonderful opportunity for her children to learn something and see the world.

It was at Woodcraft Folk that I met a pretty girl called Kate Healy, and we fast became friends. She was like nobody I'd ever met before: warm and funny with a carefree attitude to life that was energizing. She was also a proper tomboy, although there was never any doubt that she was a girl, with exceptionally large boobs for her age. Kate was one of those girls who appeared to be effortlessly sexy, and she was extremely popular. The family lived in a lovely house in Muswell Hill: her father, Maurice, had a long billowing beard and was into jazz, and he was the editor of *Which?* magazine, while her mother, Josie, was a teacher. Kate also had two sisters, Jessica and Lulu. She was a year older than I was, the same age as Vicki, and to me she had the perfect life, and the coolest, trendiest family I could imagine. Back then I assumed that they were incredibly rich, but they were actually just a nice middle-class family: quite liberal and slightly hippyfied. Maurice and Josie were warm and unpretentious, and the kids all went to state schools – just like me. The house, in

Onslow Gardens, was tall and airy with a beautiful garden and it was stylishly decorated, with wooden floors and lots of rugs rather than carpets, and there wasn't a net curtain in sight.

Suddenly, outside of school, my social life opened up and through Kate I met lots of new and exciting people. They all seemed so different from me and the other friends I had; much more cool and arty. In fact, Kate's older cousin, Jane, was an actress and I loved talking to her and telling her about my dreams of one day doing the same. Kate, on the other hand, had her heart set on going to art school and wasn't at all interested in acting or coming to the Cockpit with me on a Thursday night. She was creative but in a completely different way. One of the people she introduced me to was the owner of a hair salon called Loveland, where I ended up working as an assistant in the school holidays. It was the summer or 1976, and in those days every point in our lives seemed to be defined by a song. The big song on the radio at that time was 'Float On' by The Floaters. It seemed to be played endlessly while I was sweeping hair off the floors at Loveland and it drove me insane. I swept, washed hair and tidied around after the stylists and I got two pounds a day, which I was more than happy with. One of the stylists was a drag queen by night, and he used to bring his wig in and get me to set it with rollers while he put his make-up on. It was fairly evident that I wasn't destined to be the next Vidal Sassoon, however, when I failed to rinse some poor woman's hair properly.

'Michelle, what's this?'

The manger of the salon was attempting to blow-dry this woman's hair with thick globs of conditioner still oozing from it.

'Wash it again!' he growled, but he gave me a wink and a smile.

He was only shouting at me to look good in front of the client. I actually got quite good at doing hair in the end, and my mum used to let me blow-dry hers. Perhaps I could have been a hairdresser. It could have been my 'something to fall back on'!

In those days I'd do almost anything to earn a bit of extra cash, so Mum used to pay me five pounds if I agreed to clean the stairs and hallway of the house from top to bottom. I'd put on a vest and a little pair of shorts and off I'd go. The dust was horrendous, and there was a lot of it, but at that age I just wanted to earn some money. Vicki and I even had a little cleaning job at the house of a couple who would have been branded yuppies five years later. The truth of the matter was that Vicki used to clean while I'd sashay around the flat, making believe I lived there. If I wasn't doing that I'd be nosing through the woman's wardrobe, ogling her lovely clothes, or flicking through their record collection.

'Are you ready to do some work yet?' Vicki would yell at me.

But I was far too busy lolling around on the sofa, listening to Queen or ELO on Capital Radio. Vicki always split the money with me, though. Bless her! I was grateful to get it, too. There was always some record I wanted or an item of clothing that had caught my eye in Chelsea Girl.

After work on Saturdays, Kate would come and meet me at the salon and we'd go back to her place. She had a brilliant bedroom in the attic of the house, and there we'd get ready to go out, blasting out the latest pop songs while we did our make-up. Kate and I both loved music, and we were really into Bob Marley and Fleetwood Mac – in fact, both of us longed to be Stevie Nicks. We'd change into our oversized shirts – fifty pence from Dingwalls in Camden – our Lee dungarees (or if you were really cool, like Kate, some striped OshKosh ones from the King's Road), put on some Patchouli perfume (which I occasionally nicked from Woolworths) and then we'd be all set for our Saturday night out. In those days we were a bit too young for pubs and bars but somebody always seemed to be having a house party and we'd be the obligatory gatecrashers, or perhaps one of us might have been invited but a whole tribe of us would turn up with a Party Seven tin of beer and a cheap bottle of wine. Then we'd all dash to the kitchen to see what booze everyone else had brought that might be better than ours. Sometimes there would be so many in our gang that the petrified host wouldn't let us in, and on those occasions we just found somewhere to hang out, opening our drinks in the street. There would be Rory, Sean, Jumbo, Guy – Kate went to a mixed school so there were always a few handsome boys tagging along with us – and sometimes Melissa would come with her new boyfriend, Bennett, but I never really hung out with anyone from my own school. It didn't matter how many of us there were, though; we weren't the kind of kids who were out to cause trouble, and we ended up having a good time wherever we landed up. It's funny, we never used to have any trouble getting booze in those days, and we never got asked for ID (Kate was often the one who got sent into the off-licence or into the pub for some off-sales because she was tall and looked older than the rest of us). Even I used to get served in a pub called the Tibberton Arms in Islington, ordering large vodka and limes at the age of fourteen. Still, I don't ever remember abusing alcohol like some of the young drinkers seem to today, apart from the time when Melissa and I decided to find out what it was like to get drunk. Most of the time, though, we just hung out and had a laugh. There was no rolling around in the gutter and getting arrested and I don't recall ever staggering out of parties legless and incapable when I was a teenager. All that came later! It wasn't all fun and games, though – once Jill and I were driven to a disused car park by a rogue cab driver who locked the doors on us. We had to scream our heads off before he finally let us out, but it's well documented that some women aren't so lucky in that situation.

Things seem quite different now. I know the rules are a lot stricter on kids buying alcohol, and I'm glad, but I think if kids really want to get hold of it they will, and I do worry about my own daughter Maia sometimes. These days it's all happy hours and cheap shots, and, of course, young people like to experiment and push the boundaries.

Thank God Maia feels like she can be honest with me about things like going out and drinking alcohol rather than doing it behind my back. There were just some things I couldn't have told my mum because I knew she'd be disappointed in me, and drinking as a teenager would have been one of them. I don't believe that parents should necessarily try to be 'best friends' with their kids, but I believe honesty is crucial, particularly in a mother–daughter relationship.

Along with Kate, I used to also hang out with some of the boys from Highbury Grove, which was near to my school, and there was one particular boy (I won't name and shame him) who at some point went out with Kate, Vicki and me. What a stud, eh? He always wore Acqua Di Selva cologne, and I remember sitting in the back row of the ABC cinema on Holloway Road watching *The Omen* with him constantly trying to put his hands under my skirt. I wasn't having any of it, but I was secretly quite pleased that he'd at least tried because I quite liked him. I have a vivid memory of Kate, Vicki and me all going to see Rod Stewart at Wembley Arena with some of the Highbury boys, when he released the album *A Night On The Town*. We were all massive fans of Rod's, and I still am to this day. We were also friendly with some boys from the private schools, Highgate Boys' and King Alfred's. There seemed to be a lot of boys named John around back then, and at one point Vicki and Kate and I were all going out with different Johns, which could be rather confusing at times. I must say those private school boys were by far the naughtiest – but that's all I'm saying! I had a brief romance with the son of a well-known actor, who was the first boy to undertake the task of trying to remove my bra – to no avail. Well, I was only fifteen! In truth I was more interested in the fact that his dad's girlfriend at the time was Britt Ekland.

It was October 1977, and Kate and I had been dating two brothers, Sean and Rory. One night, the boys had a bit of a party at their parents' house and Vicki and I went along and stayed over afterwards. Kate was away on a field trip to Wales with her school at the time. The morning after the party there was a phone call, and suddenly Vicki was screaming and crying.

'Kate's dead, Kate's dead!'

'What? What are you talking about?'

The shock of hearing those words was like being hit by a car. I just couldn't believe what Vicki was saying, and when it finally did sink in I was devastated – we all were. It transpired that Kate had suffered a heart attack due to an abnormal valve in her heart. Her family had known about the condition since she was a baby, but the doctors didn't think it was anything to worry about. She'd become ill while the group she was with were on a hike miles from anywhere, and in the end Jumbo and Guy had carried her body all the way back to the place where they were staying. It was horrible and my whole world came crashing down. Experiencing the death of a young friend when you're that age is just not something you're equipped to deal with. I'd come to terms with the death of my great-grandfather, but this was something else entirely. I was in a terrible state and for weeks afterwards I was convinced that Kate was appearing in my bedroom. I remember waking up with a bolt one night and seeing her standing in the corner. Perhaps it was just my distress and overactive imagination or perhaps I just wanted so much to see her one last time, but even now I feel like she's with me sometimes. I think I always will.

Her funeral was an event that I'll never forget. I'd never seen so many young people in a church; Kate had been such a popular and beautiful girl. People could barely get in the door, it was so packed. During the service they played her favourite songs: 'No Woman No Cry' by Bob Marley and 'River Deep Mountain High' by Ike and Tina Turner. Just thinking about that makes me cry. It was hard on everyone. Her family were utterly distraught, as were all her friends, and it was tough on my mum trying to comfort me when I was so terribly unhappy. She's since told Vicki and me how difficult it was for her to help us through that terrible time because we were so young, and unaccustomed to that kind of raw grief. The following summer I felt like I was still grieving so I went on holiday to Brittany with Kate's family, hoping that spending time with them might make me feel better. It actually made things worse, for me and for them. Being around Kate's family without her just made me very sad, and for them I think my presence was simply a reminder of the daughter they'd lost. What made things even harder for me was that nobody at my school knew Kate so nobody really understood the loss I'd suffered. I felt lonely and angry and even more distant from everyone there. Why had this terrible thing happened? I'd met this amazing friend – a soulmate – and now she'd been taken away from me. It was so unfair, and one of the things that helped make up my mind to leave Highbury Hill at the end of the fifth year. There was no way I was staying on at that place. I wanted to walk away and never see it again. I was over it.

CHAPTER 7:

PUNK!

L ike most kids in the 1970s, pop music and the radio were a massive part of my growing up. Radio 1 disc jockeys were almost as famous as the pop stars themselves, and quite often my friends and I would queue outside BBC Broadcasting House on a Saturday morning in the hope of catching our favourites; Tony Blackburn or Noel Edmonds, who I had a huge crush on. In the days before camera phones, all we had with us was our autograph books. Those same DJs presented *Top of the Pops*, which was huge, and one of the few TV shows where you could see your favourite pop stars perform their latest singles. I'd secretly always wanted to be one of Pan's People, the show's glamorous dancing ensemble in the seventies, and when I was ten, my cousin Jenny and I shared a dream of meeting in Piccadilly Circus one day so we could run away to join them.

My heartthrob was David Essex: I was crazy about him. Years later he was in *EastEnders*, long after Cindy had departed. She'd have definitely made a play for him had she still been there. He'd been my childhood pop hero but his music wasn't exactly what you might call rebellious. I was also a fan of T.Rex and The Jackson Five, but certainly not Alvin Stardust or the Bay City Rollers who I thought were very uncool (plus those wide, cropped tartan trousers were very unflattering!). I also liked The Osmonds, but I kept that one quiet. I recently met Donny at the National Television Awards – what a lovely guy.

When some of my mates got tickets to see David Essex in concert in 1975, I was devastated when my mum wouldn't let me go. Just a few months before there had been a terrible crush at a David Cassidy concert at White City Stadium where one girl had died and hundreds of others had been injured, so I guess her over-protectiveness was understandable.

Punk emerged in 1976, and I think most people my age remember the Sex Pistols' appearance with Bill Grundy on a teatime news show. We'd never witnessed anything like it before: young people swearing and behaving and dressing outrageously. I was shocked, but it was great to watch. I was only fourteen at the time, and that year I went on holiday to Brighton with Melissa. The big song then was 'Dancing Queen' by Abba, which was a great song but a world away from punk. However, my friends and I were all aware of punk as a fast-growing new culture that was making a mark on the music and fashion scene. At first it seemed a bit superficial, almost violent, but as time went on there were great bands forming and a new style of dress was emerging: dramatic, edgy, and very daring. There was one girl at school who started to look a bit different, and then another couple of girls, who were quite cool, started to get into the punk scene.

Eventually I started to follow suit. Kate's death had affected me deeply and I'd become quite withdrawn at school and a bit of a loner. It was almost like punk was right there waiting for me to embrace it: it was just what I needed. I loved the music and adored the style and I started to wear black whenever I wasn't in my school uniform, buying all my clothes from second hand shops and markets and looking as moody as I possibly could.

I knew that Mum wouldn't approve, so I used to hide all my cool gear in the big old wooden sideboard downstairs in the hall, by the communal call box. Whenever I was going out I'd dress up in my nice normal clothes and then once I was downstairs I'd get changed into my more punky stuff while Vicki kept Mum occupied. Then I'd put on my lipstick, which was actually black eyeliner, and off I'd go. When I got home I did it all in reverse, breezing back into our flat looking every bit the sweet, innocent teenager that my mum was expecting. Inevitably, I got caught one night when I was sneaking back in and Mum wasn't impressed, as she hated the idea of me being a punk. Mum couldn't comprehend why anyone, including me, would want to swathe themselves in black and look so severe. At the time I suppose it reflected the way I felt. People stopped and stared at the punks, but secretly I think that was what we all wanted – attention. For other people to sit up and take notice. To many adults, punk was all about violence, shock and rebellion, and I guess that's how my mum saw it. She wouldn't let me dye my hair, either, so I persuaded her to let me henna it instead. After all, henna was a natural substance and not some damaging chemical. Using henna, however, was rather like slathering one's head in thick, unpleasant green slurry – quite disgusting. It also had quite a potent aroma and I spent much of the punk era smelling vaguely of curry.

In those days Melissa, Jill and I would go to the Hope and Anchor pub on Upper Street, Islington, where many of the coolest bands of the time started out: The Police, Dire Straits, Joy Division, The Cure, The Stranglers. They've all played at the Hope and Anchor over the years, and it was *the* place to hang out when I was fifteen or sixteen years old. I also loved going to the Roundhouse in Camden, or the Marquee, and I'd see all the best punk bands, like Slaughter And The Dogs, The Dammed and 999. On St Patrick's Day 1978, Jill and I were at the Marquee watching a band called Spud who were supporting Dire Straits. Afterwards we got chatting to two of the band's good friends, Ray Burmiston and Micky Screen, and post-gig we all left the club together. As we were walking along Wardour Street, we were randomly stopped and searched by a couple of police officers.

'How old are you?' one of them asked me.

'I'm sixteen,' I lied, nervously.

My sixteenth birthday was two months away.

'Can you take your shoes off, please?'

They checked our shoes and all our pockets: it was quite frightening at the time. Let's face it: my mother was going to kill me if I'd got arrested at the age of fifteen. Luckily there was nothing for them to find, but the experience did throw Ray and me together, and we dated for some time after that. He ended up fronting a band called The Passion Puppets in the early 1980s, and these days he's an extremely sought-after photographer, taking pictures of some of the world's most famous actors and musicians. We've worked together quite a few times, and we're still great friends today. Jill started dating Micky that night, too, and they went out for years.

Meanwhile I wasn't the only one in the family going out and enjoying myself. Mum was still very glamorous and she'd always be off out with her friends looking fabulous, top to toe in all the latest fashions of the day. She'd have her hair pinned up in ringlets – very sophisticated – and it would last for about three days with the amount of hairspray she'd put on it. Then she'd comb it all out and start all over again. I have a vivid memory of seeing all the hairpins lying on her pillow where they'd come loose in the night. Mum was a real social butterfly, and she was always out at some show or other, often at the Talk Of The Town: Shirley Bassey or Dame Edna Everage. Boxing was a very big thing and although it might seem odd now, it was considered a very glamorous night out in the seventies. Mum always loved going out to watch the fights, dressed up to the nines in one of her beautiful long evening gowns.

One night she came home with a question for me.

'Michelle, have you ever heard of a group called Skinny Lizzy?'

'Do you mean *Thin* Lizzy, Mum?'

'Yeah, that's them. I met this gorgeous young man called Scott Gorham tonight.'

'Scott Gorham! You met Scott Gorham?'

I'd always loved Thin Lizzy and Scott was the beautiful guitarist with long blond hair who I really fancied. What the hell was my mother doing mixing with my music idols?

'Yeah! He asked me out,' she went on.

I was excited and appalled all at once.

'Oh, Mum! Are you going to go?'

'Don't be silly,' she said. 'He's far too young for me.'

I couldn't believe what I was hearing, but I wasn't really that surprised that someone like him had asked my mum out. She was still young and very beautiful, and when I was around sixteen she found love again with a man called Sid who she's still with today, over thirty-five years later. Sid tells me that I completely ignored him for the first year he was going out with Mum, and given what a moody, punky teenager I was that doesn't surprise me. These days we get on famously. His friends know him as Steak – 'steak and kidney' being rhyming slang for Sidney – and he adores my mum. He's also been very good to my sister and me – a father and a friend.

After about eight years it was time for us to say goodbye to Fairmead Road. We were finally moving into our very own flat on Caledonian Road. It was a three-bedroom flat, which meant that at long last we could all have our own rooms. Before we left Fairmead Road, Mum agreed to let Vicki and me have a party while she was out getting the new place ready. I was very excited about this event and duly began spreading the word to all my friends. Little did Mum or any of us know that half the skinheads in Holloway would turn up, plus punks, teds and everyone else who had heard tell of the great party at number 7 Fairmead. God knows how they all found out about it – there was no Facebook or Twitter in those days, of course – but by eight o'clock that night they were literally queuing along the street to get in. In a short space of time our flat was rammed to the hilt and I just couldn't control it. There were fights, the police were called, and to top it all the man who lived across the road was arrested for an alleged unsavoury incident with one of the teenage girls at the party. It was bedlam. Vicki was there with me, but it wasn't her fault. She wasn't even into the punk scene; she liked Lionel Richie – that was how different we were. When my mum found out what had happened she knew exactly who was culpable and she went absolutely crazy. She was furious with me, and she didn't hold back.

'Right, that's it! You're not going out anymore. You're grounded.'

I was fifteen years old and this was in the run-up to my O-levels. To be honest I think it's what helped me pass some of them. The fact that I was grounded meant that I had to stay home and study. Apart from that I wasn't really that bothered about my exams. Like many young people in the late seventies, punk and the new wave scene had changed my life. It made me look at the world in a whole new way. I no longer felt like I had to conform and fit in with the other girls at school; in fact I was desperate to do the opposite.

After years of being a little bit withdrawn, I suddenly got a real kick out of people staring at me. Being a punk for me was like playing a role and it became an outlet for my theatrical leanings. It wasn't just the clothes, either; it wasn't shallow. Punk was about the music, which felt like it meant something, and it was about young people rebelling and having something to express in a new way.

Our new home was in Tealby Court in Caledonian Road, which was a brand new and very modern estate, and our flat was pristine. It was a lovely split-level design with a kitchen upstairs and stairs leading down to the bedrooms and living room. The first thing I did when I got into my new room was paint the floor black, and then I chucked out the bedstead. I simply wanted a mattress and a record player on the black floor and no furniture. Basic. Having new rooms didn't stop Vicki and me fighting, though. I was too interested in other things to do boring jobs like laundry most of the time, so whenever I ran out of clean knickers I'd sneak into Vicki's room and pinch hers. She ended up setting a trap with bits of thread tied to the door so she knew when I'd been in there. Then she screamed her head off at me for invading her privacy.

'She's been in my room again!'

'What? No I haven't, she's making it up!'

'Yes you have! I can prove it!'

How my poor mother put up with it I'll never know, but Vicki and I never really got on until we were well into our twenties. For some reason I felt the need to rebel and she didn't. Even when she got married, aged twenty-four, we were still trying to rub each other up the wrong way. I went to her wedding in the sexiest, tightest dress I could find topped with a bowler hat – and no bra or knickers. I'm sure it was just to annoy her, but the groom was fuming. It wasn't until much later that the two of us started to bond and become the close sisters we are today. In fact, it was 1989 by the time we decided to get re-acquainted and book a holiday together in Spain. Vicki and I hadn't really seen a lot of each other in the mid-to-late 1980s, and I think we both decided that it was high time we spent some time together. We ended up having a fantastic week: clubbing until six or seven in the morning, waking up for some Weetabix at 5pm, then getting ready to go out for dinner and doing it all over again. We did this for a whole seven days and we had such a great time together. It was year that 'All Around The World' by Lisa Stansfield and 'Have I Told You Lately' by Van Morrison came out and I remember us playing those songs non-stop on our cassette player. We'd had many ups and downs before that holiday but we've been very close ever since. These days we are the best of friends, but when we were teenagers we couldn't have been more different.

This rebellious streak in me certainly didn't pay dividends when it came to my exam results. I did OK – not brilliantly, but that was to be expected as I'd hardly done any revision. I hadn't done as well as my mum had hoped and certainly not as well as most of the other girls in my year. I took eight O-levels and I passed four, and although I'd knuckled down to some extent it just hadn't been enough. I was stubborn, though. In the back of my mind, I told myself I didn't need fantastic exam results because I was going to act. In the January before my exams I'd done an audition for a college drama course, and because I only needed to pass a minimum four O-levels to be accepted, I wasn't that bothered about the rest. It was a dangerous mix of arrogance and determination, but I could already see that there were other avenues opening up for me.

CHAPTER 8:

A DRAMA QUEEN IN THE MAKING

Kate's cousin Jane had told me about a sixth form college offering a two-year diploma course in performing arts. It was called Kingsway Princeton, and Sid Vicious from the Sex Pistols had studied there two years earlier. I auditioned with both a classical piece – Viola from *Twelfth Night* – and a modern piece by Stephen Poliakoff, both of which Jane helped me prepare. I was completely ecstatic when I got accepted. Mum had been supportive and happy for me to go as long as I filled in my time with a couple more subjects to make up for the fact that I hadn't passed all my exams. She knew how committed I was to acting because of all the youth theatres and classes I'd attended off my own bat, but just doing drama wasn't enough as far as she was concerned – so that was the deal.

Of course, I loved Kingsway from the word go, just as I knew I would. The thrill of doing acting classes every single day was incredible and I had two brilliant acting teachers, George Cornell and Sara Newman, who taught me so much during my time there. I wasn't quite so enthusiastic about some of my other classes, however. A-level English Lit was all fine and dandy, but an O-level in pottery wasn't the best idea I'd ever had and I think I only went to about two classes in the end. In fact, much of the time I was supposed to be hunched over a potter's wheel was spent in the pub.

That was the thing about college. Higher education had a whole new slant to it – it was a different world altogether. For a start I was mixing with boys, and on top of that I could wear exactly what I liked after years of sticking to a strict uniform. The other thing was that there was no one forcing you into the classroom if you didn't feel like going. If you ended up failing the course through non-attendance, it was your own fault. Kingsway Princeton was all about self-motivation, and while I had a passion for all things dramatic, I quickly got used to the idea that I could do pretty much as I pleased as far as the rest of the courses went.

My A-level English class was in an annexe of the college, which involved me leaving the building and crossing the Gray's Inn Road to get there. Well I never seemed to get past the Calthorpe Arms on a Monday afternoon, a fate that befell quite a few of the other students as well. I don't think I made it to my English class for about three months, and when I did eventually find my way there I'd beg one of the clever girls in the class to give me all her notes. I met some amazing groups of people at Kingsway Princeton; there were the Teddy Boys, and the kids who were into Northern Soul. I was really into fashion and going through a bit of a rockabilly phase at the time where everything was second-hand, or vintage as we preferred to call it. I wore drainpipe jeans, leather jackets, fifties jumpers and stilettos (I wouldn't be seen dead in flats while I was at college) and my hair was a jet-black geometric 'do' that was Mary Quant meets Siouxsie Sioux, fashioned by one of the hairdressing students at a trendy salon called Jingles. It seemed to be a place for young people, who, like me, wanted to learn but who never thrived at school. I was wide-eyed at the students smoking joints at lunchtime and kids selling *The Socialist Worker*. It all seemed so fabulous and bohemian. I was always drawn to anything like that.

It was at this time that I met and started dating Max, who was a socialist but who came from a very well-to-do family. Max was a very handsome boy with a foppish blond haircut and classic Scandinavian looks (his surname was Gottlieb). He was very funny but also exceptionally clever, and I think that's why I eventually fell in love with him. Max was quite politically motivated, and he would sometimes take me to along to Labour party meetings and rallies, and although I wouldn't have called myself an activist, like many students back then I was quite politically aware. During my college days there seemed to be a strike or a demonstration about one thing or another every five minutes, and Max and I would regularly attend anti-apartheid events and Rock Against Racism gigs, which were big social events as well as political statements. One day a large group of pupils at Kingsway Princeton went on strike and ended up throwing all their typewriters out of the windows. It was all part of being a student in the early 1980s.

Max, meanwhile, was one of the few students who could afford a car, and not just any car – Max had an MG sports. The trouble was, having such an expensive and prestigious motor was a dilemma for him, with all his socialist ideals, so he used to hide it from the other students, parking it well out of sight of the college. He was my first 'posh' boyfriend, and I suppose my first serious one, and suddenly I was in the midst of a whole new social group who hung out at the Freemasons in Hampstead, or at Maxwell's, which was a burger restaurant with a late licence. There weren't as many places where you could drink after 11pm in the early 1980s, so we could often be found there late into the night with Max's friends, one of whom was Steve McFadden who went on to play Phil Mitchell in *EastEnders*. Steve was also at Kingsway Princeton and dated one of my girlfriends, Kathy, while I was with Max so we spent a lot of time together as a foursome.

I felt as though the door to yet another world had been opened to me. Through Max I was suddenly meeting people from all different walks of life and it felt like the class divide was coming down. Most of the time I was quite happy mixing with people who were better spoken and richer than I was, but I was quietly aware of the class divide. Not that it bothered me. Yes, there was the odd occasion where I'd worry about whether I was saying or doing the wrong thing, or picking up the right spoon, but it wasn't a big deal. Max's mum and dad were always very nice to me and the difference in our backgrounds didn't seem to faze them in the slightest. They lived in a big house in Highgate and I was fascinated by some of the interesting people they mixed with. His father was a psychotherapist who practiced from home, and sometimes while I was at the house I'd spot some of his famous clients coming through the front door. I remember being quite taken aback when one of the biggest heartthrob pop stars of the day turned up on the doorstep. I was stunned to think that someone as successful and famous as him might be in need of a therapist, but this was in the days before everyone and their mother seemed to be in therapy. The family were also good friends with the late Peter O'Toole, and one evening they took me to see him in *Macbeth* at The Old Vic, which was famously savaged by the critics and on some nights apparently had the audience rolling in the aisle with laughter. I thought it was amazing, however, and after the performance we went backstage to chat to the man himself, which was a huge thrill for me. I'd often go for nights out at Ronnie Scott's with Max's family, too, where Max's dad was the in-house doctor. Max was really into film and the two of us were always at the Screen on the Green cinema in Islington or the Screen on the Hill in Hampstead, watching something arty with subtitles or anything directed by Peter Greenaway. I still love those art house films that Max introduced me to; in fact these days my boyfriend Michael often takes the mickey out of me because of it.

'Oh, she loves anything with a subtitle, she does,' he'll say to our friends.

One of my best friends in the drama group at Kingsway was a girl called Beverly Flower. She was a lot of fun, and we ended up sharing a flat in Highgate for a while after college. We shared bunk beds in one room and we lived on hummus and pita bread, just so we could afford to get cabs home when we went out for the night. We'd been told that the flat's previous tenant was a 'lady of the night', which explained why we'd constantly have men knocking on our door and asking us, 'Is Christine there? Do you do what Christine does?'

There was a broken bannister hidden under the bed, and we often wondered whether 'Christine' had kept it there just in case one of her customers got out of hand. Beverly eventually 'auditioned' to be a waitress in the early days of Stringfellow's, and she was appalled when she found out the job's criteria.

'They want me to walk around serving drinks in a swimming costume,' she said, aghast. 'There's no way I'm parading up and down in a bar like that.'

She now lives in Sydney and works for an actor's agent, but we're still great friends to this day.

All in all I had a great time at Kingsway. We put on some quite heavyweight productions throughout the two-year course, like *The Jewish Wife* by Bertolt Brecht, and it really set in stone my hunger to act and to be an actor. There was nothing else for me as far as I was concerned. Not everyone was as determined as I was, though. The thriving social scene combined with the laid-back atmosphere of the college meant that many of the students simply got carried away with themselves and forgot what they were really supposed to be doing there. There were twenty-eight students on my course at Kingsway Princeton when we started, but as time went on that number dwindled and in the end only three of us took the final drama exam.

The next step for me was drama school, and I saved up as much money as I could from my part-time job in McDonalds, just so I could audition for as many schools as possible. The audition fee for a decent drama school was about twenty-five quid in those days, so I was determined to make it count. One of the more memorable auditions was for East 15 in Loughton, Essex. Their methods of teaching were known to be quite avant-garde and 'out there', and instead of simply performing classical and modern pieces at the audition, we were expected to run around and climb trees. I went along with it but I knew that it wasn't the school for me. I also auditioned for Central School of Speech & Drama, RADA, LAMDA, Guildhall and Drama Centre. The auditions were always nerve-wracking and each one came with a new and unsettling experience. At RADA, the world-famous jewel in the crown of drama schools, all the anxious, eager hopefuls sat in a room looking blankly at one another while a phone on the desk rang and rang. Eventually somebody answered it, relaying the message that some of the candidates, including Collins, were to report to the bursar's room. As we all shuffled inside we were met with a grim announcement.

'I'm very sorry, but you haven't won a place at RADA this year. Do please try again next year.'

I was gutted, of course, but that was only the first in a long line of disappointments. I didn't get into any of the drama schools I applied for. In fact, the only one I got a call back for was Central and even then I fell at the last hurdle and ended up with a knock-back. Years later I was chatting to Peter Guinness, an actor who was married to former *EastEnders* actress Roberta Taylor and who was one of four people on the panel when I auditioned at Central.

'You were the only ones who re-called me,' I told him.

'Well obviously, darling, I was the only one with taste,' he grinned.

At the time I was completely distraught that I hadn't been offered a place anywhere, and it was a quite a shock. I'd done very well on my college course and I was considered amongst my peers to be one of the best actors: practically a dead cert for a place at one of the renowned drama schools. I decided that they must already have their quota of chirpy Cockneys and that I fell firmly into that bracket. I certainly didn't have what was considered to be a drama school accent. Maybe I just didn't have what it took to be an actress after all.

CHAPTER 9:

OUT THERE!

I really had no idea what I was going to do next, until Max suggested that I go to America with him. He had landed himself a place on a two-month summer film course at UCLA in Los Angeles. I was quite excited about the idea and after my miserable failure with all the drama schools I certainly didn't have any better offers. As it happened, a great-aunt of mine in Wales had recently died and left me a bit of money, so I thought I might as well put some of it to good use. Mum liked and trusted Max so she was happy for me to go, so in the summer of 1980 the two of us bought tickets on Laker Airways for £99 each, and off we went. When we arrived in California we stayed in a dark room in a tiny motel in Santa Monica and it felt like we were living in a movie, although not a very good one. I didn't like the place one bit, and for the first few days I was petrified: too frightened to even leave our room while Max was out at college. I sat on the bed asking myself the same question: 'What am I doing here? What the hell am I doing here?'

Everything I'd heard about America in those days led me to think it was a dangerous place, and if the TV cop shows were to be believed, there was a good chance that you were going to be robbed at knifepoint or gunned down on any given street corner at any moment. I decided that it would be much safer if I simply stayed in the dingy room watching American TV, which, with its hundreds of channels compared to the three we had back home, was the only good thing about the place as far as I could tell. I hardly saw anyone for that first week or so. I might venture out briefly to the huge McDonalds next door to grab a cheeseburger and a strawberry milkshake, but apart from that Cagney and Lacey were my only friends and I was quite happy with that.

Max, meanwhile, was working hard on his course, which focused on directing, and eventually he set about making a short film in which I starred. This led to me getting parts in some of the other students' films, which meant I at least had something to keep me occupied, and it was also good practise for working in front of a camera. It was then that I came out of my shell a bit more and started to ease into the LA lifestyle, but it wasn't all fun and glamour, moving from place to place and staying at various friends' apartments for as long as they'd have us. Max's parents were fairly well off, but he was never spoilt or extravagant, and we certainly weren't living it up the whole time we were there. I paid my way as much as I could, and Max always treated me as an equal rather than someone who was along for the ride.

Eventually we moved to an apartment on Venice Beach, which was quite a rough area back then. The place was owned by the girlfriend of Art Garfunkel, who was a friend of a friend of Max's, and it was in a nice apartment block overlooking the ocean. We never met Art, but there were a lot of photographs of him dotted around the place, which was quite strange with him being such a big star. We were happy there and I guess I was in love, but somehow even then I knew that we weren't going to end up together – I think we both did. We were young and on an adventure together, but something told me that it wasn't forever. It didn't matter, though. Despite my initial reservations I ended up having a fantastic time in LA that summer. So much so that in the end I didn't want to leave, and I sometimes wonder what would have happened if I'd stuck it out and tried to make it as an actress over there. Who knows?

When we returned to London at the end of the summer, Max rented a house in West Hampstead and I all but moved in with him and a writer friend of his, Mick Mahoney. Mick was a very talented up-and-coming writer who'd written a new play that was being performed at the Old Red Lion pub in the Angel, Islington. The theatre, which was above the pub, was a successful fringe venue where all the cool, young, local actors hung out. It was there that I first met actors like Ray Winstone, Kathy Burke, Phil Daniels, Perry Fenwick, Pauline Quirke and many others. There was so much great talent emerging and I was happy to see that they were young working-class actors like me. A lot of these actors had started off at the Anna Scher Youth Theatre and went on to great things, and I remember feeling slightly envious that I wasn't part of their gang.

It was a short-term living arrangement, however. Not long after John Lennon was shot in December 1980, Max and I broke up and I moved out. There was no big bust-up or dramatic departure, we'd just drifted apart and that was that. Max is now a very successful designer, and I always feel proud when I see his name on a movie poster or on the credits of a film or TV show. He's a lovely man and I always knew he'd do great things.

After the break-up I didn't want to move back home with my mum again because it would have felt like a step backwards. Instead I moved into a studio flat in West Hampstead after hearing about a room in a house from a guy called Paul who already had a room there. The room in question was pretty grim, but at least it was mine and I could retain my independence. The house was right next the Railway Tavern, where lots of great bands played, and as far as I was concerned West Hampstead was a very cool place. The first time Mum came to visit me, however, she burst into tears.

'You can't live here, Michelle, it's so awful,' she said.

She wasn't wrong, but there was no way I was going home so I wouldn't hear a word of it. As it turned out, my time there was short-lived anyway. An Irish lady owned the house and she appeared to be permanently drunk. She wore a wig that would regularly slip out of kilter, and she would forever be yanking back into place with a sharp tug while she was mid-conversation with you. For some reason this woman got it into her head that Paul and I were indulging in some hanky-panky under her roof, and she wasn't happy. Eventually she confronted me in a semi-drunken rage.

'That's it!' she cried. 'Get out of my house, you hussy! You're a whore!'

I guess it was a sign of the times that I didn't just tell her the truth, which was that Paul was gay. She probably would have thrown him out if I had, but instead she threw me out.

It was then that I got my first proper acting job, in Bulgakov's *The Crimson Island* at the Gate Theatre in Notting Hill. It starred James Fleet and a cast of about twenty actors, all crammed into a tiny dressing room above a pub. Along with the Latchmere in Battersea and the King's Head in Islington, the Gate, which is still going today, was one of the many fringe theatres around at the time. You never knew who might come and see the show and review your performance and as far as I was concerned it was all up for grabs. The play itself was a highbrow, satirical Russian play parodying the rise of the Bolsheviks, and to be honest I'd felt like I was a little bit out of my depth at the audition. Still, the director, a New Yorker called Lou Stein, saw something in me and I was grateful to have been given the chance. It was all quite avant-garde, and during the performance he had us running around and doing strange dances and all sorts. Very weird, yes, but I didn't mind. I was at the Gate Theatre, which was prestigious and very cool. As far as I was concerned I was on my way.

I also got into a regular satirical sketch show at the Gate called *The News Review*. The writers would take snippets from all of the news stories during the week and then concoct tongue-in-cheek skits around them which we would perform every Friday in front of an audience. I might find myself playing Margaret Thatcher in one sketch, and Marilyn Monroe in the next. The nature of the show was usually very political and always fast-paced, and as an actor you had to think on your feet. We might rehearse a show all week, but then if something big happened on a Thursday or Friday it had to go in, and sometimes we'd get a new script thrust into our hands just a few hours before we went on stage.

Having these acting jobs was a real shot in the arm for me,

particularly as I was determined not to drag myself through another round of drama school auditions. If they didn't want me the first time, why should things be any different now? Sod them all, I thought, I'm just going to have to do it all on my own.

CHAPTER 10:

THE BARGE

After a summer working in the gift shop at London Zoo, which mostly involved preventing unruly kids from nicking rubber snakes, I got a job in a market research company called Audience Selection, which was on a road just off The Strand. I needed to make money and I certainly couldn't sit on my backside waiting to be discovered – that just wasn't me. There were loads of other actors working there alongside me, either struggling ones who were waiting for that elusive big break to come or those who were 'resting'. We did shift work – nine to five or four until nine – and we got cash in hand at the end of the shift, which I thought was marvellous. The trouble was I was so broke that I couldn't even afford lunch half the time and I'd end up living on Mars bars.

All sorts of companies relied on our market research skills: banks, credit card companies, political parties and food companies. I remember ringing people up in the early days of cold calling and bombarding them with whatever random selection of questions I had in front of me.

'What brand of sausages do you eat? Who are you going to vote for? How many times a week do you have sex?'

People were quite forthcoming when it came to questions about food or their sexual habits, but politics was another matter altogether.

'I have sex about three times a week, but I'm not bloody telling you who I'm voting for!'

I met some great people through Audience Selection, some of whom I'm still very close to today. Sharon and Tim, who became my best friends (and who have been a couple ever since we all worked there) and Bunmi Akintonwa, who rented a room to another one of my friends at Audience Selection, Chris Stevenson. I also met my first gay friends there, including a lovely guy named Mark. Mark and I became really good friends, and once the drunken landlady had turned me out on my ear he asked if I'd like to find a place to share with him. At the time Mark's parents didn't know he was gay – in fact they were very anti-gay – so the deal was that I would pretend to be his girlfriend whenever I went to their house in Watford, just to keep the peace. The two of us ended up living on a houseboat, which was moored on the Thames. I'd seen it advertised somewhere, and on first viewing I thought it was amazing – I couldn't believe my luck. Right then and there I decided it would be ideal for Mark and me as long as we could find a couple more people to make up the rent, which worked out as £27 a week each if there were four of us. It was quite a lot of money in 1981 but just about manageable if we were careful and didn't eat much. I suggested the idea to two other guys who worked at Audience Selection, Eric and Phil.

'Look, guys – it's a barge,' I enthused. 'It'll be brilliant!'

Eric Van Der Veen was a Truman Capote lookalike who claimed to be a writer but spent most of his time lounging around the boat in a black polo neck with slicked-back hair, smoking Gauloises. I don't think I ever actually saw him write a single word, and he certainly hadn't had anything published as far as I was aware. Phil, meanwhile, was a photographer who was also yet to make it big. There we were, a commune of struggling artistes afloat on the river at Battersea, and when we weren't on the water we'd be hanging out at the French House pub in Soho, which was *the* place to go back then, frequented by an arty crowd that included Lucian Freud, Molly Parkin and the fashion designer Pam Hogg. We were all achingly cool and totally fabulous, and it was a really fun time, despite the fact that none of us ever had any money. The other problem was that although our barge looked marvellous at a quick glance, it was terminally damp and freezing most of the time, so not exactly luxurious during the winter months. Sometimes we'd get up for work to find ourselves stranded, the gangplank having been washed away in a storm. On those days we were just stuck out on the water, unable to contact anyone on dry land because we invariably hadn't paid the phone bill. Then there were the times I'd come home after a night out and snap my stiletto heel as it got caught in the rickety gangplank. After a few weeks of all that we realized that the reality of living on water wasn't quite as romantic as the notion, what with the constant damp and flooding. The barge was actually in need of serious repair and we were paying through the nose for it. Rather than finding a bargain, we were being exploited.

All the posh houseboats sat along the river at Cheyne Walk, but we were moored on the opposite side of the Thames, very close to a church and its vicarage. I don't know who the vicar was at the time but if his rubbish was anything to go by he certainly wasn't your ordinary everyday clergyman. We were forever spotting kinky sexual paraphernalia in the dustbins of the churchyard: leather straps, handcuffs, and some serious dominatrix tackle. We couldn't think who it might belong to other than the vicar – it was hilarious. Maybe it belonged to Eric's girlfriend, Deena, who unofficially lived on the boat with us most of the time. She was a slightly punky Marilyn Monroe lookalike from Essex who I believe worked in the adult entertainment industry – she certainly wasn't a nine-to-five girl, that's for sure – and although very pretty, she was quite mad and exceptionally stupid. I think Eric saw himself as the Arthur Miller to her Marilyn Monroe, but the only real similarity was that she was much, much younger than him. I remember coming home from work one day to find Eric smoking one of his French fags and reading his book, while Deena sat next to him, completely naked with her legs wide apart, her private parts smeared with something slimy and white.

'What on earth are you doing, Deena?' I said, horrified. 'What is that?'

'Oh it's yogurt,' she said, as matter-of fact as you like. 'Apparently it's good for me thrush.'

I had no idea what thrush even was, but I was too scared to ask.

'Well do you have to do it there, Deena?' I inquired indignantly. 'This is the living room!'

'It's too bloody cold in the bedroom,' she said. 'This is the only place that's warm.'

She was unbelievable: one of those girls that men all seemed to like but other women usually couldn't stand.

In those days we were forever answering adverts in magazines like *The Stage* and *Time Out*, which had a classified section in the back that became every actor's bible. We were always spotting something that we thought might lead to some fabulous acting job that might catapult us to stardom overnight – or at the very least help us to get our Equity Card. Mark discovered one particular opportunity in *City Limits* magazine and we decided to apply. 'Bringing Shakespeare into Soho', the ad proclaimed.

'This could be great!' Mark decided, and I agreed that it sounded quite interesting, but once we got to the 'audition', which was above a seedy shop in Wardour Street, I began to have my doubts about the idea. Things didn't bode well when we met the man behind the venture, who didn't exactly look like the next Stephen Spielberg and sounded like a cross between Ray Winstone and Danny Dyer.

'I really want to bring some class to the Soho scene,' he announced earnestly, 'but I haven't got a script yet.'

'I'm not sure about this, Mark,' I said after the meeting, 'I don't really like the sound of it.'

'Look, there's a contract involved,' Mark snapped at me. 'We're going to get our Equity Cards, so do it Michelle. Just do it!'

The Equity Card was everything. As an actor, you just couldn't move without one and as far as I was concerned it was the only thing that stood between stardom and me.

In the end I got on board with the job, just in case it turned out to be something amazing, but as soon as I read the script all my worst fears were confirmed. I can't remember the precise plotline, but one of my big scenes contained the line: 'I'll thank you to keep a civil tongue up my c**t'. I don't think I need to say any more, really.

'I can't do this,' I told Mark. 'I just can't do it. Haven't you cottoned on to what this show is?'

'It's fine,' Mark said, oblivious. 'The audience just come in, pay a fiver, get a can of lager and watch the show.'

'Exactly,' I said. 'It's a bloody sex show. They want us to take our clothes off and Christ knows what else. I'm sorry, I'm not doing it.'

Mark did it, though, and, of course, there wasn't an Equity Card in sight.

I loved my time living on the boat: there's something calming about living on the water, and it was an incredible experience even if it was below freezing most of the time. I have some brilliant, happy memories of those six months. The mix of weird and wonderful people, the wild parties, and all the fun and laughter I shared with Mark, who ended up becoming a close friend. He was a warm and generous person, but at times he could be uptight and difficult, and I think that's because life had been hard for him and he had a lot to deal with. It didn't get any easier, either. Even when Mark was dying of AIDS several years later – still only in his twenties and residing at the Lighthouse Hospice – his family could never accept his sexuality. They wouldn't acknowledge his friends, including me, as we gathered around his bed to say our last goodbyes to him, and we weren't even welcome at his funeral. I sometimes think that if he'd been born just a few years later things could have been so different for Mark. Nowadays coming out might have been easier, and the HIV drugs that are available now would probably have saved his life. By the time he died I'd lost four friends to AIDS, and soon after that I got involved with the Terrence Higgins Trust, attending fundraising events and raising awareness for the amazing work they do for people living with HIV and AIDS. I'm still a supporter of the trust to this day.

CHAPTER 11:

BEATING THE BEAT

I was still living on the barge when I answered yet another advert in a magazine for a job that would set me on a whole new path. It was for an actress to appear in the video for a song called 'Up the Junction' by the London band Squeeze. I played 'the girl from Clapham' mentioned in the song. The director of the video was a guy called Terry Iland, and while we were shooting he told me that a producer friend of his, Tot Taylor, was working with a band and was currently looking for a girl singer.

'Can you sing?' he asked me. 'You could audition for him.'

I thought about it for a moment. Jill and I had done a little bit of backing singing in a couple of our friends' bands, just for a bit of fun, but the only other time I'd auditioned for a band it had turned out to be a bit of a disaster. I was still at college, and I'd turned up for this audition and crooned my way though a Roberta Flack song, 'The First Time Ever I Saw Your Face'. Halfway through the song I realized that the person auditioning me was Malcolm McLaren, one-time manager of the Sex Pistols, and that a white teenage Roberta Flack was probably the last thing he was looking for. The job I was trying out for turned out to be the lead singer of Bow Wow Wow, and Malcolm must have thought I was complete idiot. I certainly felt like one.

'Yeah, I can sing,' I told Terry, shoving all thoughts of that previous disaster aside. Why not? Let's face it: a job was a job at the end of the day!

The audition was at rehearsal studio in north London and it turned out that one of the two female backing singers had left and they were looking to replace her. The whole look of the band was quite sixties retro, which sort of fitted in with my quirky image at the time, and Tot seemed to like the look and the sound of me straight away. I don't remember the audition being particularly thorough: I just sang through a couple of verses of something with the band and he gave me the job. I was in! The band was Mari Wilson and the Wilsations, with Mari, the Neasden queen of soul, as its beehive-haired frontwoman. Originally the band had been called Mari Wilson and the Imaginations, but they were threatened with legal action by the eighties soul group Imagination, so they had to change it. Despite the fact that I'd only really gone up for the job because I thought it would help me get my Equity Card, it was the start of a vibrant and exciting period. Before I knew it I was performing gigs all over the country, and appearing on the same bill as some really cool bands of the time. I'd always loved going to Dingwalls in Camden, so to actually play there, supporting Kid Creole and the Coconuts, was a big thrill. The only trouble there was that the dressing room at Dingwalls was so tiny that with our huge band, plus Kid and all his Coconuts, there were about twenty-five people all trying to get ready at the same time.

The great thing about our set-up was that it was more like a theatrical experience than just a band. Mari liked to put on a show, and when I was out there on stage, dolled up in fabulous vintage dresses and diamanté jewellery with my hair all teased and backcombed, I was playing a role. I wasn't Michelle anymore, I was Candide Collins and I loved it. Other backing singers during my time were Mandy Brown, who became a great friend, Lisa Clime, sister of the songwriter Simon, and a girl called Ingrid Mansfield Allman, who'd had a hit with a song called 'Southern Freeez' a year or so earlier. There were nine guys – six musicians and three backing singers – who were known as The Marines, and the two female backing singers, including me, were The Marionettes. Tot had set up his own independent label, The Compact Organization, and his other main act was his wife, the Swedish singer and former model, Virna Lindt. We put out a couple of records on Compact, 'Beat The Beat' and 'Baby It's True', which almost reached the Top 40. After that I started to feel as though we were poised for success – we all did.

Pretty soon we were appearing on TV shows like *Riverside*, which was a youth-orientated music show, and *The David Essex Showcase*, which was a Saturday night talent show hosted by David, my childhood pop idol. I was so excited on the day we recorded the show, but unfortunately David had very bad flu and when we met him he wasn't in the best of moods. I came away quite disappointed, but at least I got to look at him. He was going out with one of the girls from the hugely popular dance troupe Hot Gossip at the time, and I was madly jealous when I saw them together. Eventually the band got through to the final of *The David Essex Showcase*, coming a respectable second, and shortly after that we landed a recording deal with London Records. It all felt very exciting and once we'd signed the deal we got paid thirty quid a week as a retainer. I didn't really even look at the contract at the time. I was more interested in the fact that we were playing gigs with artists like Marc Almond and bands like Level 42, hanging out at the Camden Palace with Steve Strange, and appearing at cool clubs like Eric's in Liverpool and the Hacienda in Manchester. The Venue in Victoria was always one of my favourite places to go in those days, and we played there with Altered Images, which was a fantastic gig. We were forever up and down the motorway, all crammed into a white van, and there was never a dull moment. We'd be sitting in a Little Chef somewhere along the M1, and in would walk Dave Stewart and Annie Lennox, or Bananarama or The Belle Stars – all big pop acts of the day. We never had any money so I'd be sitting there eating Rice Krispies and Jaffa Cakes most of the time, and every stitch of clothing I had was from a second-hand shop. I had to move back home because I couldn't afford rent, and Mum would forever be feeding various members of the band. I didn't mind a bit, though; I was a budding pop star and I was having fun. We even did some memorable dates abroad, like the time we performed on a TV show in Hilversum in

Holland, which was a bit like the Dutch equivalent of *Top of the Pops*. All around the stage there were gorgeous-looking women, but there was something unconventional about some of them that I couldn't quite put my finger on.

'Phwoar! She's a bit of alright!' I heard one of the boys in the band say, nodding to some of the other guys.

On closer inspection, I realized that although they might have been gorgeous, they certainly weren't all women: we were in the midst of a large group of cross-dressers and drag queens. Still that didn't stop one of the boys in the band copping off and going home with one of the 'girls' after we'd finished the show – there's always one! These days I'd have twigged straight away, but I was only eighteen or nineteen at the time and still relatively naive. Nobody seemed to care about that sort of thing in the clubs or on the music scene back then anyway. In the days before the fear surrounding AIDS took hold in the early 1980s, it truly was a case of anything goes. Drag queens and club kids mixed with plumbers and bricklayers on the London club scene, and there was a vibrancy and creative energy in music and fashion that I don't think we've ever seen the like of since.

What I didn't know was that the rug was about to be yanked out from underneath me, and at speed. We'd recently recorded a few new songs, and one of them, 'Just What I Always Wanted', sounded like a sure-fire hit to all of us. As it got closer to the release of the new record I got a call from the band's manager, Andrew King, asking if I could meet him in the Durham Castle pub in north London for a band meeting. When I arrived at the pub I was surprised to discover that Andrew had only called a few of us: me, Mandy and some of the musicians. Mari and The Marines were nowhere to be seen.

'Look, Mari has decided to go solo,' Andy told us, awkwardly. 'She doesn't need a full-time band anymore. She doesn't need you guys anymore.'

I remember sitting there feeling stunned. Just as things were starting to take off we were being dumped. How could they do this? As it turned out, Andy hadn't exactly been honest about the situation. It turned out that he had just wanted to get rid of certain members of the band, and had advised Mari that it was the best way forward. Paying a group of twelve people every week just wasn't practical when she could simply hire session musicians as and when she needed them. Mari was the face of the band, the star, and there wasn't much we could do in protest. I was out!

It was hard to take in. As far as I was concerned we were doing really well and things were going great, but now, suddenly, it was bye-bye Candie. I hadn't seen it coming and I was devastated when it did. Being in the band had been my one shot at success and I felt like fame and pop stardom had only been a breath away. I was right, too. When a re-recorded version of 'Just What I Always Wanted' was released a few weeks later, Mari and her new band appeared on *Top of the Pops* and the record flew into the Top 20. There were no female backing singers on *Top of the Pops* that night, just The Marines, but not long afterwards Mari did hire some new girls, including Julia Fordham, who later became a successful solo artist. I'd been replaced and it was such a horrible feeling. I'd been a big part of something, doing all the hard graft to help make it happen, and now there was someone else up there, being me. Eventually the song climbed to number eight in the charts, which made me feel even worse. Nowadays I'm good friends with Mari as well as most of the boys who were in the band, but at the time it caused a terrible rift and we didn't speak for quite a few years.

Once it had all ended I tried to convince myself that being a singer hadn't been my dream anyway, and besides that I was never going to be centre stage in Mari's band. I would only ever have been the backing singer. It wasn't exactly challenging, after all. Still, the feeling of rejection was terrible, and the fear of it has remained with me throughout my career. Over the years I've done my best to turn it into a positive experience, telling myself that having such a big knockback at such a young age helped make me the person I am today. I often recount this story when I'm talking to young people who are just starting in their career: rejection needn't always be a bad thing. It made me realize that you should never become complacent or blasé about anything, and that no one is indispensable.

At the time, though, it was awful. I remember staring at myself in the mirror and wondering if it was my own fault. Perhaps the reason I'd been replaced was because there was something wrong with me. Was it the way I looked? Was I not good looking enough? Had I piled on the pounds and become too fat for potential pop superstardom? It was a line of thought that led me down a really dark path, and I didn't even realize it was happening.

CHAPTER 12:

THE SECRET

It started off with me just being a bit more careful about what I was eating: replacing bread with Ryvita, having smaller portions, that sort of thing. As time went on, though, I became more and more obsessed with food and the idea of abstaining from eating. I ate less and less – and the thinner I got, the better I felt. Then I started using laxatives to rid my body of anything I did eat, just in case it made me put the weight back on. Eventually it completely took over my life. Every time I ate something I'd have to purge it from my body as soon as I possibly could. There were times when I'd get up in the night and go through the cupboards like a locust, bingeing on as much as I could possibly get down me. Afterwards I'd jam my fingers down my throat in the toilet until I'd brought up every single scrap of food I'd eaten, then I'd go back to bed again. It turned into what seemed like a never-ending cycle: I'd virtually starve myself for days on end, then I'd binge eat before either vomiting or purging with laxatives. Soon I was doing it after every meal, it was so addictive. I felt that if I could control my body I could control my life, and in my head skinny equalled successful. I weighed myself obsessively and then punished myself if I didn't think I'd lost enough. Surprisingly I didn't find it hard to socialize, because as far as I was concerned drinking was OK; it was food that was evil. Whenever I was at dinner with friends I would order a tiny salad with no dressing and then drink copious amounts of alcohol just like them. I thought it had fewer calories than food. As time went on things got worse and by then I was drinking *instead* of eating, just so I could still go out and have a good time. I managed to go for days without any proper nourishment. When I looked in the mirror I could see that my arms and legs were scraggy and thin – in fact I had the body of a child – but in my mind I was still 'fat' and I wanted to lose more. I started taking stronger laxatives and more of them until in the end I weighed under six stone.

Although I had a lot of friends, I didn't have a boyfriend while all this was going on and I wasn't looking for one either. To be honest, I don't think I'd have been capable of holding down a relationship even if I'd wanted one, because my head was all over the place. My friends and my career were important to me, as were the obsessive control issues I had about food, and that was more than enough. I was very independent. At this point I was still working at Audience Selection in between jobs, and the offices had now moved from The Strand into Covent Garden. During that period we all used to hang out at a bar called Evergreens in Drury Lane, which held special celebration days when the Beaujolais Nouveau arrived. We'd all pile in there for breakfast at 9am (although I wasn't eating much) and immediately start tasting the new wine, staying there all day until our afternoon shift. I always thought the wine itself was revolting, but it was a lot of fun and a great social scene. The bar was opposite the New London Theatre where the musical *Cats* was playing, and one day an enthusiastic theatregoer came in and asked me if I would sign an autograph for her. I was slightly gobsmacked and wondered who on earth she thought I might be.

'Er … what do you want me to write?' I enquired.

'Just sign it "love Bonnie",' she grinned.

It turned out that the woman thought I was Bonnie Langford, who was starring in *Cats* just across the road. I didn't argue, and just went ahead and did it anyway. After all, it was the first autograph I'd ever signed and I was dead proud. 'Much love, Bonnie Langford'.

None of the people who worked with me seemed to notice how thin I was, or if they did, they didn't say much about it, and even my mum didn't really have a clue. I was quite careful to avoid her if I wasn't looking my best because I was afraid she might uncover my secret addiction, but I think because I was a young girl out socializing and partying all the time, most people thought that that was just my wasted look. I never really developed cheekbones until I was thirty anyway, so I always had quite a full face. When I got really thin Mum did take me along to a doctor, who politely suggested that I might want to put on a little bit of weight, but there was no drama about it. No 'let's rush her to the nearest clinic'. I suppose I thought if the doctors weren't panicking about my weight, then why should I?

Around this time there were a couple of actors at Audience Selection who were part of an actors' co-operative agency called Focus, which sounded interesting. I'd managed to get a provisional Equity Card through my time in The Wilsations, so I knew if I joined the agency I'd be able to start going up for professional acting jobs. Two actors, Ian Harvey and Jane Goddard, had started the co-operative and it was run out of a workshop in Clerkenwell. We had a little office with two desks, which would normally be manned by two of the actors. The idea was that there was no hierarchy, and the actors themselves ran the agency. One person would be taking calls while the other one phoned around all the casting directors to find out what was going on and what work might be up for grabs. Theoretically it was a brilliant idea, but it was often the same unfortunates who ended up manning the phones while a lucky few actors flitted from job to job. I had to go up in front of a panel of people who would decide whether I was the right sort of person for the co-operative, and one of the people who interviewed me was Tim Roth, who, as you can imagine, hardly ever had to answer the phones or work in the office. It was 1982 and Tim's career was just starting, but even back then it seemed clear to everyone that he was destined for great things.

I got quite a few acting jobs through Focus, the first of which was at the Half Moon Theatre in Mile End Road, playing an outrageous, politically-driven punk girl in a play about the music business called *HMV*. I was a bit of a Siouxsie Sioux lookalike and when the play went on there was a big picture of me in the *Time Out* listings page. All the performers in the play were supposed to be actor/musicians, so when I went for the audition I lied and told the director, Stuart Mungal, that I could play the trumpet. Yes, I had played the trumpet for a short while at school, but as I said, I left it on the bus and it was never seen again. I certainly wasn't good enough to play one on stage in front of an audience.

'Yeah, yeah,' I said. 'I can play.'

Luckily I wasn't asked to demonstrate and I blagged my way through the audition by doing a bit of singing, but, of course, that sort of lie always comes home to roost and I knew that at some point it was going to catch up with me. After all, I didn't even have a trumpet to play!

In the cast were actors like Gary Shail, who'd been in *Quadrophenia*, Gary Holton, who went on to star in *Auf Wiedersehen, Pet* and Reina James, who was Sid James's daughter. This was my first proper job so I was trying to conduct myself as professionally as I could. I was young, naive and eager to please, but some of the other cast members weren't exactly living like monks. The boys were extremely hedonistic, and I remember being petrified as I witnessed large amounts of alcohol being downed on a nightly basis, just before curtain up. I've since discovered that quite a few actors like a tipple to steady their nerves before they go on stage, but back then I found it quite shocking. I needn't have worried, though. Despite being party boys, neither Gary ever missed a line, and they never missed a show. In fact their performances as an alcoholic father and his drug-addicted son were highly acclaimed by the critics. I have fond memories of the lovely Gary Holton who did his best to look after me and show me the ropes.

''Chell, if you've got any problems, you come to me,' he'd say.

It was Gary who helped me out of the trumpet debacle after Stuart made an announcement at the end of the first week of rehearsal.

'OK, I want everyone to bring their instruments in tomorrow; we're going to start running through with everyone playing.'

I turned to Gary in shock. I couldn't believe that I'd told such a ridiculous lie and I was terrified of what might happen.

'Gary, what am I going to do? I can't do it; I haven't even got a trumpet!'

'Don't worry,' he laughed. 'I'll 'ave a word. He can't sack you now, can he?'

I wasn't convinced, but Gary valiantly saved the day.

'Michelle can't play the trumpet, mate,' he told Stuart. 'She never could. She never will.'

Stuart just shook his head.

'Oh … all right,' he said. 'Not to worry, she can do backing vocals.'

Gary went on to great success as Wayne in *Auf Wiedersehen, Pet*, but tragically died of an overdose of alcohol and morphine in 1985.

Being part of the agency was working well for me. I was going up for plenty of jobs, but the issue of food continued to haunt me, and as time went on it just got worse and worse.

Imagining that I was being terribly healthy, I would go to Neal's Yard in Covent Garden at lunchtime and buy a packet of dried figs, which was hardly enough to keep a person going for a whole day. Then I'd go home and take a handful of laxatives in an attempt to get rid of every calorie I'd eaten before doing it all again the very next day. It was a bizarre way to live, but my addiction was so serious that it became the norm. Things came to a head when I went up for an audition for a well-known employment agency called Kelly Girl, leaving the casting people less than impressed.

'She's not upmarket enough,' they told the agent who'd put me up for the job. 'She's more Alfred Marks than Kelly Girl.'

A couple of people even asked my agent if I was OK.

'She doesn't look very well,' someone said. 'Is she on drugs? She looks like a heroin addict.'

A few of the people at the agency confronted me with some gentle but solemn advice.

'Look, Michelle. You don't want this to start to affect your chances of having a career. Perhaps it's time to take things in hand; you are getting a bit too thin.'

That was an understatement. Apart from the weight loss my teeth started to look yellowy and under the make-up I looked dreadful. I couldn't sleep properly and my menstrual cycle went haywire: I think I went for months on end without having a period. The final straw came when I fell over on the way to an audition one day, ripping my tights. I took quite a tumble and I was pretty shaken up, and when I looked down my knee was bleeding badly. Deciding to skip the audition and go home I flagged down a black taxi, but the driver took one look at me and shook his head, appalled.

'No way, love,' he said, speeding off and leaving me bleeding on the pavement.

I was sure he thought I was a lady of the night who'd been in a scrap and I felt so ashamed. It was the wake-up call I desperately needed, and I realized that if I carried on the way I was, there might never be a way back.

I knew I had to change and now I was determined to do it. Deep down I knew what I was doing wasn't healthy, despite all the times I'd tried to kid myself that it was. Having an eating disorder was miserable, not to mention hard work: it took up all my time and headspace. The subject of food, or abstaining from it, was all-encompassing. It was the first thing I thought about in the morning and the last thing I thought about before I went to sleep at night. I was lucky that I hadn't got to the stage where I was so ill that I'd had to be admitted to some sort of clinic, although I think I was at the point where it could have gone either way. Fortunately, self-preservation and the fear of ruining my career took over and provided me with the push I needed to get better. For a start I joined a gym in Covent Garden, near to Audience Selection, which I saw as a way of keeping trim but being healthy at the same time, but I was almost as obsessive about that as I had been about food. Still, even I could see that being a gym fanatic was a lot healthier than starving myself. That, at least, was a positive obsession. I also went to see a hypnotherapist, which was good for me because I was able to talk openly about my problems with someone who wasn't judging me. Then I started visiting various psychics, hoping that one of them might have the answers to all of my burning questions. Would I have this terrible obsession with food all my life? Would I overcome it and have a career as a successful actress? Slowly I started to realize how skewed my ideas about my weight and how I looked had become. I'd convinced myself that being super-skinny was the route to success, and I now understood that what I was seeing in the mirror was not what other people were seeing. For a long time it was very hard to put food into my stomach without feeling the need to vomit, but I kept telling myself that if I just ate healthily and did regular workouts at the gym, I'd be OK. It was a very slow process, and not something that happened overnight. It took months to change my mindset. I had to train myself to think about something other than food, and in the end, exercise was the obsession that took over.

Some time later, when I was filming an episode of *Bergerac*, I noticed one of the actresses piling her plate high with food in the canteen.

'I'm just lucky, I can eat what I want,' she was bragging.

I can clearly remember the feeling of envy that swept over me at the time, but that night I heard her throwing up in the room next to mine. These days I think there's even more pressure on young women to look good than there was when I was starting out. Everywhere you look, there are magazines and websites saturated with stick-thin models, and, of course, girls often see that as something to aspire to. I see fifteen- and sixteen-year-old girls posting photos of themselves in their underwear on social media like Twitter and Instagram because all their self-worth is invested in their looks, and it scares me. I worry for my daughter and her friends having that kind of pressure.

Anorexia is a mental illness often brought on by trauma or circumstance, but there can be genetic links, too. When I was in my teens and early twenties it was quite a taboo subject, but we all knew the terrible stories about stars like Karen Carpenter and Lena Zavaroni. Today it's a lot more out there in the open and there's more help around for sufferers, but it's still a major problem in our society, for men as well as women. With all the glamorous re-touched images in magazines and on TV, it's no wonder so many people feel under constant pressure to conform to be the 'perfect' size. I have a friend whose daughter went to ballet school. She was a boarder there and every time she returned to school after the holidays she would be weighed. If it turned out she'd put on any weight she was put on a strict diet. As time went on she couldn't take the constant pressure to be thin, and eventually she cracked and left the ballet school, ending up in a clinic with anorexia aged sixteen. Thankfully she recovered, with her family and friends helping her through, and ultimately she realized that it didn't matter that she wasn't a ballerina because she was much happier without the all the anxiety it entailed. She's now a very healthy, lovely twenty-two-year-old.

Others aren't so fortunate, and until we can stop our obsession with being thin and believing that thin equals success, people will continue to try stupid fad diets, forcing themselves into ridiculous and sometime dangerous eating habits. I think you just have to find a way of eating that suits you and that fits your lifestyle. We have to re-educate our kids – and ourselves – about food, to make sure they know that good looks and being a size zero aren't the important things they should be striving for in life. Things will never change, otherwise.

Luckily things did change for me, and I'm probably healthier today than I've ever been. These days when I feel like I've put on a few unwanted pounds I know how to deal with it sensibly and healthily, although I'm still quite fussy about what I eat. If you've had an eating disorder it's always there in the back of your mind. It took me years to get over it and even now I don't even have scales in the house because I think it's bad for me – which is strange after all these years. I don't think it ever truly leaves you.

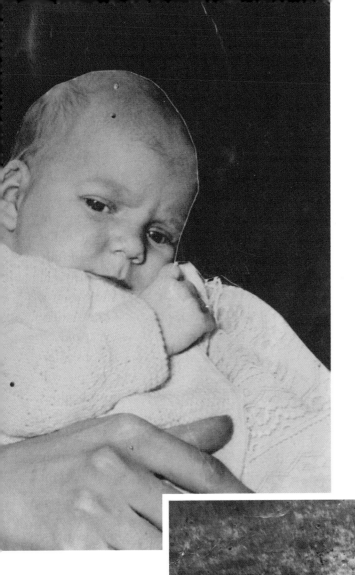

Above - Baby Michelle
– looking like Winston
Churchill!

Left - Me with my sister
Vicki at home in Highbury.

Above - Vicki and I often had matching hair and outfits growing up!
Below - My great-grandmother, Jane Bowen.

Above Left - With Kate and The Woodcraft Folk in Romania.
Above Right - Excited to be on my first school trip abroad, to Italy.
Right - Me and Sid, my mum's partner of over thirty-five years.
Below - My friend Melissa and me in matching jackets – very 1980s!

Top - Performing in my first stage play,
Reluctant Heroes.
Above - In *The Bill* in 1985, playing a burns victim.
Above Left - Me in my punky phase, with my
black bob, sitting in a plant pot on the King's Road!
Right - In my flat in Makepeace Mansions, wearing
my favourite Patrick Cox loafers.

MARI WILSON

THE COMPACT ORGANIZATION

michelle collins get ready

Above Left- On holiday in Greece –
you can see how skinny I became.
Above Right - I'm front row, far
right, with Mari Wilson and The
Wilsations.
Right - My solo foray into the
music industry.

EastEnders - I turned up in a punky outfit and I couldn't ride a bike, but it worked! Fun times with Adam Woodyatt, Susan Tully, Letitia Dean and Gillian Taylforth.

More of my favourite moments from *EastEnders*. It was lovely to work with June Brown again on *Verdict* in 1998.

Above - Mum and Sid.
Left - Does my bump look big in this?
Below Left - Me with beautiful baby Maia.
Below right - Happy times together.

CHAPTER 13:

A JOBBING ACTRESS

Between 1982 and 1988 I was a jobbing actress and I worked steadily. I had roles in popular shows like *The Bill* and *Bergerac*, and in several films, including Stephen Poliakoff's *Hidden City* and *Personal Services* starring Julie Walters. *Morgan's Boy* was my first real TV job. It was a six-part series for the BBC and I was acting alongside Gary Oldman, playing the girlfriend of Martyn Hesford (now a BAFTA-winning writer who used to write for *Corrie*). There was something about Gary that you couldn't ignore. He had a cool and edgy quality and I knew when I met him that he was going to go far. During the filming of one scene he picked a goldfish up out of a tank and everyone thought he was going to eat it. He didn't in the end, but the dangerous air he had about him was quite something. I spent quite a lot of time with him at rehearsals in the BBC studios at Wood Lane, and I suppose you might say developed a bit of a crush on him. We shot the series in Cardiff, and the night before we started filming we all went for dinner and then headed to the hotel bar for a couple of drinks. Later that night Gary knocked on the wall of my hotel room from his room next door.

'Come in for a glass of whiskey – a nightcap,' he shouted.

I was in a real dilemma for a while. What should I do: deal or no deal? In the end I decided that it wasn't a good idea. As much as I would have loved to, it was the first day of filming on my first proper TV role and I needed a clear head.

I could hardly believe that I was filming a TV show. I had an Equity Card, an agent and I really felt as though I was at the start of something good. At first I had a bit of a chip on my shoulder about not going to drama school, because at auditions directors would always ask which one I'd attended. Still, I think they liked my rawness and the fact that I didn't fit into the usual drama school mould. I suppose I was somewhat unique: I had youth on my side, with the potent mixture of naivety and confidence that brings. It was a lot better than blending in with every other actress on the scene. At least I was getting noticed. Every new job I started I saw as another opportunity and a step on the ladder. I was never arrogant and I never took anything for granted. I listened to everyone – older actors and directors alike – because I wanted to learn my trade and I wanted to do it well. At first I didn't even know how to be in front of a camera or where I was supposed to be looking, because it was something we were never taught at college. But with a bit of careful blagging and by paying attention to everything that was going on around me, I soon started to get to grips with the art of acting in front of a lens. And if I didn't know something, I just asked somebody who did.

After *Morgan's Boy*, the director, John Gorrie, employed me again in a sitcom called *Marjorie and Men* with Patricia Routledge. The show was about a divorcee who lives with her mother and is desperate to find a man, but the actress who was originally due to play the mother was involved in a car accident after the read-through. At the last minute she was replaced by Patricia Hayes, who I was totally in awe of. Patricia was a brilliant actress, but sadly not very well at all, and on a few occasions she couldn't remember her lines. It was quite sad to see such a great and well-respected actress struggling like that. The thought of not remembering my lines fills me with absolute terror; it's my worst nightmare. It's like being a builder with no tools, feeling utterly useless. That's why I admire some of the older actresses on *Corrie*; people like Barbara Knox and Eileen Derbyshire. They are pretty word perfect with their lines most of the time, and god help you if you're in a scene with them and you don't know yours.

Marjorie and Men was Patricia Routledge's first sitcom, although she was already an experienced actress, and she was very friendly towards me. I was playing a young girl called Debbie, who worked in a bank alongside her character, Marjorie, and one day she gave me a little set of keys that she said were the keys to success, and a good luck charm. To work with someone as esteemed as Patricia Routledge at such a young age was quite something. It was a great learning curve and, as it turned out, a bit of a stepping-stone. During the filming, John Gorrie offered me some helpful advice which changed my life.

'Look, I think you're really good, Michelle, but I think you need to get yourself a proper agent. There's a new agent called Michael Foster at Larry Dalzell Associates who might be able to help you. I think he'll take you on.'

Michael was one of the hottest agents in town, representing some of the brightest new acting talent. Suddenly my life seemed to be a whirl of various TV roles and lots of commercials, and I got almost every one I went up for: Kentucky Fried Chicken, Dairy Box, French Connection, TSB. For somebody of my age I was making very good money, especially with the residuals payments. I sometimes worked for Tony Kaye, an infamous director of commercials who became a respected film director, *American History X* being one of his biggest hits. One day I was called in to try out for a toilet cleaner commercial that Tony was directing. I met with him and the producer and then I had to improvise talking to a toilet cistern and telling it to open wide. I just wanted to laugh out loud, but of course I had to keep it together, and much to my surprise I got a recall for the part. Tony called me up that night and actually gave me tips on how I should play it. 'Is this guy serious?' I thought; it was only a commercial for toilet cleaner! Anyway, I did the recall but in the end I didn't get the job. I think it was around that time when I realized how crazy the profession I'd chosen could be. I even did a BP petrol commercial with Ridley Scott – I'm still waiting for him to call me back. I had a great time doing a lot of the commercials, but it was the real acting I enjoyed most.

Bergerac was shot on location in Jersey and on our first night there my cast-mate Perry Fenwick and I were excited about starting a new job in a new country, so we decided to hit the town of St Helier. We'd seen the following day's call sheet and, much to our delight, neither of us had any scenes until the early afternoon. Perry made me laugh and we got on famously, and that night we somehow managed to find a pub or a bar that was open for a bit of late-night drinking. It must have been about three or four in the morning when we finally rolled in, and we'd certainly had more than a few vodkas, but as I walked into my hotel room I spotted a note that had been pushed under my door. On it was the terrifying news that the call sheet had changed and that we were now being picked up at 5.30am to be in make-up for six. I was horrified. It was my first day on the job: what were people going to think if I turned up still drunk from the night before? Not very professional, Michelle! What made it worse was the fact that I spent the next hour feeling horribly sick in my room, and by the time the car came to collect me to take me to the location I'd only had about an hour's sleep.

That day I ended up filming in a two-man tent, which was hot and stifling, and I kept thinking I was going to throw up. To top it all, Perry and I were playing a couple of tearaways so there was a lot of dashing around involved. I had to run down the beach and then have a fight with the show's leading man, John Nettles – Bergerac himself – and all I could think of while we wrestled was 'Oh God, please don't let me throw up all over him or breathe alcohol over him!' I was only twenty-two or twenty-three and I had visions of being found out and getting a good telling-off from Bergerac. I think it was the fact that I was young and still fairly resilient that helped me get through the filming, but I eventually came a cropper when I fell over running away from John, and I had to be carted off to hospital with a badly sprained ankle. I remember sitting there in casualty thinking 'Never again. NEVER!' – I felt dreadful. Thank God I was young and could recover quickly. The trouble was, there always seemed to be some sort of social occasion on *Bergerac*, and the very next night there was a party when a new cast member arrived.

After filming *Bergerac*, I did a Screen Two drama for the BBC for a well-respected director called Michael Caton-Jones. It was called *Lucky Sunil* and it told the story of a young Asian guy who comes to London believing he's going to be studying at Oxford University but ends up at a language school in Oxford Street where he gets involved in a porn film. That's where I came in, playing one of the girls in the film – although somehow I managed to get away without showing very much. Michael then went on to direct the movie *Scandal* and I auditioned for both the lead female roles, but unfortunately I didn't get the part of either Christine Keeler or Mandy Rice-Davies. The roles went to Joanne Whalley and Bridget Fonda. I also did a workshop for the film *Sid and Nancy* for Michael, with Daniel Day-Lewis playing Sid Vicious and me as his girlfriend, Nancy Spungen. Neither of us ended up doing the film, but we had a lot of fun working together. Daniel was an amazing actor and real gentleman, but it was my old mate, Gary Oldman, who ended up getting the part of Sid Vicious.

In a TV sitcom called *Running Wild* with Ray Brooks and Janet Key, I played the sulky daughter of a man going through a mid-life crisis. It was my biggest role to date and the cast became like a real family, but sadly Janet died a few years later, still only in her forties. While I was filming *Running Wild*, I was also in the cast of a production called *Burning Point* by John Cooper at the Tricycle Theatre in Kilburn, which had a brilliant reputation for showcasing really credible new plays. The play was quite political, about the SUS laws where the police could arrest someone on sight if they suspected them of being involved in a crime, and I was really happy to be able to be back working in a theatre. Most of the cast from *Running Wild* came down to see the show on opening night, including the show's stars, Ray and Janet, and then we all went out for dinner afterwards. I think I might have done one more performance the night after that, but on the morning of 16 May 1987, Michael Foster called with some unfortunate news. I'd been sleeping in so when I first heard what he was saying I thought it was a joke.

'I wouldn't bother going in today; the theatre has burned down.'

'Oh, don't be ridiculous,' I said. 'It can't have burned down.'

'Put the news on. I'm telling you, the Tricycle's gone and that is the end of your contract.'

I immediately got dressed and went down there, arranging to meet with some of the other members of the cast. It was a terribly sad state, and some of the staff who worked there were in tears. Seemingly a nearby timber yard had caught fire and the winds were in the wrong direction. The entire stage and auditorium were badly damaged and it was left without a roof. Fire again! It seemed to have followed me since childhood … and the play was called *Burning Point*, for God's sake.

I was forever having some sort of a calamity or drama when it came to important work situations. When I was sent to meet Mickey Rourke to be interviewed about a role in his 1987 movie *A Prayer for the Dying* I was nervous but extremely excited. Typically for me, things didn't run smoothly, and this time it was, of all things, the shoes. At the time I had a little bit of a shoe shopping obsession, so there was no way I was could possibly go and meet the gorgeous Hollywood star Mickey Rourke without having a new pair, was there? Plus my agent had told me that I should dress up for the meeting because the part was for an attractive girl. I found a fabulous pair at a shop in Hampstead, but on the day of the meeting when I took them out of the box I realized that there was something amiss. Yep – one was a size five while the other was a seven! I really wanted to dress up and look sexy, though, so I threw another pair of shoes on and took the odd pair with me in a bag so I could slip them on before I went in and hope to God no one would notice. As I stepped into the room where Mickey was waiting I almost turned to jelly, he was so gorgeous. One of the most attractive men I'd ever met, in fact. Meanwhile my feet were in agony with one foot crammed into a shoe that was two sizes too small, but still I did my best to look cool, calm and composed.

'So, it's a movie about the IRA,' Mickey told me. 'Did you know that?'

I nodded. That was about all I did know, as I hadn't had much time to do any research and I hadn't yet seen a script.

'And you don't mind taking your clothes off?' he went on. 'The character has to take her clothes off.'

'Erm … no. I suppose if it's right for the character and it's done in a tasteful way … artistic … then I don't mind that.'

'And you know she's blind.'

'Oh, OK, right. So she takes her clothes off and she's blind. Yes that's all fine,' I said.

All I could think was 'Oh dear. I'm a bit flat chested. He's not going to cast someone with no boobs.'

Still, we ended up chatting for ages, with Mickey asking me about where I lived and the famous Highgate Cemetery. It seemed to go really well, and as I sat there my mind ran wild, with images of Mickey calling me and inviting me out for a romantic dinner at a fabulous restaurant even if I didn't get the part. As I left the room, however, still in my odd shoes, there was Camille Coduri waiting outside to go in after me: gorgeous and voluptuous with the hugest boobs. I was very jealous. 'She's gonna get this,' I thought. 'There's no way I'm going to get this over her'. And I was right! She got the part and I never got to have that date with Mickey.

In 1986 I filmed *Personal Services*, and it was a real highlight of those years for me. It was based on the life of the south London brothel owner, Cynthia Payne, who, amongst other things, famously accepted luncheon vouchers from elderly men who wanted to dress up in lingerie and be spanked by young women. It was directed by Monty Python's Terry Jones, who for some strange reason insisted on calling me Miriam from the moment he met me. He could never remember my name and I was much too nervous to correct him. At the time I could hardly believe that I'd got the job and was actually working on a proper film set, so I wouldn't have said boo to a goose anyway. My role was one of the waitresses in the café where Christine Painter, played by Julie Walters, worked in the 1960s.

'Christine, BCSD!' I warn Julie at the start of the film, when a large man pulls up outside the café in a red Rolls Royce. BCSD, we eventually discover, is code for 'big car, small dick'.

It was just one of many great lines in the film.

Julie was lovely to work with: very attentive to her fellow actors, and along with Shirley Stelfox, who went on to star as Edna Birch in *Emmerdale*, it was a really great cast of actors and a wonderful atmosphere. During the making of the film, the real Cynthia Payne would often drift onto the set to cast an eye over the proceedings. She seemed a really nice woman but the film's creative team, especially the director, didn't exactly welcome some of her comments and observations.

'Oh no, it's that woman again!' you'd hear on a semi-regular basis. 'She's here again. Get her off the bloody set!'

I spoke to Cynthia quite a bit and liked her: she was quite a character. She was funny and loud and called everyone 'darling'. I think she was just very excited about having a film made about her life and she wanted everything to be just right.

The film's opening night was an incredible buzz for me. It was the first time I'd ever been invited to a film premiere, and I decided to take my proud mum along with me. After the screening we partied at Brown's, and the whole night was a blast. It was a very big British movie, and such a big break for me as an actress. I couldn't wait to see what was next.

CHAPTER 14:

ROARING INTO WALFORD

n 1987 I was in a one-off drama called *Pressures*, which was about motorcycle dispatch riders and involved me riding a motorbike. Unfortunately I couldn't actually ride one, so I was just pushed in and out of shot so it looked like was in control of the bike, but for the most part I got away with it. Early in 1988, Bill Lyons and Tony Holland, who'd written the series, suggested to *EastEnders* producer Julia Smith that she should see me for a possible role in the show. He thought I had a 'raw energy and a great look' and sang my praises so much that Julia called me in to meet her. I'd already auditioned for the series once, before it was first broadcast. Back then it was called *E8* and I was up for the part of punk Mary, but by now it was huge and a great opportunity for a young actor.

I was informed by my agent that I was auditioning for the part of a girl called Corinne and that I was meeting one of the producers, whose name was Cindy. That information turned out to be upside down, because when I got there I met Corinne Hollingworth, who told me that the part I was auditioning for was a character called Cindy who ran a hat stall on the market. I was quite nervous by that point, particularly when they told me that I was going to be playing the love interest for the show's main heartthrob, Wicksy, played by Nick Berry. By the time I finally met Julia Smith I was completely petrified. *EastEnders* had made her one of the biggest names on television and she was quite a formidable woman whose fierce reputation preceded her. The last thing I wanted to do was let my nerves get the better of me and screw up my chances. Suddenly I was in a room with Julia, and although she was a little bit scary I was quite at ease once we started chatting.

'I think you'd be great for the role,' she said, matter-of-factly. 'What would you do if I were to offer it to you?'

'Er, well ...'

I didn't really know how to answer her. Was she giving me the part? Was she just testing me to gauge my reaction? I couldn't be certain, but it felt like she was.

'It's just eleven episodes,' she went on. 'Do you want to come down and have a look at the set?'

'No, I don't think so,' I said, somewhat flustered.

I was far too nervous to walk on to the set with the chance that I might bump into some of the show's big stars. They were all household names by then.

'Cindy comes in on a motorbike,' she told me. 'You can ride a bike, can't you, because I watched you in *Pressures*?'

'Yeah! Yeah! Of course I can ride a motorbike, yes,' I spluttered, terrified that if I 'fessed up about the fact that I had to be wheeled on and off the set during *Pressures* I'd lose my fabulous new role as quickly as I'd apparently got it. It was the trumpet all over again, but there was no Gary Holton to help me out of this one.

'If you do *EastEnders* it's going to change your life. You know that, don't you?' Julia said as we got close to the end of our meeting.

'Is it?'

'Most definitely. As soon as you're on screen everyone will know you. You'll be in the public eye; you'll have people writing you fan letters. Everything will change. Do you think you'll be able to handle that?'

Of course I knew how big the show was, but I hadn't really considered what it must be like to be as famous as the *EastEnders* cast were back then, even though I'd already done quite a few professional TV jobs. I nodded and smiled and told Julia that I'd be fine, but truth be told I really wasn't prepared for what was to come.

After I got the job I was due to start quite quickly. In fact, I think it was the very next week. On my first day I sat in the corridor at Elstree with Sid Owen, and although I was, at twenty-six, ten years older than him, I was just as nervous. At one point Anita Dobson, who was then seen as the reigning queen of Albert Square, breezed past us and I was completely in awe. My look then was a bit punky, with short bleached blonde hair and androgynous clothes, and on my first day I turned up in jeans and a leather jacket over a stripy T-shirt, wearing bright red lipstick. It was a strong look, and the woman who was in charge of wardrobe nodded approvingly as I walked in.

'I really like that,' she said. 'Why don't you just wear that?'

All she did was swap my jacket for a proper leather biker's jacket and I was good to go. I was ready to make my grand entrance as Cindy Williams. On a motorbike that I couldn't ride.

The day I started filming on *EastEnders* there seemed to be a mass exodus of some of the show's most popular characters, including Linda Davidson who played punk Mary Smith, and Anita Dobson, who played Angie Watts. I started on the same day as Sid Owen and Sophie Lawrence, who played the teenage children of Frank Butcher. The cast were quite a sociable bunch, and I got on very well with Sid, as well as Gary McDonald who played Darren Roberts and Nick Berry who played my love interest, Wicksy. It was the golden era at *EastEnders* and it seemed as though the entire country knew what was going on in the storylines each week. It was massive and pulling in huge viewing figures every episode. Actors like Mike Reid, Leslie Grantham and Wendy Richard were all in the cast when I arrived, and those first few weeks filming on the show felt really exciting. On my first day, however, I was given the dreaded motorbike to roar into Walford on. Someone excitedly informed me that it was the actual one that David Essex had ridden in the early 1980s movie *Silver Dream Racer*, but I remained unimpressed. Despite being a huge fan of David's throughout the seventies and early eighties, all that bike meant for me was misery and the fear that I might get into deep trouble for lying about being able to ride it. It wasn't huge, but just the sight of it was enough to scare the hell out of me. There was nothing I could do but own up to the director.

'I can't ride it,' I muttered. 'I'm sorry.'

A message went back to Julia Smith that the show's new biker girl had no idea how to ride a bike and by all accounts she wasn't happy.

'Well, just get her some lessons, for God's sake,' she told the assistant director. 'Get her some bloody lessons!'

In the end I did get on the bike to film the scene, but I was still terrified, and my driving skills were just as bad as I thought they might be. As I juddered into Albert Square I veered around wildly, narrowly missing Sue Tully and almost running over Letitia Dean. It wasn't the best start on the show: almost wiping out half the younger members of the cast. It was a nightmare having to remember my lines as well as concentrating on riding that thing, and in the end another order was passed down from the lofty heights of Julia Smith.

'Just ditch the bloody bike. Cut it!'

The green room was the hub of the *EastEnders* set, where all the cast members would gather while they were waiting to film their scenes. Back then it was a much smaller cast and everyone was very supportive of one another. I have fond memories of those early days. Gretchen Franklin, who played dotty old Ethel Skinner, always loved to entertain, and I remember her climbing up on the green room's table, almost eighty years old, and tap dancing for the rest of the cast. Mike Reid was quite a fatherly figure and always very nice to me. One morning I pulled open my car door and hit myself in the face, and by the time I got to the set I had a black eye. Mike looked furious when he spotted me.

'Who did that to you?' he growled. 'I'll 'ave 'em!'

'No, Mike, it was a car door,' I said. 'Nothing to worry about.'

'Don't give me that,' he said. 'They all say that. Tell me who the bastard was and I'll sort 'em out for you.'

You had to laugh at him. At one stage he was off work with a bad back for quite a while. The writers came up with a storyline where Frank was supposed to be upstairs in bed, incapacitated, constantly banging on the floor while his poor wife Pat ran up and down after him. All the viewers heard for weeks on end was a thumping sound accompanied by Mike's inimitable roar, which he'd pre-recorded. 'Pat! Paaaaaat!' Then Pam St Clement would roll her eyes and run up the stairs to tend to him. It seemed to go on for months.

Wendy Richard, who played the no-nonsense matriarch Pauline Fowler, was known as being quite formidable in real life, too, but I always thought her bark was worse than her bite. During my first few weeks on the show I was in the green room swigging from a bottle of Aqua Libra, which was a popular adult soft drink in the 1980s, when Wendy came in and threw me a disapproving look.

''Ere! It's a bit early in the day for that, isn't it, Michelle?' she scowled, assuming that I was on the wine.

Wendy had always been seen as very sexy and glamorous, particularly in her other famous role as Miss Brahms in *Are You Being Served*, and I think she found the transition to playing a dowdy housewife quite difficult. It's the same for many actresses who suddenly go from playing the sexy leading lady to being in the older character roles: it can take a bit of getting used to. The other thing that was hard for Wendy was the fact that the original plan was for the show to be centred around the Beale family and the Fowler family, but because Anita Dobson and Leslie Grantham had become so popular as Angie and Den Watts, they stole quite a lot of the limelight in the early days. Despite all that, I think Wendy was brilliant in the part: very gritty and very real, turning out some incredible performances. Wendy and I got on well; she seemed to warm to me and I sometimes wondered if she might have seen her younger self in me. She was a very private person, and although she never suffered fools gladly, she was often very thoughtful. She used to make a great chilli con carne, and she'd often bring it in to work in little Tupperware containers for some of the other cast members. Eventually I got to know her partner John very well and we often socialized together outside work. I also became good friends with Gillian Taylforth, who played Kathy Beale. She was always great fun to be with, and very popular with the rest of the cast.

June Brown, who still plays Dot, was another of my favourite cast members, and one day she asked me if I'd be up for going with her to visit an ex-cast member who'd unfortunately ended up in prison for a short time. As it turned out, a few of us from *EastEnders* were invited to Ford Open Prison in Sussex to attend the inmates' Christmas pantomime and to take high tea with the governor. We all went along to show our support. The panto was *Aladdin*, and actually very good: it was clear that they'd spent a bit of money on the costumes and scenery. The lead in the show was a very handsome man, apparently a big-time fraudster, and he had a catchphrase throughout the show that made me laugh.

'What's the magic word, children? PAROLE!'

Then he'd march across the stage with a great big card with the magic word emblazoned across it. The funny thing was that the magic must have worked, because a couple of months later I spotted him having afternoon tea at Fortnum and Mason. The prison governor, meanwhile, was very taken with June and after the show, when we were invited into his office, we sipped tea from proper china and ate cucumber sandwiches. It was very civilized and not exactly what you'd expect in a prison, but June was in her element. I've always admired June and enjoyed her company – she was a lot of a fun. In 1998 we ended up working together again, on an episode of a TV courtroom drama series called *Verdict*.

We had a lovely producer called Jane Fallon who'd been working on the show for quite some time but had decided to leave. I organized her leaving do, and after a nice dinner with many of the cast and crew, about twenty of us went to Brown's nightclub and had a fabulous time. Jane brought her boyfriend along, and I promised her we'd look after him as he didn't know anyone. Later in the evening, Jane was happily mingling and talking shop to everyone while her poor boyfriend sat on his own, so I went over to chat to him. He told me that he was a DJ and trying to get into comedy. I thought he was very nice: quiet, but funny and polite. His name was Ricky and he went on to become one of the most successful writer/comedians that Britain's ever produced. A few years later I worked with Jane again, on a drama called *Single*. She's a novelist now, and twenty years later she's still with the same guy, Ricky Gervais.

On the night of the transmission of my first episode, I invited a group of friends over to my then boyfriend's flat so we could all watch together before heading off to the famous Julie's restaurant in Holland Park to celebrate. There was Sharon and Tim, Chris, Bunmi, Melissa, my mum and Sid, and a few other waifs and strays. Everyone was thrilled with the prospect of me making my debut on the biggest show on television. Unbeknownst to me, they'd all made scorecards, and each time I appeared on the screen that night they held them up, comically rating my performance from zero to ten. It was such a big thing, despite the fact that I wasn't in the episode very much, and that night felt like the start of something new and exhilarating.

Even before I appeared on screen I started to get fan mail, but that wasn't uncommon. Fans of the show would know who was coming in, or they'd see your name in the *Radio Times*, and the letters would start. It sometimes still happens now in *Coronation Street* when a new character arrives. Still, I wasn't prepared for the amount of attention that an *EastEnders* actor gets, and my world changed overnight. Pre-Cindy I'd hop on and off the tube without any problem, but that all changed. Everywhere I went, people wanted to stop and talk, or ask for an autograph. It's not that I minded the fame, but if I'd tried to go on public transport it would have taken me hours to get from A to B every time I left the house and sometimes the attention could be a bit overwhelming, scary even. So from then on I had to drive everywhere, or take taxis. Twenty-five years on things have changed and now I use public transport all the time, despite the fact that I've recently been in one of the most watched TV shows again, and I've been on TV every other weekday. Maybe it's because I'm older and I've lived with it: I know how to deal with it now. Or maybe it's because fame and celebrity are much more accessible these days, and people just aren't as excited about it as they once were – particularly in London. Whatever it is, it makes life a lot easier.

The other big life change for me was being able to buy my first one-bedroom flat: 100 Finborough Road, West Brompton. It felt like a real turning point for me, like I'd finally arrived, and I felt a real sense of achievement and contentment on the day I moved in and shut the door behind me. I had no furniture, just a sound system and a pouffe on the floor, but I didn't care. 100 Finborough Road was all mine – well, the mortgage was anyway! One of the best things about the flat was its location: a stone's throw from Chelsea, with all its trendy bars, cool stores and smart restaurants. The place became a social hub for all my friends – old and new – and a real party flat. It felt like the start of a new life, a defining era, and a time when I met many of the people who became my closest friends. People like drag queen extraordinaire Yvette, who ran the most fabulous club nights at the Fridge in Brixton, where I was a regular. She shared a flat with Dr Mark Winward, who was an HIV and AIDS specialist, and the person who first encouraged me to get involved with campaigning for the Terrence Higgins Trust. He was a regular guest at Finborough Road and we became very close, and when we weren't dancing the night away at the Fridge, we'd be heading off to the gym together or wandering around the North End Road Market in Fulham. We also used to frequent Portobello Road all the time; you could always find cool, cheap clothes or furniture at the market there, and we'd always have a greasy fry-up in Mike's Café, or go to a bar or a restaurant in the evening. It was such an exciting time, and my days and nights in that little flat were some of the happiest of my life.

These days *EastEnders* is on four nights a week, but when I started it was only on for two. The rehearsals were on Saturday morning and we recorded throughout the week, and although it was hard work, it certainly wasn't as high pressured as it is now on a major soap with the amount that actors have to learn and film every week. On the studio days we'd arrive in the morning and rehearse and then start filming after lunch. In the corridors of that Elstree studio, you were almost guaranteed to bump into some of the comedy heroes of the day, like the cast of *'Allo 'Allo* or assorted members of the *Hi-de-Hi!* team. I loved filming on the days when *Top of the Pops* was being recorded, and I'd look forward to seeing which bands and pop stars might be hanging out in the BBC bar later in the evening. The lot, which included the square and all the outside locations, was about five minutes from the main studio block, and eventually we had Portakabins as dressing rooms. I got into the swing of it fairly quickly, and although initially I was only supposed to be in the show for eleven episodes, fortunately the producers saw something in me – and Cindy – so they asked if I would consider staying on and I was offered a year's contract. My agent at the time, Michael Foster, advised me not to do it, thinking a long run in the show might pigeonhole me as just a soap actress. Plus I was going to have to turn down a couple of good jobs. Michael wasn't sure I was making the right decision.

'Your career could go in one of two directions here, Michelle,' he warned. 'Think about it carefully.'

I liked the idea of staying on *EastEnders*. For any actor, the prospect of regular paid work is appealing, and I was really enjoying the job. I decided to accept the year's contract and go for it. I was lucky because I was given some great storylines as Cindy, and she became famous for being Walford's most notorious siren and all-round wicked woman. I discovered that the more I gave in my performances, the more the writers created for me, and I lapped up all of Cindy's juicy plot twists and bitchy lines. I didn't even consider the fact that it was a soap opera; as far as I was concerned, I was acting in a serious drama, the scripts were so good. It wasn't as action-packed and spectacular as some of the soaps are now, but it was more about relationships and the interaction of the characters. It was people talking. Some of the early two-hander episodes were amazing. I particularly remember the one with Ethel and Dot in the launderette in 1987: bravely written and wonderfully performed. It was almost like something Harold Pinter or Alan Bennett might have written.

In my story, Cindy was engaged to Ian Beale, played by Adam Woodyatt, but she got pregnant by another man, Simon Wicks, when they had sex on the floor of the Queen Vic pub after closing time. During her pregnancy Cindy kept the identity of the real father a secret from Ian and married him anyway, but eventually she ran off with the baby's real father, leaving Ian heartbroken. She was a fantastic character to play, and it all stood me in good stead for what was to follow. It wasn't all sex and scandal, however. For much of the time, Cindy had to earn her keep in her husband Ian's fish and chip shop, and to make it look authentic the producers sent me to do some training in a real fish and chip shop in Wembley. By this time, I was quite famous and there were so many curious people staring through the window while I sliced potatoes badly and learned to deep fat fry bits of cod that I had to wear a baseball cap. In the end, there was even a photographer from *The Sun* snapping pictures of me through the window. People must have thought I'd been sacked from the show and had ended up frying fish as an alternative career. 'Something to fall back on'.

However big the show got, there was still a great community feel within the cast. Even the extras were a big part of the show: Big Ron, Winston, and Tracey behind the bar. They all had their own defined characters, although the actors playing them are now known as supporting artists rather than extras. There was no one-upmanship between the cast and we all mixed and had a good laugh on and off set. It was a supportive family environment. Some of the boys, like Sid Owen and Nick Berry, played for the *EastEnders* football team, and we all used to go and support them at weekends – sometimes all over the country. I couldn't believe some of the girls who threw themselves at the boys, giving them their phone numbers at the end of the match – real *EastEnders* groupies. It's quite frightening what some girls will do to get to their idols. I remember one girl actually punching me out of the way to get to Sid Owen. You wouldn't mess with them, that's for sure. I think PR guru Max Clifford was even on board for a while, representing the team. That's how big the whole thing was.

During my first stint on *EastEnders*, 1988–90, the show just seemed to get more and more popular. There was even a reference to *EastEnders* in the infamous Princess Diana 'Squidgygate' tapes, where Diana compared herself to Cindy Beale, likening her situation to my character and worrying that she might be pregnant with a child that wasn't her husband's. Such was the power of the show in the 1980s and early 1990s. It's funny; there's quite a lot of snobbery around the idea of being in a soap, and some actors say they wouldn't even entertain the idea, but I think for a young actor or actress who's willing to work hard it can be a fantastic springboard and a chance to show off their talent. It certainly was for me, and I resided happily on Albert Square for the next two years before deciding that it was time to spread my wings again.

CHAPTER 15:

THE WORLD'S WORST TV PRESENTER

In 1991, being a presenter on *The Word* was one of the most coveted TV jobs around. The live, post-pub Friday night show was chaotic and anarchic and featured live music, celebrity gossip and interviews, plus gung-ho members of the public competing in surreal games and making fools of themselves just to get on television. Some of its most memorable musical moments included the television debut of the band Oasis, Nirvana performing 'Smells Like Teen Spirit' for the first time on British TV, and a very drunk Oliver Reed singing 'Wild Thing' with a live band. I was fresh out of *EastEnders* when I auditioned, and at the time I thought it looked like a lot of fun, as well as being a distinct gearshift from a twice-weekly soap opera. From what I heard they considered a huge amount of people, but they must have seen something in my screen test, because I eventually got the job.

Presenters Terry Christian and Amanda de Cadenet were already well established on *The Word*, and when I was asked to turn up at a photocall for the show, Amanda completely ignored me. She just wouldn't speak to me and I didn't have a clue why. I recently read an interview with her in *The Sunday Times* in which they asked her whether there was any truth in the rumour that she'd refused to talk to me when she first met me.

'Who's Michelle Collins?' was her answer.

If there's one thing I've learned about myself, it's that I'm the worst TV presenter in the world. Terrible. However, Charlie Parsons, *The Word*'s producer, seemed to think the whole thing would be a breeze for me, and decided to take my autocue away so that my delivery would be fresh and unpretentious.

'You're an actress,' he told me. 'You're a natural; it'll be fine.'

The problem was I just didn't have the confidence to pull it off, so most of the time it was more rabbit in the headlights than anything else. You need to be ballsy and brave to be a presenter and interview celebrities, and you need a certain amount of ego. Standing next to the super-confident Terry Christian and the young and pretty Amanda, who was known for her wild-child celebrity lifestyle and her rock star boyfriend, I felt quite vulnerable. Being an actress I was used to having a script and a director who told me where to be and what was happening, but *The Word* was steeped in chaos, because that was the essence of the show. I couldn't cope with it.

Some of the interviews I did were shambolic to say the least. When Brigitte Nielsen came on the show she was quite specific about what she didn't want me to talk about before we started the interview.

'You can ask me about anything,' she said, 'but don't ask me about my boob job and don't ask me about Stallone.'

I thought 'What the hell am I supposed to ask you about, then? The price of a pint of milk, Brigitte?' We sat there on the sofa with the cameras rolling and I nervously started asking her questions, but all I could hear was the director screaming into my earpiece.

'ASK HER ABOUT HER T**S! ASK HER ABOUT HER BLOODY T**S!'

The trouble was, Brigitte seemed really nice to me and I didn't want to offend her.

'ASK HER ABOUT STALLONE!' the director bellowed into my ear.

In the end I yanked the earpiece out and threw it onto the floor, I was so angry. It just seemed really awful to start questioning a woman about her body like that, but afterwards the production team wasn't very happy with me.

On another occasion I blurted out in a live interview with Kylie Minogue that a friend of mine who owned a shop in Kensington's Hyper Hyper had claimed they'd sold her a pair of handcuffs a week earlier. There was a sharp intake of breath in the studio, and Kylie looked at me as if to say 'That was a bit random; where did that come from?' I thought that's what the show wanted, a bit of edgy controversy, but it felt like I could never get it right. Chris Isaak, on the other hand, was the most engaging and handsome man I had ever met. He played his guitar for me as if I was the only woman in the world and I fell in love with his smooth, velvety voice. I could have fallen in love with him right there and then, but there was a rumour that he was dating Helena Christensen, who'd appeared in the steamy video for his single 'Wicked Game'.

When I was sent to interview Sting on location in Newcastle I was petrified. The idea was that the cameras would follow him around some of the places that had been significant in his past: his first school, the first place he'd worked, that sort of thing. The trouble was that there was a blizzard that day so we ended up in a room above a pub, and all the questions for the interview had to be hastily rearranged and rewritten thanks to the change of location and set-up. I was nervous enough to start with, but the fact that his future wife Trudie Styler was there and appeared to be watching over him like a hawk made it seem even worse. And I was slightly in awe of him, which is never a good thing for an interviewer, so I felt out of my comfort zone and a bit tongue-tied from the off. Sting downed a couple of whiskeys before we started and he actually seemed friendly and quite grounded, but he was clearly intent on giving me the runaround and having a bit of a giggle with me.

'So what was the first thing you learned to play on?' I opened with.

'The linoleum,' he smiled.

'Oh, what's that?' I said, intrigued. 'I've never heard of that instrument.'

'The *lino*,' he clarified.

I was mortified and some of the crew around me started to giggle. I thought 'This is going really badly'. I think Sting felt a bit mean after that, so the rest of the interview went a bit more smoothly, but by that point I'd realized that TV journalism might not be the best choice of job for me.

I was even shipped off to America to interview the kids from *Beverly Hills, 90210*, which sounded exciting but turned out to be tougher than I imagined. Luke Perry and Jason Priestley were affable and co-operative, especially Luke, who was quite charming, and they showed me around the show's set, but the rest of them were a bit more difficult. Word came back that Shannen Doherty didn't feel like being interviewed, and I never saw hide nor hair of the other *90210* girls. On the same trip I interviewed Vanilla Ice on a bus, and a famous rapper – now turned actor – who kept me waiting for hours. One minute during the interview the crew were all making dirty jokes about carpet burns and the next the rapper was preaching to me about God while we walked along the beach in the blazing sunshine. I just wanted to walk away shouting 'I don't give a damn!' I'd been given some fabulous clothes to wear on the show by the designer, John Richmond, but everything was black and there was a lot of leather, so it wasn't exactly suitable for working under the hot Californian sun.

In New York on the same trip, my favourite interview was with Harvey Fierstein. He's a rather outspoken gay actor who wrote the play and movie *Torch Song Trilogy*. Harvey was very articulate and had something to say, which was a refreshing change from a few of the people I'd interviewed on that trip. We were doing a piece about 'outing' because at that time there had been a few famous names whose homosexuality had been publicly revealed by a New York magazine called *OutWeek*. Harvey was commenting on the story, and he was hysterical. He also had the deepest voice I'd ever heard.

By the time I left America I really was over the whole thing. Most of the people I'd interviewed seemed fake to me, and on more than one occasion I'd wanted to turn around and tell someone that they were talking a load of old rubbish and I didn't believe a word of it.

As far as my interviewing technique went, I lacked the bravado to be controversial, and I had too much self-respect to be sycophantic, so I was on to a loser. By then I hated the job. I was desperate to get back to acting and I wanted out. Unsurprisingly, I wasn't asked back for the next series.

'I don't think it's really you, Michelle, is it?' Charlie Parsons said towards the end of my run.

'No, Charlie, I don't think it is.'

After that I shipped myself up to Ayr in Scotland to perform in a terrible play called *Anyone For Murder* with the late Barry Evans. It was a ridiculous farce in which I had to wear a swimming costume and a stupid wig, and for most of the show I was dragged around the stage by various members of the cast. One minute I was in a cupboard, the next I was being pulled down the stairs and shoved under a sofa. It was one of those panic jobs that I took on because I was worried about being out of work for any length of time. One of the members of the cast was a lovely woman called Carolyn Jones, who'd played tart-with-a-heart Sharon Metcalfe in the long-running soap *Crossroads*, which I'd loved and grown up with. I recently remembered one very embarrassing conversation I had with her where I remarked on the show's awful wardrobe.

'Those terrible outfits they used to make you wear!' I said.

'Darling, they were my own clothes,' she laughed.

One night during the run I stopped off at a burger stand with some of the cast after the show. All of a sudden, I was aware of a man lumbering towards me with his hands completely covered in blood. I froze on the spot but then he spoke.

'Can I have your autograph, please, Michelle?' he said.

Once I was back in London a few weeks later, the police came down to interview some of the cast about the mysterious man we'd met at the burger stand. It turned out that a short while before I'd signed his autograph he'd murdered someone at a nearby nightclub, and then toddled off to get himself a snack – seemingly without washing the blood off his hands.

It gradually dawned on me that I may have jumped the *EastEnders* ship a little too soon, and that the grass wasn't necessarily greener outside Albert Square. I'd left without really having a goal or a vision about what I was going to do next; at the time I just thought I might like to do a bit more theatre. I suppose I was worried about being typecast as just a 'soap actress', and let's face it, I was always worrying about something! So when Nick Berry had announced he was leaving the show it just seemed as though it was the right time for me to try my luck in the outside world too. I'd got itchy feet and missed the challenge of playing different roles. Since leaving I'd done quite a few plays, including a couple with Nick (*Strictly Business* in Southampton and John Godber's *On The Piste* in Hornchurch) so when the producers asked me to go back to *EastEnders* I decided to say yes. Nick and I were both offered the chance to take *On the Piste* into the West End, but at the same time as I was asked back to *EastEnders*, Nick landed his most defining role as PC Nick Rowan in *Heartbeat*, so we both turned it down and sadly missed out on a West End run. I'd really missed acting in front of the camera, and after being out in the big wide world for a while, I decided to return for another adventure in Albert Square. Cindy was back!

CHAPTER 16:

PARTY TIME

There was something special about the 1990s for me, despite the fact that the country was in recession for the early part of the decade. I was lucky enough to be working and didn't have to worry about money, I wasn't thinking about the future, and I was enjoying myself. It was 'Cool Britannia', and London was the perfect place to have fun, with outlandish raves and parties, and a fabulous social scene. In the early nineties we were all listening to the cool new wave of bands coming from the north of England: Oasis, The Stone Roses and The Happy Mondays. It was the first time since punk that music felt alive again, and it all added to the excitement of the era.

My friends and I could often be found hanging out at my friend Aldo Zilli's bar on Dean Street, the Wag Club, Kettner's or the Soho Brasserie on a Friday night, or Fred's, which was a private members' club. Brown's was a place where you could bump into Naomi Campbell, Mariah Carey or any number of other big stars on any given night, and there was a mantra that all of its regular patrons adhered to: 'what happens in Brown's stays in Brown's'. In an unlicensed after-hours drinking club called Jerry's I was partying with several members of the cast of *The Bill* one night, when suddenly there was a police raid. The guys were terrified of being photographed being hauled out of a late-night drinking den by the police – the photos would inevitably be spread all over the tabloids. How would that look to their producers and the general public seeing as they were in a TV show playing officers of the law themselves? In their inebriated state they were certain that they'd all be sacked, so as the police entered the building they dashed into the bathroom and climbed out of the window. I was almost hysterical watching a bunch of well-known actors all trying to squeeze through a toilet window. I think I must have been coming out of the same place as dawn broke one morning when my friend Damien and I thought it might be entertaining to ride around Soho on the back of a dust cart.

'Let's help with the rubbish collection,' Damien suggested.

It was one of those ideas that somehow seems hilarious after a night out. So we jumped on the back of the cart and went around helping the dustmen for about half an hour. Thankfully, there weren't that many people about at that time in the morning. What must it have looked like: Cindy from *EastEnders*, dragging bin bags across Old Compton Street and chucking them on the back of a dust cart at 5am?

Soho was a very friendly place back then; seedier and a lot less family friendly, but it had a real heart. Everyone seemed to know one another, and in those days there were different gangs for different nights. There was a Fred's crowd, a Brown's crowd, and there was always a party at somebody's house. I'd rented out my flat at Finborough Road and was I was now living in an apartment on the tenth floor of Plantation Wharf in Battersea, which had beautiful views of the river and right across London. It was a brilliant place for entertaining and I had some very interesting and eclectic social gatherings there. One party I hosted included Dale Winton, Steve Strange, Natalie Imbruglia and Pat Cash, plus my mum, my sister, my aunt and a handful of *EastEnders* cast members. I loved mixing different crowds of people together and this was the perfect place to do it. 'It' girl Tamara Beckwith came to an impromptu party there once, and I walked into my kitchen to find her in a pair of Marigolds, up to her elbows in washing up.

'Hi Tamara, you OK?' I said.

'Yes!' she said aristocratically, while staring dreamily out of the window. 'Isn't this a lovely view of all the council estates?'

Just that vision on its own kind of sums up the crazy, random nature of the 1990s for me: Tamara Beckwith washing up in my kitchen, musing innocently on the beauty of the local council flats. Tamara was always very good fun, and I also hung out with Tara Palmer-Tomkinson, who was convinced that I was psychic. In those days, after a couple of glasses of wine, I would have a crack at a bit of amateur psychometry as a sort of party trick, where I'd take a personal object from somebody and then tell them their fortune. Tara told me that everything I'd told her during my mystic readings had come to fruition, and after that I found myself in demand as a celebrity fortune-teller wherever I went. I'd be at a party or with a group of friends in a restaurant and someone would thrust their watch into my hands and beg me to tell them what might lie ahead. TV presenter Richard Bacon reminded me of this long-forgotten skill only recently when I was appearing on his daytime quiz show *Show Me the Telly*.

'I remember being in a club with you when you grabbed my watch and told my fortune,' he said.

'Really?'

'Yes, and it all came true!'

I'd spent a fortune on psychics myself when I was in my late teens and early twenties, during the worst days of my eating disorder, and I was a little bit obsessed. I think one of them must have told me that I had the gift myself, and that I should bestow it upon whoever crossed my path. 'Mystic Miche', they used to call me. It was hilarious, but I was actually very good, although I'm sure some people just thought I was completely mad.

There was an Italian girl called Anna Miani who used to have the most amazing parties at her house in Shepherd's Bush. It was there that I met the artist Harland Miller and art dealer and gallery owner Jay Jopling, who was at the cutting edge of the arts scene in the 1990s. I was forever at gallery or exhibition openings back then. There seemed to be so much cool and interesting stuff going on, and it was always great fun. I'd often find myself chatting to fascinating people at these events: painters, writers and a whole host of brilliantly creative people. It was a thriving scene and there was a lot of talent around. Most of the people I went with never actually bought anything, though; they just turned up for the free booze and a half-decent canapé.

In 1992 I even met the great David Hockney at his home in California. At that time I'd become very friendly with Michael Cashman and his boyfriend, Paul Cottingham. Michael had played one of soap's first gay characters, Colin Russell, in *EastEnders* from 1986 until 1989, and was part of the first gay kiss in a British soap opera. He later went on to become a founder member of the lesbian and gay rights charity Stonewall with Sir Ian McKellen and is now an MEP. Paul had been a regular film extra on *EastEnders* and that's how we'd all become friends, and in 2006 I was a witness at their civil partnership alongside Sir Ian.

Virgin Airways had lots of parties back then and they were always very generous if you made an appearance at one of them, often giving you flights as a thank-you. I think I'd only shown my face at one of their events, but I was offered two free transatlantic flights. That was the sort of thing that happened when you were a famous face in those days. Anyway, I asked Paul if he'd like to come along with me for a little Californian mini-break and he agreed.

It turned out to be a memorable trip for a number of reasons. On the way over on the plane we bumped into Carol Decker and her group T'Pau. They seemed like good fun, and we all started on the brandy cocktails from the minute we buckled our seatbelts. Carol sensibly went to sleep fairly quickly, but the rest of the band stayed awake talking to us for the next twelve hours. In the end I couldn't even see straight enough to fill in my immigration form. In those days you could still smoke on a lot of long-haul flights, so we were all puffing away and drinking as if we were in a nightclub. It's hard to imagine doing that now, in fact I'm exhausted even thinking about it, but that was the nineties for you. We must have still been a bit tiddly when we landed, because when Paul and I attempted to get into our convertible hire car we spent half an hour trying to yank the roof down manually, almost breaking the bloody thing. Eventually it dawned on us that all we had to do was press a button that completed the task automatically and we ended up crying in hysterics. I guess one of us must have sobered up enough to drive in the end, but I don't want to think about what might have happened if we'd been stopped.

We stayed at the Ramada in West Hollywood and we ended up spending a lot of time in various gay bars such as the Abbey on Robertson Boulevard. I'd had no idea that the area we were in was the gay haven of Los Angeles, but nevertheless more often than not I'd end up going home to bed before midnight. We certainly had a lot of fun hanging out and meeting various weird and wonderful characters along the way, though, and boy were there some characters! One night in the bar of the hotel, we met a very friendly Israeli doctor who, amongst other things, injected the penises of porn actors to keep them aroused during a long day's filming. Through him we met the famously well-endowed porn superstar, Jeff Stryker, at a party. As far as I knew I hadn't met any porn actors before, certainly not any famous ones, but Jeff struck me as a very ordinary guy and we all happily chatted the night away. At some point during the evening, Jeff kindly gave Paul a little parting gift.

'Here's a copy of my new movie on video,' he said. 'But make sure you post it! Whatever you do, don't try to go through customs with it.'

Paul took the video, not wanting to offend Jeff, and then we sort of forgot about it. This was certainly turning out to be a memorable trip.

Paul knew David Hockney, who was a supporter of Stonewall, and the two of us were invited to David's house for the day. David was charming, but he'd recently had a heart attack so he wasn't feeling all that great, and while he chatted to us he was slowly walking on a treadmill in the living room. It was all slightly surreal. There he was, this brilliantly talented and ridiculously famous artist, on a treadmill and chatting to us about his mum,

Laura, who he adored. In time, lunch was served, and although I was going through one of my vegetarian phases, I was far too self-conscious and timid to mention the fact when a plate of chicken was placed in front of me. I just kept quiet and ate it. I knew a bit about art, but I was no expert, so it was one of those times when I decided to keep my mouth shut so I didn't make a fool of myself. I knew that I loved David's work, however, and I was completely captivated by him.

David's house was incredible. It was a typical Laurel Canyon chalet-style house, surrounded by palms and overlooking the Hollywood Hills, and I think his chef and gardener lived next door. In the garden was the famous kidney-shaped pool, which had been captured in many of his paintings. At one point during the visit, Paul started nudging me, and motioning towards the window.

'Michelle,' he said under his breath. 'Go and stand over by the window and look reflective.'

'What? Why?'

'Well if David likes the look of you he might ask to paint your portrait.'

So, as nonchalantly as I could, I drifted over and stared wistfully out of the window, hoping that David might suddenly be overwhelmed with inspiration and feel a desperate need to immortalize me on canvas like Celia Birtwell, his famous muse. I don't think he even looked up at me once, so I never got him to paint me, but I did successfully bid for one of his lithographs at an auction a few years later. I'll always cherish the short time I spent with him. It was a memorable day, and an incredible experience.

I was bound to get stopped as we headed through customs at Gatwick. I'd bought a pair of shoes for the guy I was dating at the time, Gary, and I'd also bought a pair for myself, and I was lugging two great big Gucci bags with me – one on each arm.

'Are you sure you don't have anything to declare?' the customs officer asked as Paul and I breezed through the 'nothing to declare' channel.

'Well ... yes, I've got these,' I said, sheepishly.

'And what about you, sir?'

I could see that Paul looked a bit embarrassed, and it suddenly dawned on me that not only had we forgotten to post Jeff Stryker's video, but we had it with us in our hand luggage.

'Er ... yeah, I've got something,' Paul said, honestly.

'Oh no,' I muttered under my breath.

Paul took the video out of his bag and handed it over to the officer.

'What is it?' the man asked, peering at it.

'It's a porn video,' said Paul.

'What's on it?'

'I don't really know,' Paul said, 'because I haven't actually seen it yet. Someone gave it to me.'

'Well what sort of porn is it?'

'I think it's probably gay porn.'

The man nodded and then disappeared with the copy of Jeff's new celluloid masterpiece, then about half an hour later, while we waited in a room, he came back.

'It is what you say it is,' he informed us, 'but I'm going to have to confiscate it and I'm also going to have to take your passports away.'

A couple of the customs officers had recognized me, and they seemed to find the whole thing quite amusing, but I was horrified with the thought of having my passport taken.

'Look, it's nothing to do with her,' Paul heroically protested. 'It's my video and it was in my hand luggage. It's not her fault I was carrying it.'

In the end they just took Paul's passport and we had to wait ages while the whole thing was being sorted out.

Michael had been waiting for us in the arrivals hall at Gatwick ever since our flight from LA had landed, but he didn't seem angry at all, in fact quite the opposite. It turned out that Pamela Stephenson had also been on the same plane as us, and while Michael was waiting he'd got chatting to Pamela's husband, Billy Connolly, who was there to meet her. Not only did Billy later donate the proceeds of one of his shows to Stonewall, but he also introduced Michael to Elton John, who became a patron of the charity. Elton and his manager, John Reid, ended up donating £50,000 each to Stonewall. Michael always tells me that if it hadn't been for those Gucci shoes he might never have got that kind of support from Billy or Elton.

I was also a big fan of Brighton in those days, because I somehow felt a bit more anonymous there. I used to head down there regularly with a large group of friends, including my girlfriends Sharon, Debbie, Melissa and Bunmi, and we'd often head to the Zap Club on the beach front. We always seemed to find ourselves in the most ridiculous situations. On my birthday one year – it might have been my thirtieth – I decided that I wanted to have a party, and my PR managed to blag me a huge top floor suite at the Grand Hotel at a knockdown price. Mind you, I hadn't exactly been honest about what was going to be happening in the room.

'Oh there'll just be a few of us coming up,' I said nonchalantly.

There was a huge group of us, however, including Sid Owen and a big crowd from *EastEnders*, Paul O'Grady, Michael and Paul, my friends Dr Mark, Tim, and Yvette, plus all the girls. We all went to a restaurant first, so we didn't even get to the Grand until midnight, but somehow we managed to sneak in loads of crates of beer and wine, a sound system and about eighty guests. Pretty soon the party was in full swing and we got away with it for about an hour, but eventually the hotel manager put his foot down and we all got chucked out.

People were unashamedly hedonistic at the time, and in the nineties London was one of the best places in the world to party. It was fun, fun, fun, and we weren't embarrassed to show that we were having a good time. Mind you, I was never into big raves that much. I didn't fancy partying in a muddy field in the middle of nowhere. No, I liked a bit of glamour. So if the party was in some fabulously decked out house in town, or perhaps the beautifully lit grounds of a stately home, I was there, but other than that I wasn't a fan of dancing around in a kagoul and wellies, or being stranded in the middle of nowhere in the early hours with no sign of a London cab. That being said, I worked just as hard as I played. I was certainly never one to rest on my laurels, and as much as I loved hanging out with my friends at the weekend, I was always ready to start work again on a Monday morning, despite the odd hangover. I had a keen work ethic, which, I'm glad to say, is something I inherited from my mum. In many ways I think my generation has been very lucky. As well as living through some of the most vibrant and exciting decades, there's never been a war on our doorstep, and as a woman I was able to take advantage of opportunities that my mother and grandmother would never have been given.

CHAPTER 17:

THE TWO-YEAR ITCH

When I sat down to write this book I decided that I didn't want to list every man I've ever dated or had a relationship with, dedicating a chapter or section to each of them. For a start they can't defend themselves against anything I might say, and secondly I've never been keen on the idea of being defined by the men in my life. They're just part of the story. Suffice to say, there have been some relationships that have meant a great deal to me, and some that I'd just as soon forget. I know the song says '*je ne regrette rien*', but I do regret a few and I've certainly made some mistakes. Haven't we all? These mistakes usually tended to happen when my confidence was low, and I think if I'd felt better about myself at the time I wouldn't even have contemplated some of them. I'm quite old-fashioned, though, and as far I'm concerned you don't wash your dirty linen in public, as the old saying goes. There have been a few frogs in my life that never turned into Prince Charming: men who were rather less than gallant and who didn't treat me with the greatest respect. Some of them perhaps deserve less discretion than I've shown on these pages, but I just don't see the point in being vindictive. It's so negative, exhausting and time-consuming, so these days I tend to be a bit more relaxed about it. That being said, I may in some cases have forgiven, but I'll never forget. The other thing about my relationships is that none of them, so far, have gone the distance. You've heard of the Marilyn Monroe movie *The Seven Year Itch*; well my itch seems to have more of a two-year turnaround.

I remember once, before the era of mobile phones, sitting alone in my flat, waiting for my latest crush to call me. I'd stayed home all evening, completely terrified to go out in case I missed his call. Hours I sat there until I finally decided to take myself off to bed and watch TV. That was when the phone went, of course, sending me leaping out of bed like a mad woman to answer it. I was in such a panic to get to the phone that I tripped over the TV lead, knocking the damn thing to the floor with a huge crash and smashing it into bits, and by the time I picked up he'd already hung up. I didn't have his number so I couldn't get hold of him, and I took that as a sign that I probably shouldn't see him again. To be honest, I'm not sure I ever did. The most upsetting thing about it was that the TV had been a parting gift from a friend who'd moved to Australia, and her dad had told me to keep hold of it because it was cool, retro and sure to be worth a lot of money one day. Still, there it was at two o'clock in the morning on the bedroom floor of my flat in Finborough Road, in bits. A sad casualty of my desperation for a second date.

People always ask me questions like 'How do you deal with sex scenes?' or 'What was it like kissing Ian Beale?' I'm not really a person who talks about sex much, to be honest. I tried to read *Fifty Shades Of Grey*, but it really wasn't for me. Luckily I haven't had to do too many sex scenes in my career, but there have been a couple of steamy moments. Still, I can rest assured that there isn't any dodgy old footage of me out there, and there certainly won't be any Michelle Collins sex tapes cropping up. As far as I'm concerned, the first rule when doing a kissing scene is no tongues – well, it used to be when I started out but I think the rules have changed a bit now. I've always got off lucky because I haven't fancied many of my leading men, or I might have found those scenes a bit trickier. I have had some gorgeous men playing opposite me, but when I work closely with someone I tend to get to know them as a mate rather than a love interest.

In *Real Women* I had a scene where my character was raped up against a wall on her hen night. David Schofield, a brilliant actor, was terribly worried about hurting me and kept on asking me if I was OK. Eventually I said, 'Let's just go for it, shall we?' We did it all in one take, and it was pretty horrible and quite graphic to say the least, although certainly not gratuitous. Afterwards, both David and I were relieved it was all over, but we didn't speak to each other for a while because it was such a shocking thing to act. We knew it had worked, though, and the director was very happy.

On another occasion I was doing a drama called *Perfect*, where I played a serial bigamist called Julie. Nicholas Gleaves (later to star in *Scott and Bailey*) was one of my husbands, and we had a scene where we had come through the front door and strip each other's clothes off as we went up the stairs. We'd been both dreading it for a while, and decided that on the night of the shoot we'd bring in a miniature shot of alcohol each for a bit of Dutch courage. After all, there was no dialogue to remember, just lots of heavy petting. So just before the cameras rolled we took a swig of whiskey each and just went for it. We had flesh-coloured underwear on so no one was going to really see anything, and this was ITV primetime, not *9½ Weeks*. Again, we did it in one take with a cameraman following us up the stairs, filming us throwing our clothes off as we went. It went so quickly I can hardly remember a thing about it, apart from the fact that it was bloody cold. The director loved it, though, which was a huge relief.

I've been very lucky to work with some wonderfully charismatic leading men over the years – Brendan Coyle, Martin Kemp, Stephen Tompkinson and Stephen Moyer to name just a few – but I've not always been so adept at picking out the leading men in my real life. I once went out on a date with a guy called Paul, who I met through a mutual friend. For our first date he asked me to go for dinner at the Blue Elephant Thai restaurant in Fulham, and although I didn't know much about him, he seemed like a really decent, attractive single guy. As we approached the door of the restaurant that night I was aware of someone shouting close by, but I couldn't see anyone.

'You bastard! How can you do this?'

All of a sudden a woman jumped out of the bushes leading up to the restaurant, wearing her pyjamas and screeching like a banshee.

'You've done it again, you bastard!'

Paul didn't even look that surprised.

'Oh God, what are you doing here?' he said as she dashed towards us. 'I told you it was over.'

I was stunned, but clearly not as stunned as the woman was when she came face to face with Cindy Beale off the telly.

'Oh God! It's you!' she said, blinking at me. 'Oh no, no! Cindy from *EastEnders* ... why? I always really liked you. No!'

Paul was desperately trying to calm her down and stop her making fools of all of us outside a busy restaurant, but by then she was far more interested in me than she was in her apparent ex.

'Well I wouldn't bother with him; he's a real bastard! A complete and utter shit,' she said. 'He told me he wasn't seeing anyone and here is with Cindy from *EastEnders*.'

In the end, Paul calmed her down and got her to leave, but then he acted like nothing had happened.

'Sorry, that was just an old girlfriend,' he said, calmly. 'Shall we go in?'

Dinner was quite strained, as you can imagine. I couldn't believe he'd just dismissed this woman, who he'd clearly been having a relationship with, and then treated the incident as if it was nothing. Paul clearly wasn't the man for me and I never saw him again after that night, but I did bump into the woman again, strangely enough, one night in a bar some years later.

'I was that mad woman who came screaming out of the bushes in my pyjamas,' she said, blushing.

We ended up chatting, and she was fully dressed this time.

'Well he was a bit of a weirdo, wasn't he?' I giggled over a glass of wine.

'Yes, I told you not to go out with him, didn't I?' she said. 'Although I think I was more upset by the fact that I liked you in *EastEnders* and thought you were too good for him!'

It was a lovely moment, and the two of us laughed our heads off about how ridiculous the situation had been.

It wasn't the only weird date I've ever had, either. On another occasion a guy I went out with asked me if I'd kept the red bathing suit I wore on TV.

'What red bathing suit?' I asked, confused. 'I haven't got one.'

'The one you wore on *Baywatch*,' he smiled.

It turned out that he'd looked me up on the internet before our date, and got me confused with an American actress of the same name.

A lot of girls I knew had the dream of meeting the perfect man and having a big white wedding, but I was the complete opposite. I never wanted what everyone else seemed to want, including Vicki, who married quite young. She had her own ambitions of working with children and she achieved that. My dream was to be an actress, and I knew I was going to have to forfeit quite a lot of other things in life if I was going to make it happen. It wasn't that I wanted to be famous, and I certainly wasn't thinking about money. I was just passionate about the idea of being on stage or in front of a camera, and I felt like acting was a part of me. Other things were going to have to go, and that's probably why I put my career before any relationships that came along. I suppose in a way I was far too selfish. When you're an actress you have to be slightly selfish if you want to succeed, especially when you're starting out. That can be detrimental to any relationship. Whenever I did get involved with someone romantically there always seemed to be something that stopped me from going the distance. Perhaps it's because I've always believed that a failed relationship isn't as bad as a failed marriage, or perhaps it was Vicki always telling me that you should date a man for at least two years before you even consider marrying him. Whatever the case, the fact remains that although I've been engaged a few times, I've never made it all the way to the altar.

In many of my relationships I've been the chief breadwinner, and I sometimes wonder if it's my own insecurity that draws me to men who aren't as financially secure as I have been over the years. I've shied away from dating anyone famous, and I couldn't stand the thought of dating another actor. I think the clash of fragile egos might be too much. I've known couples that were both actors and despite the fact that things have come a long way, it's often the woman that has to compromise her career simply because she's the one giving birth and looking after the children. I read recently that Helen McCrory's pregnancy cost her the role of Bellatrix Lestrange in the *Harry Potter* movies. It's nobody's fault, but just the way things are.

Even when I was younger, the idea of dating someone who wanted to 'look after me' was unappealing. It wasn't that I didn't like the idea of having a bit of money, but it had to be money that I'd earned myself, not something that had been handed to me on a plate. I'm fiercely independent and have always looked after myself. I guess you might say I'm a feminist at heart. Maia has recently displayed the same attributes.

'I want to earn my own money, Mum,' she says. 'I don't want to get married just to be kept by a man.'

It makes me happy that she wants to be her own person, but I hope it doesn't stop her from finding happiness. I sometimes think that my stubborn determination to stand on my own two feet has been a millstone. I also believe that being a woman in the entertainment industry isn't always conducive to a happy, healthy relationship. It certainly hasn't been in my case. I'm usually the one in a relationship who's always busy, who's always travelling, who's trying to have a career while being a single mum, and sometimes there isn't an awful lot of time for much else. That's me, though. I'm a doer and I try to work hard and I can't see myself changing. Even when I've been with a partner I've still considered myself a single parent. I want to keep things happening all the time, and I want to make sure the people around me are being looked after. Deep down I'm probably a bit of a control freak: scared of letting go of the reins for a second in case it all goes to pot. I went back to work much too soon after Maia was born, and that's why I've always got the fear hanging over me that my next job could be my last, so I want to keep moving. Some men find that hard to deal with, I suppose.

Maybe that's why so many of my relationships have been doomed to failure or have fallen at the last hurdle – just out of earshot of those much-heralded wedding bells. Perhaps if I'd chosen another profession, things might be different. Perhaps I'd have gone for a different type of man – who knows?

In the late eighties I almost made it to the altar ... well, sort of. I was in my late twenties, dating a man who was a nightclub owner living in Spain. We'd met while I was on holiday with Vicki and still working on *EastEnders*. During that time I would finish work on a Friday and dash straight to the airport to catch a plane out to Fuengirola to see him. We were together for about eighteen months, and we were even engaged for a while once I'd left the show. There were all sorts of exaggerated stories about us oversleeping and missing our own wedding, but the truth is we didn't even get as far as booking it. We'd planned to get up and go down to Marylebone registry office one Saturday morning to book the big day, but in the end we never got out of bed so it simply never happened. I think that says a lot about my attitude to weddings in general! Even if I did get married, it would probably be something I'd do quickly and without too much fuss. I can't imagine myself planning a big fancy wedding; I'd be more likely to jet off into the sun and get married abroad. Like many long-distance relationships, that romance foundered because of the space between us. I couldn't move to Spain and he didn't want to move over to England, so we decided to call it a day.

CHAPTER 18:

FABRIZIO

One man who did have a very big impact on my life was Fabrizio Tassalini. The first time I set eyes on him I was in Miami with my stylist pal David Thomas and his partner, Ollie, my friends Caroline Sterling and John Barrett, plus a few other good mates. I loved hanging out in South Beach, and I took several trips out there with my friends in the mid-1990s. I was at the height of my *EastEnders* fame, and sometimes I preferred having nights out there because nobody really knew me apart from the odd British holidaymaker. I appreciated the anonymity of being in America, and felt like I could let my hair down a bit more because nobody was bothered about who I was or what I was doing: a far cry from my life in London. In Miami I was free to be Michelle. Nobody was staring at me or shouting out 'Cindy' every five minutes as I walked along the street. Don't get me wrong, I loved the fact that people in Britain were enthusiastic about my television persona, but sometimes I needed a break. I wanted people to like me for me, not because I was on the telly.

A few friends had recommended South Beach to me, and as soon as I got there I fell in love with the place. It seemed to be full of vibrant, crazy people on rollerblades and skateboards, dressed in the coolest clothes. The bars, restaurants and clubs were fantastic, catering for a real mix of ages, and there were stylish new hotels cropping up everywhere – even Jack Nicholson had a hotel there.

It was the place to be. We'd usually stay at the Raleigh on South Beach, which is a beautiful art deco hotel, and my friends and I would all take suites and adjoining rooms on the top floor. It was such great fun and I always had the most fabulous time.

It was on my third trip to Miami that I met Fabrizio, around Christmas 1995. We were all at a club called Bash, which was part-owned by Mick Hucknall and Sean Penn, when I spotted him across the room.

'Oh my God! Who is that gorgeous guy?'

He was so striking it was impossible not to notice him. David looked over and smiled.

'I'll go over and get him for you if you like,' he said.

'No, no, don't do that,' I said, slightly flustered. 'I was just saying how handsome he is; don't go over there.'

'It's fine,' David assured me, heading towards the unsuspecting man. 'Leave it to me.'

The conversation didn't last long. As far as I know, David simply said, 'My friend really likes you, would you like to come and join us?' Not that clever, but certainly efficient! The next thing I knew, Fabrizio was sitting at our table and we were talking – although not in any great depth because he was Italian and neither of us were particularly accomplished in the other's native tongue. Still, we did our best and it was clear that we were getting along very well. Fabrizio was from Milan and working as a mechanic for Harley Davidson. He was in Miami for some kind of motorbike convention and I told him I was an actress, playing the whole thing down as much as I could. He seemed so nice, and was even more handsome up close. Dark hair and brooding eyes: I remember thinking that he looked a bit like Rudolf Nureyev. Real movie star looks! It was virtually love at first sight as far as I was concerned, but for a moment I was haunted by the grim memory of a previous romantic encounter in the same glamorous setting.

A year or so earlier, I'd dated a London taxi driver called John. Not my usual type, but very handsome and quite charming in his way – or so I thought. During the first few weeks we were dating

I'd planned a trip to Miami and I invited John to come with me, even offering to buy his ticket. John was very enthusiastic about the idea of the two of us going away together, and as I stepped onto the plane I pictured the two of us sipping cocktails and enjoying a wonderfully romantic time beneath the sunshine and palm trees. Things didn't get off to a great start, however, when we had a huge row on the very first day. It was all over something stupid, but John ended up storming out of our hotel room and to my surprise he never came back. I was quite taken aback, but what could I do? It was clear that we weren't really a good fit and I should probably never have invited him. Looking back I think he saw me as a bit of a meal ticket, rather than a girlfriend, but I'd just been too naive to see it back then. I had no idea where John had gone or what he was doing until couple of days later when I was shocked to see him walking along the beach with a Swedish girl, apparently without a care in the world. I was furious, of course, but I was also very hurt. I couldn't believe that someone who I'd been dating could come away on holiday with me and then go happily waltzing off with another woman without a single backwards glance. At the time I thought it best to ignore him. I felt like he'd just used me to get to Miami and then disappeared, and I was angry and embarrassed. What made it worse was the fact that I got flu and ended up spending the next few days in bed, alone in my hotel room. I was fed up and feeling very sorry for myself. As soon as I was feeling better, I headed out to a nightclub with my friends in an attempt to put John behind me. Unfortunately, John had decided on a night out with his new girlfriend in the very same club. This time I saw red, marching over and giving him a left hook, right in front of his girlfriend. The smile disappeared from his face and I ran outside: shocked at what I'd done but secretly quite pleased.

After that I just wanted to forget all about John and our disastrous trip, but a couple of days later he called me at the hotel.

'What time's the flight back to London?' he said, as though nothing had happened.

I couldn't believe the cheeky sod was expecting me to meet him at the airport with his ticket home. For a while I considered leaving him stranded in Miami, but one of my friends said that might be a step too far. In the end we flew home together and I was stunned when, during the flight, he suggested that we picked up right where we left off the moment we touched down in London. I was appalled at the thought, but looking back it doesn't surprise me. John was too handsome for his own good, completely narcissistic, and a serial womanizer.

Of course I was hoping for much greater things when I met Fabrizio, and for the first four or five days after we met, we were inseparable. In those days, in South Beach, nobody ever seemed to go to bed, so we all hopped from one restaurant, club or hotel bar to another each night before spending the day on the beach, and Fabrizio and I never left each other's side. After a few days, however, my gang of friends decided that the weather was so terrible that we should head to sunnier climes, and somebody rustled up a swift package deal to the Cayman Islands, which is about an hour and a half away by plane and a bit like Blackpool for Floridians. The trouble was, I didn't want to go. I'd come over all 'lovesick teenager' so the last thing I wanted to do was leave my gorgeous new man. I wasn't about to abandon my mates, though, so off I went, but as soon as I got there I wanted to get the plane straight back to Miami. The place seemed to be chock full of overweight Americans and all everyone wanted to do was eat. Meanwhile there I was, totally lovesick – and to top it off, the weather wasn't that much better than it was in rainy Miami. It was back in the days before everyone had mobile phones, and the whole time I was there I was desperate to get in touch with Fabrizio. I only had the number of the small hotel he was staying in, so it wasn't easy, but when we eventually spoke I told him that I was coming back to Miami and we planned to spend New Year's Eve together.

I don't remember exactly where the party was that New Year's Eve, but we were all outside on a beautiful terrace and I had an amazing time with Fabrizio. It was all a bit of a blur because by that point I was completely head over heels in love with him and it was all I could think about. He was charming and incredibly handsome. In fact, I used to get a bit miffed when we walked along the street together because he'd be turning so many heads – both male and female. When he left to go back to Milan I was very sad, but despite my strong feelings for him we didn't really make any solid plans, simply promising to keep in touch. It seemed implausible that we could make any sort of relationship work. For a start, he didn't speak great English and I spoke virtually no Italian, we lived in different countries, and I was full on with *EastEnders*. How would it ever work? Practical or not, deep down I knew it wasn't the end of Fabrizio and me, and once I was back in London I couldn't stop thinking about him. We talked on the phone every day that first week I was home.

'Shall I come over and see you?' I asked him during one of our lengthy calls.

'Yeah, OK!' he said.

The following weekend I was on a flight to Milan, and when I got there nothing had changed.

Fabrizio rode an old Norton motorbike, which was odd because he'd once been on the Ducati riding team until an injury prevented him from riding. He also had a huge motorbike in his living room, just for show, and a beautiful big dog called Jack. He lived in a nice flat in a really great part of Milan, which wasn't the prettiest of cities in my opinion, but it was more exciting than Battersea and I happily whizzed around Milan on the back of Fabrizio's bike like Audrey Hepburn in *Roman Holiday*. Everything seemed perfect. The language barrier, although tricky at times, didn't seem to be an issue. We were in love and that was all that mattered. Then about two months into our relationship, and after three trips to Milan, I started to feel a bit sick and I had a constant metallic taste in my mouth. I felt very odd; extremely tired and nauseous. I knew something wasn't right, so I did a pregnancy test without saying a word to Fabrizio. Then I knew for sure: I was pregnant. I was both nervous and excited at the same time, and for the rest of that day I walked around with butterflies in my stomach. I just didn't know what to do next. Although I felt ecstatic I was worried on so many levels. What would Fabrizio say? What was I going to say to my mum, who hadn't even met the father of her future grandchild? And then there were my bosses at *EastEnders* to consider. Were they going to have to weave my pregnancy into the storyline? Whatever was about to happen, I was certain of one thing. My life was about to change forever.

CHAPTER 19:

BABY ON BOARD

'd had a strange feeling on the night I met Fabrizio. It was almost as if I knew he was going to be the father of my child. I'd heard a few women say that and I always thought it sounded ridiculous, but here it was, happening to me. There was an amazing connection and chemistry between us right from the start, and now my mysterious premonition was coming true. Once I realized the pregnancy test was positive, I actually felt fine and surprisingly together about the situation. I decided that whether or not Fabrizio supported me, it was going to happen. I was going to have this baby with or without him, and I was quite prepared to be a single mum. I was thirty-three years old and I felt like I was ready. In fact, I'd been getting broody for a while and I felt like my body clock was ticking. Sure, there was work to consider, but by then I was already feeling a bit restless, and I'd started to feel like I needed a change and that something was missing from my life. It wasn't like things were bad by any means: I had a great job, good friends, a lovely flat and a full social life, but I'd had no serious relationship to speak of for ages and work suddenly seemed less important. Maybe this had come at exactly the right time; it was as if the last pieces of the jigsaw puzzle had finally come together.

Still, I had no idea what Fabrizio was going to think about impending fatherhood. He already had a ten-year-old son from a previous relationship, and at thirty-six, he was settled into a happy single life, living alone with only his beloved dog Jack for company. When I broke the news to him on the phone, he too was surprisingly calm. There was a long silence, and then he said:

'Michelle, are you sure?'

'I am sure, yes.'

'OK,' he said. 'Whatever happens, we can deal with it. It's fine. Maybe I should come to London.'

'No, it's fine,' I said. 'I'm OK. I don't need you to rush over. I'm just going to carry on as normal.'

I didn't really have a game plan as such; I only knew that I had some important decisions to make.

I decided to hand in my notice at *EastEnders*, but when I told the show's chief producer, Corinne Hollingworth, I was quite nervous. Cindy Beale was a big character in the show, and I knew that she wouldn't be keen on losing her. Corinne was nice enough, but she was a tour de force, and certainly no walkover by anyone's standards. Still, when I broke the news she was surprisingly relaxed about it, congratulating me on my pregnancy and assuring me that they'd give me a great exit story – which is exactly what they did. Then I told some of my fellow cast members, the first being my on-screen husband Ian, played by Adam Woodyatt. He immediately told me to take folic acid and said it was the best thing that could have happened to me. Then I told other friends in the cast like Gillian Taylforth and Michael French, who were both full of congratulations. Once they all started joking about knitting me bootees I felt like a huge weight had been lifted from my shoulders.

Although Fabrizio knew that I appeared in a very popular TV show, he had no idea quite how popular that TV show was, or how famous the cast were. As our relationship grew and news of my impending motherhood hit the papers, things got difficult. It all started when I was travelling back and forth to Italy to visit Fabrizio during my pregnancy. The paparazzi tailed me everywhere, and on one occasion a group of reporters even followed me onto the flight to Milan. This was in the days before phone hacking, but somehow the press always seemed to know where I was and what I was doing. The air stewardess was very apologetic because it was clear what was going on, and she asked if I'd like to sit in the cockpit with the pilot. Once I got to Milan the airport staff put me on one of those little golf carts so I could make a quick getaway. It was ridiculous, really. The trouble was, it didn't stop there. Fabrizio and I would come out of a restaurant or the door of his apartment and there would be photographers waiting – we couldn't get away from them. They even started going to his place of work when I wasn't around. This didn't go down well with his boss, especially when a reporter started calling and hassling him for information. It got so bad in the end that Fabrizio lost his job. It was very sad, totally unfair, and I felt terrible. He'd lived a pretty down-to-earth life before I came along, but now his personal life was being raked over and he couldn't get his head around it. They seemed to want to dig up everything they could about his life: his ex-partner, his son. All things I already knew about, but it made life difficult for both of us and I just didn't know what I could do to stop it.

I think I might have been the original innovator of the handbag that got bigger and bigger with the baby bump. I like to think I paved the way for pregnant actresses with that particular idea. Not that I wanted to cover my pregnancy up. Apart from the occasional paparazzi pictures of me looking tired and awful, I really loved being pregnant – it suited me.

I actually didn't care about the photos anyway; I was comfortable within myself and with my growing bump and I felt a huge surge of contentment. It was a very happy time, and even though Fabrizio wasn't with me every day I felt very settled. I decided to move out of my rented flat in Battersea and stay in North London, closer to the *EastEnders* set. The producers told me that they were going to give me a really heavy storyline leading up to my exit, so there was a lot of filming on the cards. Being closer to work would make life a lot easier, and in the end I decided to stay with friends until I found somewhere I wanted to buy: a proper home for my baby and me. I lived with David Thomas in Bermondsey for a while, and then I stayed with my friend Marie Barrett in Highgate. Marie was a masseuse who gave massages to a lot of the *EastEnders* cast, which meant I was lucky enough to get one every night. I felt happy and satisfied. I was being challenged at work, living healthily, and being pampered by all my friends. I was excited about being a mum and about where my journey was going to take me after *EastEnders*. Not having a place of my own meant that I had no responsibilities apart from working and looking after the baby growing inside me. Life felt very simple.

In the story, Cindy was having a major affair with David Wicks, played by another of the show's heartthrobs, Michael French. He was very popular and a real pin-up, and over the course of the affair I had lots of intimate moments with Michael in a Portakabin. We worked closely together right up to the end of my time on the show, but it wasn't always easy and we certainly had our ups and downs. Michael had a good sense of humour, though, and he often played tricks on me. On one occasion I'd just had my teeth whitened and Michael drew a daft picture of a great big set of gnashers, which he kept flashing in front of me every time I went to say a line. In the end I gave in because I just could not stop laughing. I did see the funny side of it that time. Sometimes I went along with his jokes, and sometimes I didn't – especially when I was pregnant, hormonal and less tolerant that I'd normally be. Still, we got through it, and eventually our paths crossed again when I did a five-episode guest spot on *Casualty*, in which Michael played a surgeon. We had a good chat about the old days, and it was lovely to see him again. I'm glad he's back in *EastEnders* now – he plays David Wicks so well.

The great storyline I had in *EastEnders* seemed to go on and on, and I started to wonder when I might be able to stop work. Some of my scenes were quite hazardous, too. In the story, Cindy was fleeing the country with her lover and children after hiring a hit man to shoot her husband, Ian. In one scene Barry Evans, played by Shaun Williamson, was driving us across London to catch the Eurostar. In the midst of all this, Shaun announced that he only had a provisional driving licence, and I suddenly found myself hurtling around the Waterloo roundabout with one of the worst drivers I've ever been in a car with. I sat there, white-knuckled, thinking 'He's gonna kill me. He's gonna bloody kill me!' Shaun, meanwhile, thought it was hilarious. Around the same time I also remember trying to lift up the two kids (Cindy had twins) and feeling a painful twinge as I did. 'I can't do this anymore,' I thought; 'I need to stop now.' Until then I'd still been working out at the gym, despite being shouted at by an old lady one day who insisted that I shouldn't be doing exercise while I was pregnant. Once I felt that pain, though, I knew it was time to take it easy. However, filming a big exit storyline involving planes, trains, automobiles and babies was always going to overrun, so the producers asked me if I'd mind staying on longer to finish it off. In the end, the production team put me up in a nearby hotel, just so I could be as close to the set as possible. They wanted to do everything they could to help me and I was very grateful. They were even kind enough to provide me with a driver to take me to and from the studio: a lovely young man called Oliver Kent, who was then a runner at the BBC and is now the executive producer of *Holby City* and *Casualty*.

I was getting up in the morning, going to work, and then sleeping as soon as I got back to my room. I was exhausted! I even fell asleep at one of my antenatal classes because I was so tired. Despite that, I did what I consider to be some of my best work during that busy time. I was utterly focused on work and on my baby, and that was it. My gynaecologist, Richard Sheridan, was wonderful, but he wasn't happy with my heavy filming schedule, and in the end he laid it on the line after measuring me during a visit.

'You're really small, Michelle; you need to stop work. It's getting too much.'

By that time I was in the middle of completing on a new house, so what with that, the pregnancy and the huge work commitment it was all getting a bit stressful. Thank God I had my friends all rallying round to help me. I went to the producers of *EastEnders* and told them that I needed to stop as soon as possible, and by the time I did I was eight months pregnant.

As soon as I finished on *EastEnders*, Fabrizio came over to

London. He had no job to keep him in Milan now, and we both decided that it was time for us to become a proper family, ready for our new arrival. He moved into my new house in East Finchley and for a while we were living in one room while the place was being done up. My mum, my sister and my friends all loved Fabrizio, and I did my best to make him feel like part of my family. I couldn't believe how lucky and euphorically happy I was because I had something that success or money couldn't buy. Some things, however, weren't as simple as that. Even though Fabrizio knew I was a well-known actress and that I was in a popular British television show, I don't think he realized quite how massive the furore around *EastEnders* was until he landed in London. Once he'd moved in with me, photographers and reporters were constantly following us, and Fabrizio found that very hard to take. I'm not sure I fully appreciated his dilemma at the time. Not only was he living away from his home environment in a foreign country, but he'd also been thrust into the public eye as someone who was dating a soap star, having his every move scrutinized by the press and media. It was clear quite early on that he found my fame difficult to deal with, and looking back I can't blame him. Eventually my publicist suggested that if I went to one of the papers and gave them the exclusive about Fabrizio and me, perhaps their curiosity would be satisfied. This seemed like a sensible notion to me. It was early on in our relationship and I thought if I gave them what they wanted now, they might leave us alone. By that point I was ready to do just about anything to end the constant intrusion and speculation about my private life. Fabrizio wasn't that keen, but I guess even he could see the logic behind it. In the end I went to the editor of a national newspaper, and Fabrizio and I did an interview together.

Unfortunately the piece didn't turn out the way I wanted, and I realized it hadn't been such a great idea after all. I naively expected the article to be a nice low-key piece about the two of us and our excitement about becoming parents, but sadly that's not what people want to read and the whole thing felt very sensationalized and frivolous. For a start it was all over the front page and then spread across a double page inside for three days, and the way it read made me sound like a complete idiot. I felt embarrassed and exposed, as if everyone was laughing at me. It was as if the lovely little romance that I was enjoying was being ridiculed, and I felt very let down by it all. The editor of the paper found out I wasn't happy and sent me a big bunch of flowers with an apology attached. It was at that point that I realized that you can never really control or court the press and there's no point trying. One of the reasons I'd done the interview was because I felt so guilty about Fabrizio losing his job, but if anything I'd made it worse and only added fuel to the fire. Nothing changed after that; in fact it got worse.

Despite all this, it was a very exciting time for me. I was deliriously in love and I was really looking forward to becoming a mum. My waters broke at five o'clock on the morning of Saturday 28 September, and I woke Fabrizio to tell him that we needed to get ready to go to the hospital, which was in Watford. This was quite a long way from home but it was near to the *EastEnders* set, and one of the hospitals where Richard Sheridan was based, so it seemed easier to have the baby there. I was lucky enough to be able to have my own private room in an NHS hospital and to have the same person looking after me throughout. Sadly this isn't always possible, but I think it should be every woman's right to have that continuity of care throughout her pregnancy. It can be a scary time as well as joyful, and it was a real comfort to me to have the security of that one-to-one relationship from start to finish. The problem was, I hadn't really worked out the timings of getting from my house to the hospital, and after first getting lost on the way we then got stuck in the most terrible traffic. In fact, by the time we got to Watford the whole place seemed jammed with cars. I remember going round and round this one roundabout, trying to find the hospital and thinking 'I've known for months that I was going to have a baby, so why do I now feel so disorganized and in a complete panic, lost in Watford?' I was in absolute agony by the time we got there, and as far as I was concerned I was ready to give birth. The nurses that greeted me, however, had other ideas.

'You're only two centimetres dilated, Miss Collins,' one of them told me. 'Go home.'

'I'm not going anywhere,' I protested. 'I'm staying here.'

'Oh don't be silly, you've got ages!'

'I'm not going home!'

Still, they wouldn't give me any pain relief even though I was in a lot of discomfort. They gave me a hot bath, a TENS machine and then gas and air, but by then I was in no mood to hang around, and typically, everything I'd been taught in my antenatal class went straight out of the window. As soon as Richard got there I was given an epidural, and by this time my mum, Sid and Vicki had also arrived – although poor Mum popped out to get something to eat just before I gave birth and missed it all. My daughter was born at 2.30pm, weighing in at 6lb 14oz. Fabrizio was there throughout, and Vicki counted all her fingers and toes as soon as she was born – just to make sure.

It wasn't the easiest of births, though, and in the end Maia was delivered with forceps. I won't go into too much detail, but I could barely sit down afterwards and had to stay in hospital for a week. Most people get flowers or fruit when they're laid up but my friend Debbie Arnold, who later played my sister in *Real Women*, bought me a huge cabbage instead.

'Darling, you've simply got to have this. Your breasts are going to be very painful. You need to stick it in the fridge and then put the cold leaves around your boobs to take the swelling down. It works wonders.'

She was right as well, and although it didn't smell too hot it was very soothing. Whenever one of my friends has a baby now I'll always deliver them a cabbage rather than flowers. It's far more useful and much cheaper.

I got so many cards and bouquets after Maia was born and you couldn't move for visitors every day. Fabrizio stayed with us the whole time, sleeping on the chair next to my bed throughout the night. When I eventually left the hospital with my little girl, I was on cloud nine. It was hard to take in. I'd gone into the building with this bump in my tummy, and now here I was leaving with a real life-sized person in a little tie-dye yellow babygro from Portobello Market. Two had become three. As I carried Maia in her car seat I realized that I didn't even know how to strap her in, it was all so alien to me, but once she was safe in the car we made our way home: me crying with joy all the way because I had so much love for her. It was a bit surreal, but there she was: Maia Rose Tassalini Collins. Our daughter.

CHAPTER 20:

SAY HELLO, WAVE GOODBYE

Six months before Maia was born I'd signed up to do panto at the end of the year. I guess I'm a workaholic and I get a bit panicky when I haven't got any work lined up, which was the case after leaving *EastEnders*. I thought I'd be fine bouncing back to work just two months after Maia was born, but boy was I wrong! In fact, with hindsight I can't imagine what I was thinking. The pantomime was *Dick Whittington* at the Orchard in Dartford, Kent, and I was to star alongside Toby Anstis and Warrior from *Gladiators*. Not exactly a defining stage role that was going to ensure me a place alongside the acting greats. No, this was purely a money job, and, as it turned out, too much too soon. I had no idea how knackered I was going to be after having Maia, and even during rehearsals I felt completely exhausted. Everyone in the company was very nice, but despite my role being quite small – I was playing Alice Fitzwarren – I found it hard to cope with the workload. During rehearsals I had Maia in a papoose and a script in one hand, and I'd be trying to breastfeed every couple of hours. When I wasn't actually feeding Maia I was leaking into my costume while the kindly man at the stage door would do his best to rock Maia to sleep as she sat in her car seat. It was crazy.

Meanwhile, Fabrizio and I were still being chased by photographers everywhere we went, and I was still under the misguided impression that if I gave them a little bit of what they wanted then they'd leave us alone. That wasn't the case, however: I was just courting them. Along with my unending exhaustion and Fabrizio feeling displaced, there was a lot of pressure on the two of us. Our relationship began to suffer and we started to argue more and more frequently. Fabrizio was that archetypal Italian man: very proud, masculine and strong-willed. I think he was beginning to feel like 'Michelle's other half', vulnerable and undermined. He had no job, he was living in a strange city, and he was getting fed up with living in my shadow. At one point he was offered money to sell his own story to the press, but to his credit he never took it. He'd always found the celebrity thing hard to deal with, especially all the hype surrounding the cast of *EastEnders* at that time. I remember him coming home with a tabloid newspaper one day and throwing it down on the table in front of me.

'Look at how ridiculous this country is,' he yelled.

I looked down at the front page of a national newspaper to see a photograph of me as Cindy standing over Ian Beale, who was lying on the floor, seemingly shot dead. Above it was a screaming headline, just as if it was a real-life piece of news. Fabrizio was horrified that a British newspaper would have a scene from a soap opera as its front-page story. He found it all very shallow. I knew, of course, that he wouldn't have reacted quite so excessively if it hadn't been me on the front of said tabloid, but I could see his point. If you hadn't known any different you'd have thought it was a photo of someone who'd actually been gunned down in the street in cold blood. It took up the entire front page. That's how big the show was at the time.

Maia was a joy, and Fabrizio adored her just as much as I did. She was the most gorgeous, happiest child you can imagine, despite not sleeping for what seemed like an entire year.

Still, Fabrizio seemed very low, and looking back I think he just felt helpless and homesick. Apart from the fact that he wasn't working, he was still struggling with his English, despite having some lessons, and he found it hard to cope with the ongoing press intrusion. The fact that I'd gone back to work so quickly after having Maia didn't help matters either. I was tired and low myself, and felt under pressure to keep everything running smoothly, and when the sleepless nights stated to take their toll, Fabrizio and I would be arguing at the drop of a hat. I was preoccupied with Maia and with work and I guess he felt like there was no place for him, and as time went on our relationship got more and more strained.

At Christmas we went to my sister's in Essex. I only had one day off from the panto, and on Christmas Eve we all went to a beautiful church for the carol service. On Christmas Day Fabrizio and I had a really huge row that just got worse and worse as the day went on, and ended with him walking out and going to stay with a mutual friend. After that he went back to Milan. It was over.

The trouble was I had no time to grieve or even think about what was happening, despite the fact that I felt devastated by Fabrizio's sudden departure. I remember thinking that I was losing the plot at one point because I was working such long hours as well as looking after Maia. I'd agreed to do a photo shoot for a well-known high street fashion store, along with Debbie Arnold and a few other women. I was still breastfeeding at that point, and by the time I arrived at the studio for the shoot my breasts were swollen and I was in agony.

'My boobs are really hurting,' I told Debbie. 'I've forgotten my breast pump.'

They say it takes a whole year for you to regain your memory and get yourself back to normality after having a baby: you seriously lose your marbles. Anyway, I kept running out of the studio for a bit of respite but a couple of the women were clearly getting ticked off because I was holding up the shoot. In the end I was in so much pain that Debbie came to the rescue once more, dragging me upstairs to the bathroom with an idea.

'I'll have to milk you,' she said, straight-faced.

'What?'

'Take your bra off, I'll do it,' she said.

I looked at her like she was mad but seconds later there she was holding my boob and milking me like a cow, squeezing all the milk out into a coffee cup. Eventually we went back downstairs, but we had to repeat the process again half an hour later, much to the annoyance of the other women. It certainly relieved the pain, but it wasn't exactly the most glamorous thing that's ever happened to me, being milked like a dairy cow.

On one Saturday, as well doing our usual three shows in Dartford, I appeared on the kids' TV show *Live & Kicking*, which meant that I had to be up at seven in the morning to get to the BBC studios. I'd had very little sleep and by the time I got to the second panto performance of the day I didn't know whether I was in *Dick Whittington*, *Cinderella* or *Jack and the* bloody *Beanstalk* – I was all over the shop. I thought I was going crazy. Then I started to notice the inevitable scathing articles analyzing my break-up with Fabrizio: many of them written by women.

'What does she expect?' was the general tone. 'Did she really think it would last?'

It seemed I'd worn my heart on my sleeve a little too much and perhaps been too honest about how Fabrizio and I had met and the whirlwind nature of our romance. Mind you, these days I'm a bit more cynical – and hopefully wiser – and if I read an article like that now I'd probably think the same. At the time, though, I was upset and hurt by some of the things that were written about me. I may have been naive, but I hadn't hurt anyone other than myself.

Once *Dick Whittington* was over I decided that I would stop work for a while, and I also took on a fabulous nanny called Alice, who helped me out no end. After much soul-searching, Fabrizio came back to London and we got back together, desperate to make things work for the sake of our daughter. This time he got a job as the maître d' of an Italian restaurant, but unfortunately that didn't last very long. He also went to school to perfect his English, but that didn't last very long either. So even though he'd come back to give our relationship another chance, things were still pretty rocky between us.

In the summer of 1997 I went up for a great role in a three-part BBC drama called *Real Women*, which was to star Pauline Quirke,

Above - Me and my glamorous mum.
Left - With Jason Donovan during my short-lived stint as a TV presenter on *The Word*.
Below - Appearing in panto is exhausting!

Above and Left - The cast of *Sunburn* including Anita Dobson and the wonderful Peter Polycarpou.
Below Left - With Pauline Quirke and Gwyneth Strong in *Real Women*, which I loved working on.
Below Right - With Ramon Tikaram in *Daylight Robbery*.

Above - Taking a break while filming
Lloyd and Hill with Philip Glenister.
Right - Celebrating my incredible friend
Michael Cashman's CBE at the Ivy.
Below - Filming *Rock Rivals* in 2007.

Above - Maia aged two. Look at those gorgeous lips!
Left - Maia and Sid.
Below - On holiday in Monaco.

Right - Ready to go to Scotland to film *Two Thousand Acres of Sky*. Our car didn't turn up!
Centre- The wonderful cast, including Paul Kaye, Sarah Stockbridge and my niece Charlotte.
Below - Ray Brooks with Karen Westwood and Monica Gibb, who helped me out by buying all the newspapers in the village.

Above Left - Me, Michael and Paul visiting Mo Mowlam at Hillsborough Castle.
Above Right - With Marquinhos in his tribal dress in Brazil.
Below Left - Ready to speak in front of thousands of people at Glastonbury on behalf of Oxfam.
Below Right - Meeting Tony Blair at 10 Downing Street as part of an education campaign.

Above - The girls from the orphanage near Nairobi that I visited with Oxfam.
Left - A selfie with Maia.
Below Left - On set outside the Rovers.
Below Right - Me and my *Coronation Street* co-stars Sue Johnston and Jane Danson.

Above Left - Fabrizio and me in Italy in 2013.
It's great that Maia got to spend some time with her
Italian family.
Right - My incredible friend and right-hand man,
Simon Frost.
Below - The Collins girls! Maia, me, Vicki,
Charlotte and Mum. With thanks to Ray
Burmiston.

Frances Barber, Gwyneth Strong and Lesley Manville. Actresses I really admired, with a fantastic script by Susan Oudot. To be honest I didn't think I was going to get it, what with coming from a soap plus all the press stories there had been about my private life. By that time I was desperate for a really good role, but I was worried that people were starting to see me as a celebrity rather than an actress. I was convinced that the director of *Real Women*, Phil Davis, was going to overlook me.

The series centered on a group of friends and it was gritty, real and had a huge heart, and I desperately wanted to play Susie – the bride-to-be with a secret past. I thought the role was perfect for me, but after three auditions I'd almost given up hope of getting the job and felt a bit low. One afternoon, when Maia had gone down for her nap, I got on the running machine in my room, and that was when my agent, Jane Brand, called me.

'You've got it!' she said.

I screamed for joy and nearly fell off the running machine: Maia must have thought I was a crazy lady. I was ecstatic. I suddenly felt as though I'd been validated as an actress and not just somebody who was in the papers all the time. The trouble was, Fabrizio and I were in the midst of breaking up again, and by the time I started filming *Real Women* – which was shot all around Islington – there seemed to be photographers popping up everywhere we went, hoping to get a candid shot of me looking upset. I was mortified and I felt like some of the people around me were getting a little peeved. In my mind's eye, I could almost see the other actresses rolling their eyes and hear them muttering 'Oh God, here we go' every time it happened, and I hated feeling like I was the odd one out. They were all serious actresses, so the stakes were high and I felt like I had to prove myself. I didn't want anyone thinking I was encouraging or courting the press attention.

One morning Maia's nanny was ill so I had to take her to the set with me until my mum could come and pick her up. While I was having my make-up done she was sitting on my lap, and one of the supporting cast actually complained about it. I should have told her where to go, after all it was an emergency situation, but instead I apologized profusely and said it wouldn't happen again. I must have been so worried about what everyone thought of me.

Somehow I still managed to get swept up in the work. I worked hard and we all had a brilliant time. I don't think I've ever laughed as much as I did shooting *Real Women*. Even after filming had finished for the day, we often stayed on in our trailers, gossiping and laughing and putting the world to rights. We all knew there was something special about that job, even before we'd finished filming it.

After a year away from *EastEnders*, I agreed to go back and do another short stint as Cindy. The idea had been discussed when I'd left, and I said I'd do six months and see how it panned out. I was terribly nervous about going back and not sure whether it was what I really wanted, but the producers seduced me with a great returning storyline so I thought, why not? I couldn't believe it when I read the script – talk about coincidence. Cindy was supposed to be living in Italy with her children, and in the story her ex-husband Ian went out to find them and bring them back to Albert Square along with Phil and Grant Mitchell. I was over the moon about the prospect of filming my initial scenes in sunny Italy, and by some strange coincidence the chosen location was the village where Fabrizio's parents had a holiday home: Bellagio. Not only that but I ended up filming on the exact street where they lived. Fabrizio had, of course, told his parents that I was an actress, but there I was suddenly filming right outside their front door. Bellagio is a beautiful place and often called the pearl of Lake Como. While we were filming there we stayed in a rather posh hotel, which had very strict rules about dress etiquette. One day during the shoot, Steve McFadden was in the hotel dining room in a pair of white shorts when a snooty member of the hotel staff approached him.

'You can't wear shorts in here, sir,' he said, patronizingly.

'All right,' Steve said, grinning.

Then he yanked his shorts down in front of all the staff and guests in the dining room. He was always a bit of a joker and we all thought it was very funny.

Once I'd started back everything felt different and I realized fairly quickly that I'd made a big mistake. Although it was great working with Barbara Windsor and Adam Woodyatt again, there was a new producer as well as new cast members and I just didn't feel as though I belonged there anymore. Some of the cast weren't particularly welcoming, either. I remember feeling quite upset when one of the young female cast members, who'd been very nice to me in the past, had a birthday party. It seemed like everyone was invited except me and I couldn't for the life of me work out what I'd done wrong. I'd just come from a job that I'd thoroughly enjoyed, and where everyone was professional and worked together as a team, and now I was in an environment where there always seemed to be someone throwing a tantrum or creating a drama. The show had changed, but then so had I, and being there was making me unhappy. *EastEnders* was going from strength to strength as a show – it was an institution – but as far as I was concerned there were just too many egos under one roof.

It was around that time that *Real Women* was broadcast, and everyone who'd been involved with the production was very nervous about how it would be perceived and whether it would be a success. I'd so enjoyed working on a show where I'd had the luxury of plenty of rehearsal time and a cast that felt like a small family without any backbiting. Filming a drama was a far cry from the experience of being back on the *EastEnders* set. It was a completely different way of working and I missed it. On the day after the show was aired I was at the gym near my house when my agent called me with great news: the ratings were great and the critics loved it. I burst into tears, I was so happy. It was such a relief to get good reviews for doing something other than being Cindy, and just what I needed. 'I can do this,' I told myself. I felt like I could move on and do other things and I could make it as an actress outside *EastEnders*. Not long after that when my contract was due for renewal, the show's producer, Matthew Robinson, took me out for dinner at Joe Allen in Covent Garden.

'Look, we'd love you to stay,' he said. 'We've got some great ideas for Cindy.' I thanked him and told him that I'd have a think about it, but the next morning I woke up certain that staying on wasn't the right thing to do. That was it. My days as Cindy Beale had come to an end, and a few months after I left, she died off-screen.

As Cindy finally disappeared from my life, so did Fabrizio. I don't think it was any one thing that signalled the end for us; it was the culmination of a lot of things. When I look back at it now I feel like we never really knew each other, or perhaps we'd just met at the wrong time and it was doomed from the start. I was very sad. Fabrizio had been no angel, it's true, but I'd had my moments too, and towards the end we just weren't making each other happy. Like many turbulent couples with a child, we'd got back together time and time again just to try to make it work for Maia's sake, but it wasn't to be. Love at first sight all sounds very romantic, but at the age of thirty-three I probably should have known better. I don't regret it, though. Together Fabrizio and I had a beautiful daughter. We'll always have that bond and whatever happens, Maia makes it all worth it.

CHAPTER 21:

SUNBURNT

Once I was finally finished with *EastEnders*, my agent Jane advised me to be very selective about what I did next. For a start we decided that we needed to avoid anything that would be seen as a 'bad girl' role. Jane said that she wanted to take me away from Cindy so that the public could see me in a different light. Cindy was a great character to play, but essentially bad. The perception of Michelle Collins was that she was just like Cindy Beale: a femme fatale, a siren. My friends and family knew that wasn't me at all, but Jane thought it was time I showed everyone else another side, too. *Sunburn* was a TV series about the lives of holiday reps with an ensemble cast, commissioned by the BBC's controller of continuing drama, Mal Young, and the part of Nicki Matthews appeared to be the perfect role for the new and 'likeable' me. Mal had been a producer while I was working on *EastEnders* and had always been very supportive of me. I thought he was a breath of fresh air as far as drama at the BBC went: he was from a working-class background and had worked on *Brookside* in its gritty heyday. Coincidentally, he also ended up falling in love with my old bandmate Mari Wilson and they've now been together for over ten years.

I was excited about doing *Sunburn* despite the fact that the logistics were never going to be easy. Fabrizio and I were well and truly over by the summer of 1998 when shooting was due to start over in Paphos, Cyprus, but he was still living in London, and wasn't happy about the prospect of me whisking his baby daughter off abroad for four months. We'd been arguing a lot, and by then communication between the two of us had all but broken down, but I was under pressure to come up trumps with a great TV role post-*EastEnders*, and this was it. I hated the idea of not working and I knew that this could be a big opportunity, and the fact that I was able to have Maia with me was the icing on the cake. It was too good a job to turn down.

Maia's nanny, Alice, came with us to Cyprus, and my mum planned to come out to visit at various times while we were there. It all seemed like an ideal set-up, with a great cast that included George Layton, Peter Polycarpou and Rebecca Callard. In the second series, former *EastEnders* actor Sean Maguire was one of the leads. Anita Dobson also turned up in a cameo role, which I was happy about, as I'd never had the chance to work with her on *EastEnders*. Although there wasn't supposed to be a starring role, I was sort of seen as the lead, and with that came responsibility. I was the girl fresh off the biggest TV show on the BBC, and so, rightly or not, I felt like there was a lot of pressure on me to make *Sunburn* work. Most of the cast stayed in a hotel, but because I had Maia and Alice with me we were set up in a villa in another town, which was all very nice, but it did make me feel segregated from the rest of the cast and crew. I spent most of the time wishing I was hanging out with the rest of the gang – feeling like I was missing out – and after a few weeks I even began to feel extremely homesick. The constant friction between Fabrizio and me had worn me down, and despite having an exciting new job, I had far too much time on my own, mulling over everything that had happened. I had to face the fact that my relationship was over and I was on my own, and I was clearly more cut up about it than I knew. Now that the dust had settled, it dawned on me how heartbroken and lonely I was. I felt like a failure and found myself sinking lower and lower as the days went on, until in the end I couldn't seem to pull myself out of the hole. I just couldn't work out why I felt so empty. I had a great job and a beautiful daughter – it was crazy. I now realize that I was seriously depressed, but at the time I didn't know what that meant because I'd never experienced it. When you're in that state, your mind just isn't your own. It talks to you in ways you couldn't even conceive ordinarily, and if it takes over it can be deadly.

Most people might think that working in a hot climate in a gorgeous holiday resort would be wonderful, but trust me, when you're in it every day for hours on end, ninety-degree heat is oppressive and exhausting. We finished late most nights, and because I had Maia I didn't go out and socialize with the rest of the cast all that much, affording me even more lonely hours to let the dark thoughts and self-doubt creep over me. I was out of my comfort zone in a strange country with the burden of carrying a new and untested show on my shoulders, and I was guilt-ridden because I hadn't been able to make things work with Fabrizio. If it had been any other relationship I might have picked myself up and dusted myself off as usual, but he was the father of my child and now we were separated. I felt terribly lonely and lost. What I should have done is talk about it to someone; I know that now. The trouble was that I never wanted to admit to any of the people around me that I was vulnerable. I wanted people to see me as strong and as someone who could cope with everything that had been thrown at her. I was supposed to be spearheading this show, and I didn't want to let people down. I certainly didn't want them to think I was cracking up, so I put on a front. A far as everyone else was concerned, I was fine. As an actor, when you're ill but you know you still have to get through a performance, everyone says 'Doctor Theatre, darling!' The show always has to go on.

When an old family friend came over to visit me on location, he persuaded me to go out for dinner and then a few drinks at a local bar in Paphos. Maia was back in London for a visit, so it seemed like a good idea to go out, relax and have dinner in the company of a good friend. As it turned out, drinking was the worst thing I could have done, but when I found myself feeling slightly merry I decided to stay for a couple more after my friend had gone back to the villa.

Pretty soon I got talking to a group of friendly people who'd just arrived at the bar, and before I knew it I was happily playing a game of pool with a couple of young guys. It was all very innocent and I felt like I was enjoying myself for the first time in ages. Quite out of the blue, one of the guys made a joke about the way I looked and about my age. One minute he was being friendly, and the next he was showing off to his mates and turning a bit nasty. I don't even remember what he said, and on another occasion it might not have bothered me, but whatever it was must have triggered something inside me, because suddenly my whole mood switched. I calmly put down my pool cue and left the bar without saying goodbye, feeling dreadful. I was only thirty-six, not exactly over the hill, but at the time it hit a raw nerve and I knew I had to get out of there. I walked all the way back to the villa in a semi-trance: emotional, shattered and really not very well at all. It was late at night, so wandering around on my own wasn't the safest thing to do, but I wasn't thinking straight, in fact I wasn't really thinking at all. I felt like I'd been tipped over the edge. My mind was cloudy and all I wanted to do was sleep, and the potent cocktail of alcohol and exhaustion sent me into a very dark place.

When I got back to the villa I felt like I could hardly breathe, let alone think coherently. The question that kept going through my mind was 'Would anybody miss me if I wasn't here?' and foolishly I somehow decided that no one would. It was ridiculous. I had my mother, my sister and my daughter and all my friends back in London, but that didn't seem to make any difference at the time. The next couple of hours are a bit of a blur. I remember thinking that I wanted to sleep and deciding I should take some paracetamol to stop me having a headache in the morning. My next thought was that I should just take all of them and that it didn't matter. I remember swallowing some pills, but that was about it. There was no definite plan or explicit decision behind my actions, it just happened. Then I woke up being violently sick, and thank God because it turned out that I'd taken a large handful of paracetamol. When I think about it now it all sounds very melodramatic, but I guess that's the nature of depression.

The next thing I knew, I was calling one of the actors from the show, Peter Polycarpou.

'Oh God, what have I done? I've taken all these pills and now I can't stop being sick.'

Peter rushed straight over and was wonderful. Being from Cyprus he knew the area and he drove me to a little hospital nearby and made sure I was seen by a doctor straight away. The main concern with large doses of paracetamol is the damage it can do to a person's liver, so after checking me over the doctors decided that it was best if they kept me in hospital on a drip. They told me I was very severely dehydrated and unwell. I needed complete rest. I felt so stupid and couldn't even fathom that I'd done such a thing. What the hell had I been thinking? Unintentional or not, how low must I have been to do something like that? It was unthinkable. My mum was horrified when I told her what had happened – I felt like she needed to know – but as soon as she knew I was going to be OK, she really let me have it.

'Don't you EVER do something like that again. What did you think you were doing?'

That was just it: I didn't know what I was doing. I'd never got to that point of utter despair before and I'm glad to report that I haven't since. I certainly wasn't in my right mind, and in hindsight it was another case of me jumping into a job, head first, without really thinking about it. I hadn't stopped for a second to consider how fragile I was after Fabrizio, and uprooting my life and alienating myself from all my friends back in London had really taken its toll. When I came out the other end of it I realized how lucky I'd been to be surrounded by such good people in my life. That was the irony of it, really. I'd spent all those weeks feeling desperately lonely when, in fact, I was surrounded by people who cared about and loved me.

I ended up staying in the hospital for four days, and while I was there four or five other members of the *Sunburn* cast and crew were brought in. It had been such hard going working under that relentless sun every day that they were all dropping like flies, and the hospital became like a casualty zone for people from *Sunburn* with sunstroke. This turn of events turned out to be something of a blessing for me. Peter had taken control of the situation, telling my producer that I'd been rushed to hospital with serious dehydration and that I'd be off for a couple of days. With everyone else getting sick, nobody even considered that there was any more to it than that, and no one asked any awkward questions. In fact, I've never really told anyone else until now. I remember thinking at the time that somebody up there must like me.

A little while after I returned to London, I still wasn't feeling a hundred per cent better, but before *Sunburn* went to air, Mal Young asked me if I fancied recording the theme song for the show. The plan was to release it as a single to coincide with the series.

'Really? Oh my God!' I was so surprised to be asked.

I was quite taken with the idea of doing a bit of singing again. In the early 1990s I'd started a band with my friend Bunmi, aided and abetted by teen heartthrob Ben Volpeliere-Pierrot from the band Curiosity Killed The Cat, who was a friend of hers. He introduced us to a producer friend and we recorded a cover version of Barbara Acklin's 'Am I the Same Girl'. We even shot a video with the director James Lebon, but it was never destined to top the charts. At the time we thought we were going to be like the next Brand New Heavies but my heart wasn't really in it, and to be honest it was never going to happen with Cindy Beale in a posh dress on the mic, was it? It was the same when a pop producer called Brian Rawlings persuaded me to record a solo single, 'Get Ready', in 1992 – I should have known better. There had been a few ex-soap actors who'd tried their luck in the music business, but it rarely worked out. I did a big radio tour, plus performances at the Fridge and on *Blue Peter* to promote it, but I never felt comfortable in the role of a chanteuse; in fact I was a bit embarrassed about the whole thing. I think when you're in the entertainment industry you need to know what you're good at, and I was an actress at heart, not a singer. I did get a much-prized possession out of it, though – a *Blue Peter* Badge!

Still, recording the theme tune to a show that I was starring in sounded like a bit of fun, so I didn't need too much persuading. I went along to Red Bus Studios to record with producer Steve Levine, who'd been the man behind many of Culture Club's hits in the 1980s. The song was extremely cheesy, fun and very catchy, but I got to make a video and I was flattered to have been asked to do it. The most exciting thing about it was that 'Sunburn' went to number twenty-eight in the charts on the week of its release, and the next thing I knew I'd been invited to attend the 1999 Brit Awards at the London Arena.

A couple of days before the big event, however, I started to feel unwell. I was wiped out and felt like my throat was on fire. Throat troubles seem to run in my family: my mum, my sister and my niece all get something called quinsy, which is abscesses behind the tonsils, and I'd been prone to the odd bout of tonsillitis when I'd been run-down, too. Like many actors, when you're full-on with a physically and mentally demanding job you just keep going, no matter what, often ignoring any warning signs that you might need to slow down. Then when you do finally stop, your body screams out and you get really sick.

I'd felt ill for a few days, and when Mum arrived at my house on the morning of the Brits she took one look at me and dragged me to the hospital as fast as she could. The doctors thought I must have caught some weird disease while I was working in Cyprus, so I was put straight into isolation in a special unit for infectious diseases. It was pretty scary, especially when the doctor informed Mum that my fever was so bad that I probably would have died if she hadn't brought me in as quickly as she did. Nobody had any idea what was wrong with me and I had to just lie there wondering how much worse things might get before they got better. After a whirl of examinations and blood tests, the diagnosis changed and it turned out that I had a serious case of tonsillitis that had developed into a nasty streptococcal infection. I ended up staying in hospital for five days, and although I was extremely happy to be feeling better, I'd missed a great night out at the Brits.

That whole period was a bit of a wake-up call for me to start looking after myself, not only physically but mentally, too. Things worked out well with *Sunburn* in the end, as it was hugely successful and we ended up filming a second series in Portugal. But after what had happened in Cyprus I decided that I needed to bite the bullet and go and see a psychotherapist for some counselling. I needed to try and get to the bottom of why I was always so hard on myself, why my relationships didn't last, and why, after so much apparent success, my self-esteem was so low. Looking back it wasn't exactly rocket science. I was trying to be all things to all people, juggling too many balls at the same time and not wanting to let people down. I was still trying to learn how to be a mum, I'd gone back to work too soon because I was fraught with the idea that I might not be able to provide for my daughter, I'd been in the midst of a tempestuous relationship and I felt like I'd failed both Fabrizio and Maia when it came to an end, and I was anxious about being on the wrong side of thirty-five. It was for all these reasons that I continually felt as though I had to fight for my place in the world, both as an actress and as a woman. In the end, a friend of mine recommended someone at a well-known clinic who would be very helpful and discreet, so I nervously went along. As it turned out, I found that talking about all that stuff really helped. I wasn't keen on the idea of numbing my pain with anti-depressants, so it was the perfect solution to me and I kept going to therapy for as long as I thought I needed it. It was somewhat of an epiphany – just the kick up the backside that I needed, in fact. Right, I thought. That's it now. It's time to grow up, stop feeling sorry for myself and get my act together. And that's exactly what I did.

CHAPTER 22:

THINGS CAN ONLY GET BETTER

hadn't really ever thought of myself as especially political, although I was a staunch Labour supporter and always had been. I grew up with a mother who bought the *Daily Mirror* every day as it was considered a Labour paper – although she now reads a broadsheet! Even to this day, I couldn't see myself voting Conservative. It was my friendship with Michael Cashman that got me thinking about how I could use my voice as an actress and 'celebrity' in a positive way. Through Stonewall, the equal rights charity set up by Michael and Ian McKellen, I got involved with speaking out against Clause 28 (also known as Section 28), which was an addition to the local government act stating that local authorities were no longer allowed to 'promote homosexuality' and that schools were not allowed to promote the acceptability of homosexuality as a 'pretended family relationship'. The fear and prejudice surrounding the spread of HIV and AIDS had been largely directed at the gay community, and somehow this clause – which seemed ridiculous then and seems even more so now – was passed in Parliament and became law in the late 1980s. One of the things it meant was that any sort of positive message about being gay was banned from being taught in schools, so effectively there was to be no support for young lesbian and gay students. Along with Michael and many other people, I spoke out and campaigned against the clause, which was spearheaded by Margaret Thatcher and the Tory government. I also appeared in a party political broadcast for the Labour Party with Stephen Fry and Hugh Laurie around that time.

Paul Cottingham worked for the celebrity unit of the Labour Party, which encouraged people in the arts and show business to get involved in campaigning for the party. The first thing I signed up for was called The Big Event, a fundraiser show at the Piccadilly Theatre featuring stars like Judi Dench and Joanna Lumley amongst many others. We performed various songs, sketches and monologues, and it was like a who's who of London's West End. There seemed to be quite a lot of actors throwing their weight behind the idea of getting rid of the Tories, who'd been in power ever since I'd been old enough to vote. Apart from anything else, Labour seemed to be much more involved with the arts at the time, while the Conservative government under John Major appeared to be winding down funding and taking grants away from theatres and arts organizations.

Suddenly in 1994, when Tony Blair took over as leader of the Labour Party, there seemed to be a glimmer of hope that things might change and we might actually have an alternative government after so many years. Blair exuded flair and charm and seemed to have an aura about him that gave people confidence and hope. Knowing my political views, Michael Cashman asked me to show my support by speaking at roadshows and rallies, which I've since done alongside John Prescott and Gordon Brown amongst others. I'd always been quite cautious about that kind of public speaking before, because I'm someone who likes to know exactly what I'm talking about. I have to be properly briefed and have all the information about a particular subject before I even open my mouth. I'd never want to be seen as someone who's jumping on a soap box just to get her face out there, but at the same time I do have a strong belief that if you have a voice and a public platform, it's important to try to do something positive in society where you can. Not only in politics, but for other causes that you might feel passionate about. I've always considered it a privilege.

On 1 May 1997, the night of the general election, we were all so excited because we knew that it might well be the start of something new. I was with a group of friends, including Michael and Paul, who gathered on the South Bank waiting for the results to come in. I remember feeling so patriotic and proud being a part of it, and when it was announced that Labour had won with a landslide victory, there was the biggest spontaneous celebration you can imagine. We ended up singing and dancing up and down the street with Peter Mandelson until the very early hours of the morning, and then we were interviewed live by the *GMTV* crew. I was absolutely exhausted from being up all night, but I didn't care because I was still on such a high. We all were. To this day the song 'Things Will Only Get Better' by D-Ream rings in my ears when I think about that night.

Once Tony Blair was in office, I was one of the campaigners who were invited to go to Downing Street, which was a big thrill. I was struck by how grand it was, with its tall ceilings and all the beautiful furniture and paintings of past Prime Ministers. It reminded me of a stately home, and as I looked around I could picture heads of state gathering in the rooms for important conferences. I heard that one of the invited guests stole a toilet roll – how common! I pinched a biro. On another occasion a smaller group of us were invited to go to the Blairs' private flat, which was at the top of the building. Tony often held these informal forums with people in the public eye who'd supported him. He wanted to know about the things that we felt were important, and to hear our views on various government policies on the arts. It was quite an honour, and felt a bit like being one of the chosen few. I remember going up the stairs and almost tripping over baby Leo's pram, which was on the landing outside. Tony was always attentive and charming, and I had the utmost respect for him. I also liked Cherie, who I've met on numerous occasions over the years. Sheila Hancock was there that night: a woman whose work I'd always admired. She was very concerned about the problems facing women in prison and how so many of them were being incarcerated for petty crimes such as shoplifting, which often led to them turning to drugs and more serious crimes after being in prison. She really gave Tony Blair a hard time that night, and I admired her dedication to a cause she felt so strongly about. Aside from being one of our best actresses, she's an amazing and impassioned woman and as I listened to her laying into the Prime Minister, I decided that I wanted to find out more about the subject myself. Later that night, I was going to the Ivy for dinner and Sheila kindly offered to drop me off.

'Come on love, get in. I'll give you a lift.'

I was really taken with her, because to me she's a great role model. An intelligent woman who's down to earth, does great work, and who's true to her chosen causes. She's very passionate about the causes she champions but I'd rather someone was slightly outspoken than had nothing to say. Sheila is somebody I'd love to work with one day.

After that I got more involved with the plight of women prisoners through a charity called Smart Justice, who, amongst other things, focus on the huge cost to society resulting from the sometimes avoidable imprisonment of women, and the urgent need for an alternative. The woman who introduced me to the organization was its director, Lucie Russell, who explained to me that one of the most common offences women are locked up for is shoplifting. They're not really a danger to society but after a spell in prison, rather than being rehabilitated, many of them end up going down a path of further crime or become dependent on drugs. Their children are put into care and their families are torn apart. She believed that education and rehabilitation was a better deterrent than just punishment, and that everyone would benefit if these people were doing some sort of community service rather than being locked up for twenty-three hours a day. I started to visit some of the women's prisons in London, and it was quite an eye-opener. I met quite a few women who were covering up for men who hadn't even been sentenced. The mother and baby unit in Holloway prison was quite heartbreaking, with all the buggies and prams lined up outside the cells. They also had a large photographic mural of a leafy green park on one wall, and in front of it was a park bench. Some of the young girls who hadn't told their families that they were in prison would sit on the bench while the prison wardens took their picture. That way they could send photographs of what looked like a happy outdoor scene to their families, who would be none the wiser.

Mo Mowlam was somebody who made a huge impression on me during my time campaigning for the Labour Party. I met her at a party thrown by my friends Charlie Parsons and Waheed Alli, who were my producers when I'd worked on *The Word*. Even though they hadn't exactly been enamoured of my skills as a presenter, we'd still remained friends and they always invited me to these infamous and fabulous affairs at their beautiful home in Kent, which they threw every other year. Charlie and Waheed had the best parties back then, and they were inevitably a who's who of the entertainment industry, featuring an assortment of actors, comedians and politicians. They had a full disco and even a funfair in their huge garden. On the night I met Mo, who was then Secretary of State for Northern Ireland, I'd not long ended my relationship with Fabrizio and I was a bit down in the dumps. She was surrounded by bodyguards, which was a bit weird at a private party, but it was all part of the territory given the sensitive nature of her job. Eventually, Mo and I got chatting and she seemed so amiable and friendly. We were getting on like a house on fire, and suddenly, sensing that I might need a bit of a pick-me-up, she came up with an idea.

'Darling, why don't you come to Greece with me and Jon?'

'What?' I was a bit gobsmacked. 'When?'

'Tomorrow morning! Don't go getting yourself in a state about men. Come with us. Meet us at the airport, we're all flying off to Greece.'

I didn't take her up on her offer, but I was quite taken with her lovely manner. One of my funniest memories of that night is of Mo and Peter Mandelson line dancing in the garden, but I don't think she made it to Greece the next day, because the party was the night before the Omagh bombing.

After that night I became quite good friends with Mo. She invited

Michael Cashman, Paul Cottingham and me to Hillsborough Castle, her official government residence in Northern Ireland, and then I started helping out with a charity she'd set up called MoMo Helps. The aim was to provide easy access to small amounts of cash that could assist with holidays and respite care for families of disabled children as well as helping ex-drug users reintegrate into society. Her husband, Jon, was an artist and during that time she invited me for dinner at her house, and we'd talk about everything from art to politics to life in general. She was a great hostess and very down to earth. She lived in Hackney and people from the area quite often knocked on her door if they had a problem or a grievance. She was always very accessible, despite her perilous job, and willing to help them out in any way she could. Considering how clever, sharp and politically aware she was, she was one of the most down-to-earth people I'd ever met. It was such a tragedy when she died in 2005, and Jon died four years later, aged just fifty-three.

CHAPTER 23:

A GOLDEN GIRL

etween 2001 and 2004 it seemed as if I was the golden girl and the jobs just seemed to keep on coming: second series of *Real Women* and *Sunburn*, two series of *Daylight Robbery*, *The Sleeper* and *Two Thousand Acres of Sky*. All great roles, but I'd become a workaholic and I hardly gave myself time to breathe. Still, nobody wants to turn a good job down when they're on a roll, and that was my mindset at the time. By the time I shot *Perfect*, which was a Susan Oudot-penned two-part drama about a serial bigamist, I'd just about run myself into the ground. I played Julie, a woman who was addicted to weddings and married one man after another without bothering to divorce the previous spouse. We were filming in the winter and I felt dreadful, and I looked in the mirror one morning only to be faced with the most humongous cold sore I'd ever seen. As the day went on, it just kept getting bigger and bigger until it almost entirely covered my mouth; I looked shocking. Still, there was no way any amount of make-up was going to cover it up, and the schedule was much too tight to be halting the filming until I looked human again. The show had to go on and there was a deadline to meet. In the end it was decided that the post-production team would get rid of the offending blemish in the edit, cleverly wiping it away with whatever trickery it is they use to achieve such magic. I didn't care what they did, as long as it went. It must have been more difficult than anyone had imagined, because the next thing I heard the special effects people from *Walking With Dinosaurs* were being drafted in – that's how bad it was. It ended up costing tens of thousands of pounds just to get rid of my hideous cold sore.

The Illustrated Mum, which I filmed in 2003 for Channel 4, was one of those parts that doesn't come along all that often, and it was a joy from start to finish. Based on Jacqueline Wilson's book, it's the story of two young girls who live with their multi-tattooed, bipolar, alcoholic mother, Marigold, which was my character. It wasn't a particularly well-paid job and my agent warned me that I'd have to work right through the summer holidays if I did it, but as soon as I read the book I knew that I had to have the part and I went all-out to get it. I found out that one of the film's producers, Julia Ouston, was represented by the same agency as me, Independent Talent, so I got them to arrange a meeting with her and the director, Cilla Ware. At the time I was working on a series called *Sea of Souls* in Scotland, so I had to get a car to Manchester just so I could meet them for dinner. We got along very well and by the next morning I had a text telling me that I had the job. I was over the moon. There were plenty of jobs I'd had to do just for the money – the bread and butter jobs – without a great amount of creative satisfaction, but this was the opposite. It was never going to make me rich, but I felt like it was the part that I'd been waiting for.

The girl playing one of my daughters, Holliday Grainger, has gone on to do very well in Hollywood, starring as Lucrezia in *The Borgias*. In fact, quite a few of my screen daughters over the years have gone on to big success in America. Ophelia Lovibond, who played my daughter in a TV series called *Single*, went on to star in *Mr Popper's Penguins* and *Nowhere Boy*, and Romola Garai, who I worked with on *Perfect*, is a very big name these days. Despite being seen as a children's film, *The Illustrated Mum* was a huge success, winning one BAFTA for Best Schools Drama and another for Debbie Isitt, who'd written the screenplay. We also won the Prix d'Or at the Monte-Carlo Television Festival, and an International Emmy, which was presented to us at a ceremony at the New York Hilton by Lenny Kravitz. I was very proud that night.

My other favourite job of that period was playing Abby in *Two Thousand Acres Of Sky* alongside Paul Kaye. It was the story of a single mother from London who takes a life-altering job running a bed and breakfast on a remote Scottish island. It ran for three series between 2001 and 2003 and was set on the fictional island of Ronansay off the coast of Skye, although we shot it all on location in the tiny seaside village of Port Logan. Writer Tim Prager, who had also written shows such as *Dangerfield* and *Silent Witness*, wrote it with me in mind, and I loved the character and the story right off. It was almost like a reinvention for me as well as a new start because Abby was a million miles away from backstabbing Cindy Beale. It was hard being away from home for four months of the year, but there was a real family atmosphere, with many of the cast and crew bringing their spouses and children up while we were filming during the summer holidays. Maia was only four when I started so I was able to have her with me throughout the filming, and Vicki came up, too, because her daughter, Charlotte, was playing one of my children in the show.

On the day we left for Scotland, Maia and I sat outside our house in Hampstead along with Maia's nanny, Karen, waiting for the cab to take us to the airport. I have a lovely photograph of Maia sitting on top of all the suitcases, ready to start her new adventure. Unfortunately the cab never arrived, so in the end the BBC had to send a car to drive us all the way to Scotland because by then we'd missed our flight. By the time we arrived at the farmhouse where we were staying it was very late, but when I woke up the next morning I opened the window and took in a deep breath of fresh, clean air. There were cows plodding about outside, tall trees everywhere, and lots and lots of green. It felt as far removed from London as I could imagine: a breath of fresh air. I suddenly felt as though my life was running in parallel to the character I was playing in the show. Abby had moved out of a big city to start again in the wilds of Scotland, and, in a way, so had I. It was life imitating art. On one of the first nights there was a ceilidh in the church hall of the village of Portpatrick, the village where we were staying. A ceilidh is a traditional Scottish social gathering with lots of music and dancing, a bit like a barn dance, and it turned out to be a wonderful night. All of the cast and crew joined in, and it was the perfect way for us to all get to know one another. In that part of Scotland it barely gets dark in the summer, and that night was especially beautiful. As I sat there enjoying the music with my new colleagues, I thought, 'I'm going to love this. This is just what I need.'

Other than that I hardly ever went out when I was in the middle of filming something with a heavy schedule, and while we were filming in Port Logan there weren't exactly many places to go anyway – just a few restaurants and a couple of pubs. I was happy staying in our cosy home, where we always had plenty of visitors. It was a two-hour drive to Glasgow and then a plane back to London to get home, so we hardly ever went home at weekends, either. One night I did go back to London for a few days off, and I went to see Madonna performing her 'Drowned World' tour at Earl's Court with a group of mates. The funny thing is that after that night there were all sorts of stories in the press about Madonna and me being best friends, and there was one article that suggested Madge and her daughter Lourdes were coming up to visit Maia and me on location in Port Logan and that we were going for a drink in the Port Logan Arms. It was all complete nonsense because I'd never even met her, so God only knows where the rumours came from. After Madonna's show we headed off to the after-party, and it was to be the first time I'd been caught on camera looking the worse for wear. I was decked out in a beautiful Missoni dress for the occasion, but unfortunately at the precise moment I was snapped by a paparazzi camera, one of my boobs fell out of my dress while I was in the back of a car on the way home. It wasn't exactly the classiest look in the world, I have to say, but once that camera flash has popped, there's very little one can do about it apart from praying it's not too hideous. A couple of days later I was walking past a newsagent's in Muswell Hill when I stopped dead my tracks. There I was, plastered across the front of one of the papers, looking dreadful. The worst thing was that they'd done 'before' and 'after' pictures, which somehow made it even more upsetting. It was a case of: at one point in the evening Michelle was all pristine and glamorous ... and now look at the state of her. I can't remember exactly what the caption was, and I certainly didn't want to read the story inside, but I later discovered that the picture was coupled with a piece about me looking exhausted and frail. I was completely mortified. It wasn't as if I'd never been tipsy before, but I'd certainly never been photographed like that, and the fact that my boob was hanging out for the world to see was just horrendous. I just didn't do things like that, and as a working actress it was the sort of publicity I could have done without.

The next day I was due to open a new swimming pool at a local primary school. I was certain that it was going to be full of shocked parents and disapproving teachers, and the worst part about it was that it was the school that I was hoping to get Maia into when she started.

On the Sunday of that week I was due back up in Port Logan to open a village fête. What would the local people think? It was a national newspaper so everyone was bound to have seen it. But I arrived back in the village to discover that two of the actresses on the show, Monica Gibb and Karen Westwood, had gone to every shop in the village and bought as many copies of the newspaper as they could get their hands on because they knew how embarrassed I'd be. It was such a kind and thoughtful thing to do, and typical of the camaraderie of the show's cast. Those who had seen it just giggled and had a bit of a laugh about it.

'Och, Michelle, is that what happens on your day off? You'd better stay up here, you're safer!'

That's what I love about the Scots: they can always see the funny side.

There was a lot of heart and warmth surrounding the whole project, and of all the characters I've played, Abby Wallace was probably the one I identify with most. During the third series, Paul Kaye said that he didn't want to do a fourth, so Tim Prager decided to kill his character off. The chemistry between Paul and me had been such that I didn't feel the show would work without him, so at the end of series three we called it a day. *Two Thousand Acres* was one of those great jobs that I took for granted at the time. Although I thoroughly enjoyed doing the show, I'm most definitely a London girl and I missed my home and my friends down south when I was away for months on end. It's probably the most popular drama I've done with audiences and people are forever asking me when it's coming back and telling me how beautiful it all looked. Mind you, people always seem to struggle with the title, calling it 'a thousand acres of something' – which makes me giggle. It certainly had a great charm and was brilliantly written. It's the one series that I'd secretly love to come back, just so I could do it all over again.

CHAPTER 24:

OPENING MY EYES

I first got involved in Oxfam's Education Now programme in 2000. The idea behind the campaign was that every child should have the right to an education, and I was invited to travel to Brazil to help raise awareness about the charity's work with disadvantaged communities in the country and their projects to fight poverty in education and to get children into school. There were about four different issues that Oxfam were involved with, and they included helping an indigenous tribe who were in danger of losing their land to rich landowners who were illegally selling off the land. The idea was that I'd travel over with a photographer and a group of people from the charity, and then do lots of TV and media highlighting the various causes and issues when I got back. I loved the idea of doing something positive, and so I asked my friend Stephen D Wright if he fancied making a documentary about what we were trying to achieve out there. Having never been on a trip like this before, I took two huge cases with me: one for my clothes and one for my shoes and make-up. I had no idea what I was going to need for filming, so I just took everything I could carry. As it turned out, the bag with the shoes and make-up never arrived in Brazil so I ended up going to a local shop and buying a pair of flip-flops and a bit of concealer to dab on my face. The suitcase eventually turned up in Lisbon, two weeks after I got back from Brazil. I'll certainly never pack like that again.

Brazil was one of the ten richest countries in the world, but no other country had such a massive divide between rich and poor. It's such a vibrant, colourful place, with pink, blue and yellow buildings everywhere you turn and music coming out of every window and from every street corner. It's as if it's always carnival time, with caipirinha cocktails and salsa dancing night and day. Then when you're sitting having dinner at a nice restaurant, you notice the bouncers who are there to keep the wretched, imploring street kids away, and you realize that there's more to it. In the city of Recife, some of the kids I saw were as young as three or four, and some of them had lost limbs where they'd fallen down in the street chasing a car in an attempt to procure a small offering of money or food. They were often mixed up in drugs or prostitution, and the majority of them were into glue-sniffing. In fact, a lot of people merely thought of them as vermin, shooing them away and cursing after them, and worse still they were killed like rats on a daily basis – at least four a day. I was there to raise awareness and show people back home what was going on, and my eyes were well and truly opened. Oxfam's objectives there were to get these kids off the streets and into schools by highlighting the issues and campaigning, but it was a mammoth task.

We travelled towards the Ororubo Mountains to meet the Xukuru tribe, and I discovered that the chief had recently been assassinated in the fight to reclaim his tribe's land. Now his twenty-one-year-old son, Marquinhos, had taken the crown, and when we met the boy he was all decked out in his finery and feathers – a bona fide customary tribal outfit. It was quite a shock when his mobile phone rang while we were chatting to him.

'Hi,' he said, answering it with a light American twang. 'Yeah, OK, I'll call you later.'

Then he hung up and carried on talking to us. The next time we met him he was dressed just like a regular kid, with trainers and a football shirt. We stayed in Marquinhos' father's empty stone hut, all sleeping together under a net because there were mosquitos everywhere. On the wall loomed a huge portrait of the boy's dead father, his eyes staring down at me all night. Very spooky!

When we visited one of the country's sprawling slums, known as favelas, the kids were all laughing at my flip-flops. I didn't understand why until someone explained that they couldn't understand why I was wearing such cheap shoes, being a famous actress from England. They expected me to be clad head-to-toe in designer gear. I played football with some of them and they kept asking me questions about some of our most famous footballers.

'Do you know David Beckham? What about Michael Owen, do you know him?'

When you're in a deprived area like that, where people are literally struggling to survive every day of their lives, it's always best to remember that you're there to try to help and to do a job. As a celebrity you can't go on those kinds of trips because you think it might broaden your horizons or help your career. I heard about an actress who did a trip for WaterAid and insisted on a first-class ticket – what's the point of that? You need to be committed and you have to totally immerse yourself in what you're doing. You also have to try not to cry, which isn't always easy. You mustn't be patronizing, just honest. I like to think being a mum helped me along the way, because I could in some small way identify with all the mothers who were just striving to look after their children in the best way they could. That's something universal.

The Brazil trip gave me such an incredible life experience, and when I got back to London I'd been so moved by everything I'd seen that I organised a charity event of my own to raise some money. It was at a restaurant called Sugar Reef, owned by a guy called Mark Fuller – an old mate from the London party scene – who agreed to let me use the space for nothing. David Thomas and I came up with the idea of a fashion show with glamorous models wearing clothes that all came from Oxfam. David styled the event, bringing in his friend Bruno Tonioli to choreograph the show for free – he was fantastic fun. Then I gathered together as many celebrities and as many journalists and photographers as I could and charged fifty pounds a ticket for the show. It was a roaring success and we raised quite a bit of cash for the charity that night. It was certainly a little stressful to organize, but very rewarding.

On another trip to South Africa I was due to meet Nelson Mandela, but unfortunately he was sick when we arrived. Oxfam's mission there was to try to make it legal for generic HIV drugs to be sold. The big pharmaceutical companies had a monopoly on the life-saving drugs, and were, at the time, resisting the introduction of cheaper alternatives. We visited the Chris Hani Baragwanath Hospital in Soweto, which is the biggest hospital in the country, and the third largest in the world. Some parts of it reminded me of pictures I'd seen of the field hospitals of World War One, with people lying on gurneys and makeshift beds waiting to be seen. There just weren't enough doctors and nurses to tend to everybody. While we were there, we took a *GMTV* camera crew along to the women's unit where we met a girl of eight who was HIV positive and had lost her mother to AIDS. The girl was thin and frail, but along with her aunt she'd walked the long twelve miles from her home to the hospital in the hope of getting some life-saving drugs. After she'd been seen and had received the drugs we offered them a lift home – none of us could stand the thought of them walking another twelve miles that day – and they accepted. When we asked our driver if it would be OK to take the little girl and her aunt in the car with us, he looked uncomfortable.

'Do you have to?' he said, coldly.

To say that I was taken aback was an understatement. Here was this seemingly intelligent Afrikaner – a solicitor in fact – but he simply refused to have the little girl in the front seat of the car and insisted that if we had to bring her at all, she'd have to travel in the back. There was still such deep-rooted racism there and it was quite shocking to witness. When we got the girl back to her home in the Soweto slums, we asked her aunt if she thought that her niece would get better, and she seemed full of hope now that she had the drugs. The following week I appeared on *GMTV* to talk about our trip and the accompanying film we'd made, but before the show went to air we found out that the little girl had died. It was devastating news, and it really hammered home the importance of what the charity was trying to do over there.

In Kenya we visited the Mathare slums in Nairobi, which was probably the worst example of poverty I've seen in my entire life. Again, our purpose was the education campaign, to help enable kids to have access to schools, particularly girls who seem to suffer more than boys in times of poverty.

More recently I've tended to stay on home turf with the causes I support, like the children's charity Barnardo's. It's a homegrown charity so I get to see the results first hand, and I also like the fact that they help a lot of young adults as well as children. They've recently launched a campaign to encourage more people to foster children who are in need of good homes and families. There are more than 90,000 children in need of foster care or adoption, and there are many people who don't even realize they'd be eligible to become a foster parent. Vicki now works for Essex County Council, in the fostering service, and she's very keen for me to support her in some fundraising for the fostered children. I'm determined to help her in any way I can because it's a cause I'm passionate about.

CHAPTER 25:

BOLLYWOOD IN BRUM

When I tell people that I was in a Bollywood musical, I can see their excited faces light up like Christmas trees.

'Wow! That's amazing!' they'll generally enthuse. 'What was it like filming in India? Which parts of the country did you go to?'

'I didn't go to India; I went to Birmingham,' I tell them, and then I watch their faces fall like stones.

Yes, my Bollywood film was set in Soho, which is an area on the borders of Birmingham and Smethwick. Not that there's anything wrong with Birmingham, but it's not exactly the place you think of when you envisage the glamour of a Bollywood musical, is it?

Two renowned casting agents, Suzanne Crowley and Gilly Poole, offered me the part and it came totally out of the blue in 2006. The story was sold to me as being a bit like an Asian version of *The Commitments*, and I was to play the mother of a young man who was trying to make it big in the music business. Rishi Kapoor was the very famous Indian actor who was going to be playing my husband and although I hadn't heard of him, I was told that his family were a prominent dynasty with a long history in Hindi cinema. Not only that, but he was distantly related to Felicity Kendal. The cast also included Ray Panthaki as my son and another famous Bollywood actor, Sunil Shetty. It all sounded quite exciting and very different from anything I'd done before, and on top of that the company making the movie were paying very well, so it was a bit of no-brainer as far as I was concerned. I was totally on board for *Don't Stop Dreaming*.

My character in the film, Jessica, was a British woman married to an Indian man, and although I got to wear some gorgeous saris, I didn't have to speak very much Hindi apart from the odd 'good morning'. It was a different way of working for me, because I'd been used to doing take after take until everyone was happy on most of the things I'd worked on, but with this they only shot precisely what they needed and everything seemed to be done at lightning speed. It wasn't exactly a big budget production, either, and although I was put up in a very nice hotel in Birmingham, there wasn't much in the way of on-set catering apart from curry, which everyone seemed happy to eat all the time – even for breakfast. I'm not that great with anything very hot, and from what I'd been told most of the food would have blown my head off, so I didn't eat much on set most of the time. One day for lunch we were at least offered an alternative: it was either curry or a kebab, and as the majority of the men on set were big burly crew members, they were quite happy with that selection.

Most of the crew didn't speak much English, but there was a lovely director of photography who I got chatting to, and the director seemed affable enough, too, even though he didn't seem to have done all that much before. My on-screen husband, Rishi, was charm personified; fifty-four years old and very good-looking. But my God, he was a diva. I don't think it was his fault; he just had so many people running around after him all the time that he was used to being treated like a superstar, and that was all he knew. The list of people attending to him and the way he looked was quite astonishing. He had someone to do his eyebrows, someone to look after his clothes and shoes, someone else to do his make-up and then another person doing his hair. In India the Bollywood stars are almost godlike, and Rishi was one of the biggest. We got on very well, but some of his antics on set did make me chuckle. Whenever we were about to go for a take he would whip out the most enormous mirror you'd ever seen and glare into it at close proximity, just to make sure everything was perfect. Then he'd thrust it in my face.

'Do you want to have a look?'

'Ooh, God no!' I'd say, leaping backwards as my own giant reflection hurtled towards me. 'I'm fine as I am, thanks, Rishi.'

After about six weeks of filming I got a call from my agent saying that production on the film had been halted, but nobody really knew why. Apparently they were going to get back to us soon but there wouldn't be any filming in the immediate future. It was a bit of a shock, but there wasn't very much I could do about it. Then a week or so later I heard a rumour on the grapevine that the production had run out of money, so I imagined that would be the end of it. No more Bollywood for me. Eventually my agent found out that the director had apparently disappeared and the film had been canned. It was five or six months later when I received a call from the production company with more news.

'*Don't Stop Dreaming* is back on,' they enthused as if they were talking about *The Jewel In The Crown*. 'If you still want to, we'd really love you to do it!'

I mulled it over for a moment.

'Fine. OK. Is Rishi still in it?'

'Yes, he is. The cast is the same, but now Richard Blackwood is in it, too, and we have a brand new director.'

On my first day back on the set, however, I discovered that things had changed quite a bit on the movie. For a start I no longer had a son; I now had a daughter who wanted to make it in the music business.

'What about all the stuff we've already filmed?' I asked, slightly flabbergasted. 'What's happening with that?'

'Scrapped,' I was told. 'We're starting again. We're throwing all that away and we're starting again.'

'Oh. Right.'

The new director was a cousin of Rishi's and was older and a lot more experienced than the last. The actress playing my daughter was called Sigga, who was a stunningly beautiful girl with jet-black hair and piercing blue eyes. She had the perfect look to be a Bollywood star but she was more of a model than an actress … and she was Icelandic. So we had an Indian father, a mother from North London and a daughter from Iceland, who, for some unknown reason, had all chosen to settle in Birmingham. Confused? I certainly was. Sigga had an accent that reminded me somewhat of Björk with the odd American pronunciation thrown in. It sounded neither British nor Indian, but nobody on the production crew really seemed to think it mattered.

'But she's my daughter and she's speaking with a completely different accent than me and her father,' I protested.

'It doesn't matter,' I was told. 'We'll sort it out afterwards.'

That seemed to be the answer to everything. We'll sort it out afterwards.

I knew it was a load of rubbish while I was doing it, but there wasn't much I could do by then. I just kept my head down and tried my best to communicate with my on-screen daughter without laughing at the ridiculousness of it all. I did end up seeing the finished movie and it was possibly the worst thing I've ever seen on screen. To add insult to injury, when I watched the trailer I realized that they'd done something to my voice in post-production that made me sound like I'd been sucking on a helium balloon. It was like watching one of Pinky and Perky, so I couldn't even bring myself to watch the whole film. I just had to console myself with the fact that at least I wasn't doing any singing. I didn't see many reviews of the film out there, but I did find one that suggested that the cast of *Don't Stop Dreaming* might want to head for the hills, adopt a new identity and deny ever having any involvement in it.

I would dearly love to go to India one day and star in a real Bollywood movie, but *Don't Stop Dreaming* is the film that you'll find in the bargain bin at the supermarket for £2.99. Actually that might be pushing it, let's call it a pound.

CHAPTER 26:

OUT OF FASHION?

When I first went up for the part of Ma Baker in the Boney M-inspired musical *Daddy Cool* I had high hopes. Writer Gurinder Chadha – who was one of the writers of *Bend It Like Beckham* – was involved and it seemed like it was going to be a really wonderful and exciting project. I met Gurinder and the show's producer, Robert Mackintosh, in the tearoom at Fortnum and Mason and she completely won me over, but by the time the show went into production she was no longer involved and I started to wonder whether I'd made the right decision saying yes.

With each passing day leading up to the start of *Daddy Cool* rehearsals, the pressure was mounting. For a start, I was really panicking about the idea of doing a full-on West End musical, especially the singing, which was out of my comfort zone, and I was sent off for singing lessons with the renowned and formidable singing coach Mary Hammond, who taught from her house in Camden. I'd also just come out of a long-term relationship, which had ended painfully and not very amicably. I was upset and struggling to get over it, and the timing couldn't have been worse. It's often been said by my friends that in the Collins world there's either been a drama, there's a drama happening, or there's a drama about to happen, and at that time it felt like it was all three at once. Everything seemed to be spiralling out of control, and by the time the first day of rehearsals arrived I wasn't in a good place at all. The day started with me having a very scary panic attack and completely freaking out. I was shattered and emotional from all the rows I'd been having with my ex-boyfriend, and suddenly I just couldn't face the idea of starting a new job and meeting new people. I wasn't ready.

'I don't know why I'm even putting myself through this,' I told myself. 'No. I'm not going to do it.'

It's very unlike me to be unprofessional and to even consider letting an entire company of actors and a creative team down, but that's how I felt at the time. I just couldn't think straight. In the end I sent a text to the director, an American guy called Andy Goldberg, telling him that I was sorry but I felt terrible and couldn't come in. I'd warmed to Andy immediately and I felt like I could trust him. Not long after I fired off the text, he called me.

'I'm having a really bad time,' I said, bursting into tears suddenly. 'I'm so sorry, I just don't think I can do it.'

I didn't have any confidence in myself. The idea of getting up on stage in front of an audience seemed unimaginable in the state I was in. Andy was sympathetic and gentle with me.

'Look, just come and meet me for a chat, and I'll tell the rest of the cast that you're not coming in today,' he said.

We met in a café near the Welsh Centre in King's Cross, which is where we were rehearsing, and Andy couldn't have been nicer.

'You can do this, Michelle, I know you can. You've just got to give yourself a chance.'

He convinced me to come in the next day but I still didn't feel great, so I made an appointment to see a doctor as soon as I possibly could. I didn't really like the idea of taking anti-depressants, but I needed to feel better quite quickly if I was ever going to step out on to that stage. In the end I gave in and took the pills he prescribed, but unfortunately they didn't agree with me at all. I know they say you sometimes feel worse before you feel better but I couldn't cope with the way the pills were affecting me. Half the time I felt as though I was having some kind of strange out-of-body experience, and in the middle of a rehearsal I'd be dazed and unfocused to the point where it was unbearable. I knew that I had to pull myself together and that these pills weren't right for me, so I threw them away and resolved to throw myself into my work. In the end, I quite enjoyed the rehearsal period. We had an amazing choreographer called Sean Chapman, who gave me such confidence with my singing and dancing, which were the things I was the least confident about.

The show was a love story about two young lovers who came from opposing families, a bit like a modern-day *Romeo and Juliet*, and I played the mother of the girl, Ma Baker (as in the song title). I had an unforgettable line.

'Hi, my name's Margaret Baker ... but you can call me Ma!'

There was some amazing raw talent in the show, and it was actually a great story. In fact, once I got into the swing of it, I started to feel a little better. It dawned on me that I'd simply had too much going on to really appreciate and enjoy the experience and low self-esteem had got the better of me. I'd let my personal life impact on my work and it was clouding everything. As the opening night drew near I decided to pick myself up, dust myself down and get on with it. I needed to put my heart and soul into it, just like I did with all my other jobs. I really wanted it to work. On opening night I sat in my dressing room at the Shaftesbury Theatre, staring out of my window at the bright lights and all the hustle and bustle of theatreland. This was the West End and I was about to make my debut in a proper musical. It was quite an amazing feeling, and I felt lucky.

After a small hitch, where we had to postpone the opening because the theatre roof collapsed, the show made its debut with reviews that weren't too bad at all. It wasn't enough, though. Although I believed it could have been a really good show given half a chance, it felt as if it was doomed from the beginning. Despite the great music and performances, the production was surrounded by bad press and seemed to be more infamous because of all the gossip surrounding two of its stars, who were said to be having an affair. I'd never worked on a West End musical before, but one of the things that amazed me was the amount of time that some of the cast seemed to take off. It seemed like every day there was an understudy or a swing on for one of the main actors because somebody was sick or just hadn't turned up, and I found that quite shocking. Although a few of the of the actors shone and worked hard, like Ricky Norwood who went on to play Fatboy in *EastEnders*, and Melanie La Barrie, who had an incredible voice, not everyone in the cast shared the same enthusiasm and dedication it takes to put on a great show. On top of all that there was so much in-fighting and behind-the-scenes backbiting and bitching that it became quite wearing. In the end I called the show's producers, pleading for a bit of support and offering an ultimatum.

'Please sort this out or the show is going to fall apart. If someone doesn't step in and lay down the law, I'm going to walk the minute my contract is up.'

By the time someone got back to me it was too late and nothing changed; there just didn't seem to be anyone on the production who was holding things together. When I arrived at the theatre on Boxing Day 2006 I was the only lead actor who'd bothered to turn up, and for me it was the final straw. I went on holiday to Bali on New Year's Eve, left my agent, and never went back to *Daddy Cool*. Of course the producers weren't happy, but I'd been quite clear of my intentions if somebody didn't step in and sort out the mess the show was in. It was quite unlike me to walk away from a job, but as it turned out, the show didn't run for much longer anyway. It was a great shame really because I thought it had such potential.

While Maia and I were on holiday, spending a relaxing time in the paddy fields of Bali with my good friend Caroline Sterling, I got a call from a producer called Phil Collinson, who I'd worked with on *Sea of Souls*. He was interested in me playing a part in an episode of *Doctor Who* and I was thrilled at the prospect and excited about working with David Tennant and Freema Agyeman. Chris Chibnall, who went on to write *Broadchurch*, wrote a fantastic episode called '42', which was about a spaceship that was hurtling towards an alien star, with forty-two minutes before impact. I hadn't done science fiction before, and this wasn't just any old sci-fi series: it was *Doctor Who*, one of the biggest shows on TV. I was more accustomed to playing down-to-earth women, so I wasn't exactly sure how to play it. As I was portraying a very capable ship's captain, Kath McDonnell, I thought I might take inspiration from Sigourney Weaver's character, Ripley, in the *Alien* movies, but I felt like needed a bit of advice from an expert.

'How do you play it?' I asked David Tennant on our first day on set. 'Do you go over the top? Are there different rules and boundaries for sci-fi?'

'Just do honesty,' he said. 'Play for the truth, as if you were doing any other drama.'

He was such a lovely, giving actor to work with, totally professional, and I really enjoyed working on *Doctor Who*. Freema had only just started on the show, so she was fresh and still a bit nervous, but I also warmed to her very quickly – she's a great girl. She was changing agents and I recommended her to my previous agent, Independent. It turned out to be a good call because her career has soared ever since; in fact she's recently been in a big American television series called *The Carrie Diaries* – a prequel to *Sex and the City*.

In the episode we were supposed to be sweating to death in a steaming hot spaceship that was plummeting towards a star. Meanwhile, it was the middle of winter and we were filming in a freezing cold warehouse just outside Pontypridd in South Wales. To keep me looking hot and sweaty the make-up people slathered me in baby oil the whole time, greasing my hair down and stripping off any make-up.

'Oh please,' I'd beg the lovely, late Pam Mullins, 'Just a little dab of mascara, for God's sake.'

'No, you can't,' Pam would say. 'No make-up at all on this one.'

It was brilliant fun. I spent most of the time running around in Doc Martens, combat trousers and a vest and it was an incredibly liberating experience. I was working with a lovely cast with a great script and I was enjoying myself. I even got used to not having any make-up on ... once I resolved not to look in the mirror.

My next project, *Rock Rivals*, was a show based around a TV talent show like *The X Factor*. In fact, Simon Cowell was one of the people behind the series, created by Shed Productions: the company behind *Footballers' Wives*. I played opposite Sean Gallagher as one half of a husband-and-wife team who were both judges on the fictional talent show, and the plot centred on their turbulent relationship as well as the lives and loves of the contestants. The idea was for the show to be multimedia and an interactive experience for the audience, with the public actually voting for the ultimate winner of the competition. Nobody in the cast or the production team would know the outcome until the votes were in, and we had to film two different endings to accommodate either eventuality. It all sounded like such an interesting and novel idea, but there were problems right from the off. Simon Cowell didn't like the actor playing the lead male contestant, and after about ten weeks of shooting the actor was fired and replaced, meaning that the rest of us had to reshoot a ton of scenes. The rest of the cast, including me, thought that the fired actor was great and none of us could understand why Simon didn't like him. His face obviously didn't fit and that was that. The whole thing left a bit of a bad taste and from then on, something didn't feel right to me. It was another project that I felt should have turned out a lot better than it did, but sadly the public didn't warm to it and it didn't do as well in the ratings as everyone thought it would. It's quite tough when that happens because when you're the lead in a TV show you tend to feel responsible if it's not a success. There were a lot of talented people in the show and we were all disappointed when we didn't get a second series, but I try to view experiences like that as a learning curve rather than a failure.

At the end of 2008 I did panto again. This time I was the wicked stepmother in *Cinderella* at the Bristol Hippodrome. I enjoyed the experience, particularly as Maia and my family came and stayed up there with me all over Christmas. The cast included my old mate Peter Straker as Dandini, Bobby Davro, and Hollywood legend Mickey Rooney playing Baron Hardup. Mickey, who was eighty-seven at the time, had been a child star who had gone on to appear in movies alongside Marilyn Monroe, Audrey Hepburn and Judy Garland, and everyone in the production was quite excited to be acting in the presence of a real live Hollywood legend. His eighth wife Jan was also in the show as Baroness Hardup, and she was a lovely woman. Mickey was a very sweet and charismatic guy, but he had his bad days, too. One minute he'd be charming you with the most fabulous stories about Frank Sinatra and all the Hollywood legends he'd worked with, and the next minute he'd be really grumpy and you couldn't get a word out of him. He also had a terrible habit of trying to upstage the other actors in the production, sticking his tongue out and pulling monkey faces while they were trying to deliver their lines. I guess he thought it was all part of the fun, but it could be quite annoying, even in a pantomime. One day the director told him off after he'd pulled silly faces behind me during a matinee, and Mickey wasn't happy. In fact, for the next couple of days he didn't really speak to me, that was until he found out about the special guest I had coming to watch my performance one evening.

I'd met Sir Ian McKellen through Michael Cashman twenty years earlier; they lived a couple of houses apart. In fact, from Michael's window you could see right onto Ian's roof terrace. Ian hadn't seen me perform on stage for years, and as he was staying in the area for Christmas he came to see the show. Meanwhile, Mickey got wind of Ian's visit and broke his silence to come and speak to me about it.

'Michelle!' he rasped. 'Is Sir Ian in tonight?'

'Yes, Mickey, I think he is.'

'Well can you bring him to my room?'

'Er ... OK. I'll ask him, but I don't see why not.'

'Great!'

After the show I told Ian that he had been invited to meet Mickey and he was thrilled.

'I'd love to meet him, absolutely,' he said.

'Well I'll take you up to his room and we'll go and say hello,' I said, and off we went.

I knocked on the door of Mickey's dressing room and it swung open, with Mickey beaming a big smile and offering the cheeriest of greetings.

'Hey! Sir Ian!'

Then Mickey yanked Ian into his room and slammed the door

shut in my face, leaving me somewhat stunned in the corridor. That was the last I saw of Ian for about forty minutes. It was actually very funny, and I didn't really mind. Ian obviously enjoyed meeting Mickey, and at the end of the day he is a bona fide Hollywood legend. I guess if anyone deserves to be treated like a star it was him. He was in his eighties and doing his fifth panto in the UK. Hats off to him!

I must admit, I wasn't feeling particularly great about the way things were going in my career by then. Performing in a good panto could be quite lucrative, but it wasn't exactly all that satisfying creatively. I began to analyse and assess things, wondering what I should do next. I'd been working, yes, but there was nothing very thrilling on the horizon and I wasn't being offered any roles that excited me. Like so many actors, I panic if I don't work for a month. When you're a single parent there's no one else to fall back on. It's my responsibility to support and look after Maia, and I've always put pressure on myself to work hard and be the breadwinner. As far as I'm concerned, there are few things better than having a bit of money behind you and knowing that you've worked hard and earned it. Whenever that stability is threatened I find it hard to cope. At the end of the day, I knew that I just wasn't happy with myself. It's that age-old thing: you can't love anyone else until you learn to love yourself. It might sound corny, but in my case it was an adage that certainly seemed to ring true. All my life I've been trying to feel good about myself, to love myself, but I'm fundamentally quite insecure. I've often wondered if this is because I'm an actress, or perhaps there's something more deeply rooted: maybe that self-doubt is in my DNA. It's most likely a bit of both.

For years after my first defining role as Cindy Beale in *EastEnders* I was afraid that people wouldn't take me seriously. I always felt like I was up against it, that there was something holding me back. As much as I was and am eternally grateful to Cindy, she was also my albatross. I recently heard Clare Grogan from the band Altered Images being interviewed on the radio. She was talking about the band's massive and much-played hit record 'Happy Birthday' and saying that for sixteen years after its success she couldn't bear to hear anyone mention it, let alone listen to it herself. I was the same about *EastEnders* for a long time. Whenever people mentioned it in my presence I'd silently explode inside.

'I want to move on,' I'd say dismissively. 'I want to be taken seriously as an actress, not just a character from a soap.'

I had a rather big chip on my shoulder, and it took me a long time to accept that *EastEnders* was a massive and important part of my life. It was ridiculous, really. I landed some really good and credible dramas after I left the show and I should have been riding high, but unfortunately, whatever good things might have been happening, my insecurities would always win the day and I'd end up telling myself that I wasn't good enough. Now, for the first time in my career, I felt like I wasn't really 'in fashion' as an actress and it scared me.

CHAPTER 27:

THE ROOMS

I t didn't take much for those anxieties to bubble to the surface. I'd been bruised by *Rock Rivals* and the fact that it failed to get picked up for a second series, and I wasn't sure what to do next. I was in my mid-forties and I felt like I was floundering. Then, a friend of mine in California suggested I head out to LA for pilot season, which is the period between January and April when the TV studios create, cast and produce all their new shows. My agent warned me that I'd hate it, but that made me even more determined. I needed a change and I was always up for a challenge, so after much thought I decided to give it a shot. Why not? As far as I was concerned it was a positive move forward rather than sitting back and waiting for something good to fall in my lap.

After a couple of trips back and forth I'd managed to get my O-1 visa, which would allow me to work in America for up to three years, and I decided that this time I was really going to make a go of it. I think some people who knew me thought 'Good God, what's she doing that for?' I could see it in their eyes when I spoke about it. For me it was a chance to try my luck as an actor in a place where nobody had any preconceived ideas about me. It was a chance to reinvent myself, and that felt quite appealing at the time. On previous, shorter trips to LA I'd stayed in boutique hotels – sometimes with Maia – but that burnt a serious hole in my pocket. However, I was lucky enough to have plenty of generous friends to stay with, like Mari Wilson and Mal Young, who had a beautiful house in Beverly Hills. My friend Ollie Pickton-Jones lived there, as did Shirley Greene and her husband Ramon, who I knew from London. Shirley became like my surrogate mother in LA and she really looked out for me, particularly when I was out there alone. I was never short of somewhere to lay my hat. Of course, I always missed Maia terribly when she wasn't with me, so I decided to take her along for five weeks. Perhaps she might love La La Land and we'd make it our permanent home. It meant pulling her out of school and getting her a private tutor for the duration of our trip, but I thought she'd find it exciting and get a kick out of it.

Trying to make it big in Tinseltown is most definitely a young person's game and you have to dedicate yourself to it fully to be in with a real shot. You also have to have a brilliant agent to help ease your way along, and although mine wasn't bad, they simply didn't have the clout needed to get me through all the right doors. Once I got settled in I found myself in a whirl of auditions and meetings. I met the casting directors of *Desperate Housewives*, *CSI*, *Bones*, and quite a few other big US shows. There were no specific roles on offer; they were very general meetings to find out what I had to offer. They all seemed very positive on the surface, but you can never really tell whether it's going to work out or not. After I did one audition, the female casting director called my agent with what she felt might be a 'helpful' suggestion.

'You gotta tell that girl to ditch that terrible perfume. It's disgusting. It made me feel sick!'

'It was Clinique Aromatics and I only had a tiny squirt,' I protested to my agent. 'What a cheek!'

The woman had been a nightmare during the interview, too.

'Why do ya wanna work in Hollywood anyway?' she drawled. 'You're quite old!'

She was no spring chicken herself, but maybe she wasn't far off the mark. The place is literally brimming with young starlets and beautiful women, and you can bump into a gorgeous A-list actress in every coffee shop or hotel bar. In the matter of a couple of weeks

I sat next to Cameron Diaz in Chateau Marmont having a cup of tea, stood behind Jennifer Aniston in the queue at Starbucks, saw Courteney Cox shopping at The Grove, and Nicole Kidman jogged past me in Coldwater Canyon while I was out power-walking one day – a very LA pastime! One day I was working out in the gym next to the gorgeous Hayden Panettiere from the TV show *Heroes*. She was so beautiful and her body was so amazing I could hardly believe it. I was on a Power Pilates machine at the time, and I was so busy staring at her that the machine's elastic strap came of its hook, pinging back and slapping me in the face. So that's what I was up against!

Still, there was no point being an actress in LA if I wasn't going to network. After all, the old adage about getting on in the entertainment business – it's not what you know, it's who you know – couldn't have been more accurate there. So as well as my gym classes, dialect classes and the odd acting lesson (which everyone seemed to do but which I hated) I found myself in a whirl of dinners and social events around town, which more often than not involved alcohol. It's funny; I found it was the Brits and the Aussies who lived there that partied the most. They were the ones who seemed to have all the best house parties. There's even a little society there called Brits in LA, which is run by Craig Young and Eileen Lee. They have a breakfast club at Cecconi's restaurant in West Hollywood every Tuesday and Saturday, where ex-pats and people who are working in the city long-term get together for a meet and mingle. There's always HP sauce and Marmite on the tables, and Eileen's a great host. One of the downsides of the place is that you sometimes end up just talking to other actors moaning about the fact that they can't get a job, which can be a bit of a downer. Yes, it was good to touch base and a great idea for people who lived there, but I didn't see much point in coming to Los Angeles just to hang out with the people from back home.

One night I went to Elton John's Oscar party, where I was shunted off the red carpet in favour of someone far more famous than I was. I was asked if I had a plaque with my name on it, so I could hold it up to show people who I was. It felt like an identity parade. No thanks, I thought, I'm not that desperate.

As the weeks went on I started to get bored saying the same things to different people at all the parties and dinners I was attending. Sometimes I felt like I needed a drink just to get me through the evening. Everyone drives in LA as it's very hard to get cabs and the public transport system isn't anything like the ones in London or New York, so I found myself worrying about whether or not I'd be able to have a drink at this event or that, if I then had to drive home. Suddenly it began to dawn on me how much importance I was putting on alcohol. Was I relying on it too much? When I thought about it I realized that nine times out of ten when I'd ended up in a screaming row with a boyfriend, alcohol was the catalyst. I'd often get over-emotional when I'd had too much to drink, and that was when things usually spiralled out of control. I was suddenly faced with a blinding truth: Chardonnay made me crazy.

Along with this revelation came reflection. People always seem to be analysing themselves in LA, but being away from my life in London made me take a long, hard look at myself and I started to wonder what I was running away from. I was a small fish in a very big pond and on top of that I was lonely. I knew that something had to change and that things just couldn't carry on the way they had been. One of my friends came up with a suggestion, which, at first, sounded shocking.

'Look, you're not happy, Michelle. Why don't you come along to an AA meeting?'

Alcoholic? Me? I wasn't one of those people who got up in the morning and had to have a drink; in fact I could go for days or sometimes weeks without having one. The problem was that when I did go for it, I tended to drink quite a lot in a short space of time and that's what was getting out of hand. At the end of the day I just wasn't happy, so perhaps it was time to do something about it.

I was nervous to say the least. The only other time I'd been to an AA meeting was for research, when I was playing a recovering alcoholic in the TV series *Sea of Souls* in 2004. I thought it might be beneficial to see exactly what went on in 'the rooms' so the show's production manager found a meeting in Muswell Hill that I could attend.

'Will you be all right going on your own?' she asked.

'Yeah, I'll be fine.'

As the evening of the meeting drew nearer, however, I got very nervous. Would I get recognized? Should I go in disguise and pretend to be someone else? What would I say if I was asked to speak? When I got to the room where the meeting was being held it all seemed very quiet and I considered just turning around and going home. In the end I gathered myself and knocked on the door, and when I walked in I was surprised to find just one solitary man.

'Hello,' I whispered, nervously. 'My name's Michelle and I'm from the BBC.'

God only knows why I said that, but I did.

'Er ... is this the AA meeting?' I went on.

The man looked up at me.

'No, love,' he said. 'This is the Boys' Brigade, alcoholics are tomorrow.'

I ended up going to a meeting in the King's Road, but inevitably the press spotted me and it was all over the papers the next day that I had a secret drink problem. I was furious.

The first meeting I went to in LA was above a bar (actually a lot of the meetings were above bars, which struck me as a bit odd) and I burst into tears the minute I got there. I was petrified, and for some time I didn't dare speak, praying that nobody would notice me and ask me to tell my story. Everyone who speaks has to introduce themselves with the customary mantra: saying their name and acknowledging that they are an alcoholic. The trouble was, I didn't really believe it. Even though I did finally pluck up the courage to open up, I felt like I wanted to say, 'Well, I'm saying it but I'm not really. I'm just a bit lost.' That's how I truly felt but, of course, you can't say that. I stuck with it, though, turning up to meetings every single day, and in the end I actually started to look forward to them. Whether or not one agrees with the almost religious approach that the organization adopts, it's a very positive environment that helps so many people the world over to see things more clearly and get their lives back on track. In LA I found it particularly relevant, because it helped me to see the whole Hollywood scene for what it is. People can get so caught up in the aspirational lifestyle and the glittering facade that they lose themselves. Like many people there, I found the meetings grounding and they helped me to see through the smoke and mirrors. You need that or you can go crazy out there. I found that sharing my fears and troubles rather than shutting them away was therapeutic, and listening to other people's stories made me feel humble and realize how lucky I was. It helped me put things into perspective and sort out what was what. I soon realized that alcohol was just a small part of a bigger problem ... and that bigger problem was me. Instead of celebrating my triumphs and feeling grateful for the things I'd achieved in life, I spent the majority of the time beating myself up about the things that hadn't worked out. The negative voice in me always triumphed over the positive and that was the demon I really had to overcome.

Almost all of the people I met in AA were there for genuine help with their addictions and, like me, they got a lot out of the meetings, but I soon realized that there were a few people who went to 'the rooms' simply to network. After all, there was no telling who you might find yourself sitting next to at a meeting around Beverly Hills or West Hollywood, and it was quite often the easiest way for eager budding actors or screenwriters to bump into some of Hollywood's big players. It was like having a captive audience. If the actor could come up with a decent monologue beginning with, 'Hello, my name's Bill and I'm an alcoholic,' tinged with just the right amount of pathos and emotion, it could serve as a worthy audition piece in front of the right crowd.

After six or seven weeks in America I could see that Maia wasn't happy. She was just thirteen at the time and really missing home.

'Mum, they're all so fake here and I really miss my school and my friends.'

She was right in many ways. After a few weeks of meetings and promises and dashed hopes I was starting to feel a bit desperate touting myself around all over town. The realization was creeping over me that if you're not young, beautiful and connected in Hollywood then it's probably not the place to be, and I had no intention of being one of those people who outstayed their welcome and ended up turning bitter. It's a place where, as an actor, you can slip off the radar and disappear forever. On top of that I felt incredibly guilty for dragging Maia out of her home environment, especially now I knew that it wasn't as much fun for her as I thought it would be. Of course I'd love to have been offered some amazing role in an American film or TV series, and it's certainly something I wouldn't rule out in the future, but then wasn't the right time. I couldn't stand the thought of my daughter being unhappy any longer and so the two of us headed home.

Once I was back in the UK it hit me how much I'd missed London and I fell back in love with it all over again. Coming back had provided me with a new motivation, not to mention the kick up the backside that I sorely needed. The funny thing was that as soon as I got back I landed a great part on *Miss Marple*, with Julia McKenzie and Edward Fox, playing a rather stern and dowdy housekeeper called Miss Treadwell. This was something quite different for me, character-wise, and my first ever costume drama, but it came exactly at the right time, setting me off on a more positive path again.

I still carried on going to AA and continued to find it a fantastic support. I was quite taken aback, however, by some of the snobbery involved in who went to what particular meeting and where it was situated. There were certain people I met who would only go to the Mayfair or the Portobello meetings. They certainly wouldn't be seen dead going to the one in Holloway Road because they thought that some of the attendees were too rough.

'Too many drunks, darling!'

I thought they were missing the point.

I didn't touch a drop of alcohol for about two years, and eventually I didn't feel like I needed to go to the meetings anymore. I felt like I turned a corner and that I'd given myself a fresh start. It was an experience that changed me for the better, and although I do have a drink now, AA taught me to keep a check on myself and stay focused when I'm working. That means no socializing or getting even tipsy while I'm in the middle of something, and certainly no letting my personal problems infringe on the job at hand. And definitely no Chardonnay!

CHAPTER 28:

DOING THE RIGHT THING

In the winter of 2009 I was in the Take That musical *Never Forget*, which was co-produced by Charlie Parsons, who I'd first met when I worked on *The Word* in the early 1990s. The show was on in Croydon over Christmas, and I was playing Babs, the mum of a northern boy who was starting up a band. It actually turned out to be good practice for getting my Lancashire accent right, ready for *Coronation Street* which I started a year or so later. The run-up to the holiday period hadn't been the best of times. My mum's former partner, Mickey, was now dying of cancer and receiving palliative care at home. I'd stayed close to him over the last few years, and by then he was in a pretty bad way. Seeing Mickey so helpless and frail had made me realize how lucky Maia and I were, and I thought that it might be good for the two of us to do something other than just stuff ourselves with turkey and open presents that year. My next-door neighbour was quite involved with the local church, so I asked her if there were any organizations she knew of who might need a couple of willing volunteers on Christmas Day, which was my one day off from the show. She put me in touch with a friend of hers who ran a church soup kitchen in Crouch End. They were serving food to the people who were homeless or down on their luck at Christmas and were happy for Maia and me to come along and help out, so that's what we decided to do.

On Christmas morning, Maia and I went over to Mickey's house to visit him. He looked terrible and it was quite hard to take. Mickey had developed a cancerous tumour that had taken over almost the entire right side of his face. By then you couldn't even see his eye anymore; it was heartbreaking. A few weeks earlier, I'd taken him out Christmas shopping for the afternoon in Holloway.

'I want to buy Vicki a watch,' he told me. 'And I want to buy you something too, before I die.'

It was a tragic thing to hear from someone who'd once been such a lively and vibrant character. At one point that afternoon we sat in Argos waiting for a light fitting that he'd ordered to be brought down from the stock room, when I suddenly realized that everyone was staring at him. I was still getting used to the way he looked but to other people it must have been quite shocking. Poor Mickey looked incredibly hurt and I felt terrible. Then he turned to me, despondently.

'This is the last time I'm ever going out,' he said. 'I'm not doing this again.'

He died the following March.

After our Christmas morning visit to Mickey's, Maia and I headed over to the church hall, ready to help doing whatever it was the organizers needed us to do. It was mostly OAPs, but there were a few younger people there, too. While Maia and I were waitressing that afternoon I noticed a woman sitting very quietly with her four children. She had three girls and a boy, aged between about four and eleven, and as I watched her I became curious about what her story might be and how she came to be at the soup kitchen on Christmas Day. I got chatting to a woman called Anne who worked for a Christian-run housing organization that helps homeless families in Haringey. She told me that the woman – I'll call her Gina – lived in one room with her four children but no father, and nobody was quite sure where she was from because she didn't seem to have a passport. She desperately needed re-housing and the charity was trying to help her. Gina seemed nice but she hardly said two words, and the kids seemed very sweet and well behaved. After dinner when everyone had been given their Christmas presents, Maia went over to play with them. The oldest girl was quite chatty but the younger ones were pretty shy. Suddenly I had an idea, which I put to Anne.

'Do you think the children would like to see a pantomime?'

Letitia Dean was starring in *Snow White and the Seven Dwarves* at Fairfield Halls, where our show was also playing.

'The show I'm in might be a bit grown up, but I could take them to see an afternoon matinee of *Snow White* before my evening show.'

I asked Gina what she thought, and she nodded.

'Yes I think they'd like to go,' she said, quietly. 'That would be lovely.'

'Well why don't I give you my number and then you can text me to arrange something,' I suggested, not wanting to come across as pushy or patronizing.

Gina agreed, and a few days later she called and said that her children would love to go to the pantomime and would it be possible for me to collect them at an address in Tottenham. She wasn't able to bring them herself because she was pregnant and feeling very sick. I had a matinee myself that day, so I had to send a taxi to pick them up and bring them to Croydon, and there was some discrepancy about where they actually lived. Anne had given me one address but Gina gave me a completely different one. Still, I didn't think much about it at the time, and eventually the children turned up and, along with Maia, happily went to watch the panto. I popped in to see them during the interval and they were jumping around and looking so happy. It was great to see. Gina texted me the next day and told me that the kids had really enjoyed the show and thanked me very much for organizing it, so a couple of weeks later, after I'd finished my short run in *Never Forget*, I thought I might take them out again. My friend Sharon and her husband Tim, who are both teachers, were round at my place with their teenage son one afternoon.

'Why don't we take all the kids to see *Avatar*,' I suggested.

I knew that Gina's children had never been to the cinema so I thought it might be fun for them to see a big blockbuster movie, especially as it was in 3D. Once again Gina said that the children would like to go, so I jumped into my jeep with Maia and headed over to pick them up, with Sharon and Tim following behind in their car. The address I'd been given was a very run-down building that served as some kind of church, and the area wasn't the sort of place I'd have fancied wandering around on my own late at night. Gina came down with the kids and a man in tow, who didn't say much, and I thought for a moment that the two of them might want to come along with us.

'Gina, I'm really sorry, I don't have enough room for everyone,' I said.

'That's fine,' she said. 'I'm not feeling that well anyway.'

The children didn't look especially tidy and well turned out and there seemed to be a quiet melancholy about them, which unsettled me somewhat. Once we were all in the car I asked them who their mum's friend was.

'Oh, that's our dad ...' one of the girls began, but suddenly stopped herself.

'I'm not supposed to say that,' she muttered.

'He's a preacher at the church,' another one of the girls said.

She looked quite cagey, and I remembered Anne telling me that there was no father in the picture, so it all struck me as a bit odd. What concerned me more was that the children then told me that they'd never been to school before.

'Our mum takes us to the library every morning,' one of the children said. 'There's nowhere else for us to go.'

I didn't really know what to say, so I just nodded and listened, but there was something disconcerting about the children's story and their manner that sent alarm bells reverberating inside my head.

At the cinema the kids enjoyed wearing the 3D glasses and filling themselves up on popcorn, but they all ended up falling asleep during the long two-and-a-half-hour film. Afterwards they wanted to meet my beautiful white Samoyed dog, Jingle, so I took them all back to my house for some tea, texting Gina to tell her that I'd drive them back later that evening. I made them pizza and they played with Maia in her room and they all seemed happy and contented for a while, without a care in the world. When I drove them back to the church building, Gina came down to meet us and one of the girls invited me inside. I followed Gina and the children inside and up some stairs to the back of the building, eventually walking into a barely lit room with a massive TV screen on one wall. There was no sound coming from the TV, just footage of what looked like large groups of people shouting at one another, and the room had padded sound insulation all around its walls, like you might see in a music studio. It was a strange set-up and the atmosphere unnerved me, but then the man that I'd met earlier came over and shook my hand, firmly. I smiled and said hello, but made my excuses and left pretty quickly: it was dark outside and I just wanted to get out of there. Something wasn't right, and after that day I never saw the children again.

A few weeks later, I started getting emails from Gina telling me that her kids were geniuses and that she needed money to help get them educated. I felt sorry for Gina and her situation but something just didn't add up, and being a teacher my friend Sharon was particularly worried that the kids weren't going to school. When the housing charity called me to say that they were trying to rehome the family and they desperately needed stuff for the new house, I managed to get hold of a computer and a TV for them, but nobody ever came to collect it. I really didn't know what to think, especially after the emails asking me for money continued. I called Anne again and asked her advice.

'There's something odd about this whole thing, and there was something about that man I didn't like, too.'

Anne agreed that things weren't right and suggested that I call Social Services.

'I think the family should be on their radar,' she said.

Friends I'd spoken to had said much the same, but it's not an easy decision to get involved in someone else's business when you don't know the whole story. In the end, my concern for the children won the day, and I made the call.

'I think someone should check out what's going on,' I told the woman on the other end of the phone. 'The children aren't going to school and I'm worried that they're not being looked after properly.'

'Thank you; you're not the first person who's spoken to us about this family,' she said. 'We'll be looking into it.'

I still had no reason to think that Gina was anything other than a loving mum who'd got herself into a bad situation and who needed help, but then in 2010 I got a letter from a human rights organization, telling me that the children had been taken away from their parents and asking me if I knew where they were. Of course I had no idea, and I got the shock of my life when a lawyer representing Haringey council called me. She said that Gina and the children's father were taking me and the council to court because they believed there was a conspiracy between us to take their children away so I could adopt them. The accusation was that the whole idea of me going to help out at the shelter on Christmas Day was a set-up, and that I was there specifically to manipulate Gina and her children so that I could eventually adopt them for myself with the council's blessing. I was astonished and at first I thought it was ludicrous, but I was then subpoenaed to attend a family court and suddenly it all seemed a lot more real and frightening.

When the day of the court hearing arrived I knew I hadn't done anything wrong, but it was a nerve-shredding experience all the same. I was still none the wiser when I left the court that day, though, because the family didn't even turn up. I think the judge thought it was all a bit ridiculous and after that things went quiet for a while. I thought it was over. A few months later, however, I opened my front door to a man who I'd never met before, firing questions at me as if I were a criminal.

'The children have been taken away from their parents and we want you to tell us where they are,' he barked.

'I don't know what you're talking about,' I told him. 'It's nothing to do with me where they went.'

'I don't believe you; you must know where they are.'

I was taken aback and scared, but I was also furious that

someone was standing on my doorstep questioning my integrity. I couldn't get him to go away so in the end I phoned the police and he disappeared. Some time later a second man turned up, but this time he had Gina and her husband with him. They were sitting outside in a car and they looked as though they were in a terrible state.

'We know you know where these children are!' the man yelled. 'You need to tell us.'

Once again I called the police and they were cautioned, but it didn't stop there. Over the next few weeks I started to get anonymous hate mail through the door, and then photos of me leaving my house started to appear on the internet, accusing me of stealing the children.

It was never-ending, and every time I thought it had all died down, so it would rear its ugly head again. The following year, after I'd started on *Corrie*, I found out that as well as writing to all the newspapers, Gina had rung up the show's producers and told them that I was trying to abduct her children. I became distraught and confused; no matter how ridiculous it was, I couldn't bear the idea that people might think I would try to take away someone's kids. I kept thinking, 'Please God let this be over, I can't take it anymore!' I was desperate. Then I started getting more hate mail through my letterbox, and as Christmas approached in 2011 I received cards containing cut-up photographs of the children with grim messages written inside.

'How can you enjoy Christmas when you've taken away our children? You are disgusting.'

It was scary stuff, and completely draining, but at that time no charge against the parents had come to court. That all changed when Gina's new baby, who hadn't previously been taken away from the couple, was given an overdose of morphine and had to be saved by the doctors at St Thomas's. After that they were arrested and charged.

The day that I was due to appear at their trial at Wood Green Crown Court was a very strange one, because in a way I was on trial too. The couple were still persisting in their allegations that I had plotted to steal their children and I had to take to the stand to prove my innocence. What made it even stranger was the fact that I was due to appear as a judge at a TV festival in Monte Carlo that night. I had a suitcase with me and a date to meet Prince Albert of Monaco, yet here I was fighting to save my reputation and clear my name as an alleged child snatcher. What could I do? I was in a child abuse case. I couldn't exactly say, 'Excuse me, M'lord, but do you know what time I might be able to get out of here and flit off to the French Riviera to meet royalty?'

My mum came with me for support, and although I'd appeared in court a few times on TV, the real thing was far more distressing and intimidating. As I took to the witness stand, the judge addressed the jury.

'You may know this woman from seeing her on television, but try to put that from your mind when you listen to her evidence,' he said.

I was being accused of something so ridiculous, but so serious, and I'd never felt so nervous. It didn't matter that the allegations were false; I felt like I was fighting to save my reputation, not to mention my sanity. As the questioning got underway, the couple's defence lawyer let me have it with both barrels, inferring that I might have received some sort of financial compensation for adopting the children and that that had been my motivation.

'People who want to adopt don't do it because they get paid,' I protested. 'They do it because they want children.'

'So you, out of the goodness of your heart, took these children to the cinema and paid for them all?' he went on.

'Yes.'

'Why? Why did you do that, Miss Collins?'

'Because I thought it would be a nice thing to do.'

'A nice thing to do? How ridiculous!'

'There are people who still do things out of the goodness of their heart,' I said, 'but it's a sad indictment of society that you can't anymore, because this is what happens.'

In the end I broke down and cried. It had all been too much

and I just couldn't hold it together any longer. I'd just tried to do something kind and good by taking some kids on a couple of outings, and through my naivety I'd ended up in this mess. I found myself blurting out the most ridiculous things through the sobs.

'I do charity work for Barnardo's! I love children!'

I was desperate to convince the jury that what these people were saying was a lie, and my mum sat upstairs in the gallery, furious that I was being put through such a nightmare. She'd told me all along not to get involved with the family, and now her warnings were coming home to roost.

In the end, the catalogue of terrible abuse that came out during the trial helped me to see that I'd done the right thing by calling Social Services that day. The situation within the family was worse than I had ever imagined, and things had come to a head after they were re-housed and the eldest daughter threw an SOS note out of a window, which was found by a neighbour who handed it over to the police. It read: 'My mum is the worst mum ever because she can't cope with five of us, her broken hand and being pregnant. She always leaves me out so I always starve and I am forced to work. If I don't get enough housework done, I am beaten without mercy with the wooden end of a broom. I have scars all over me to prove it. I can't stay here. I would like a new mum.'

Gina and her husband claimed that the children were possessed by evil spirits. She had hit the eldest girl with a cable, a broom, and a vacuum cleaner. Then, in an attempt to get rid of the evil inside her, her father had tied her hands behind her back and her legs together and dangled her by her feet down the stairwell. The seven-year-old had a stick-shaped bruise on her thigh when she'd been taken into care, and had later drawn pictures of her father beating her and told stories of going without food. The couple were found guilty of cruelty to a person under sixteen, and went to prison for seven years. In his summing up, the judge said: 'You alleged a conspiracy involving a well-known actress, who had done nothing but show your family generosity and kindness, a member of a housing charity, social workers and foster carers.

'Those who had taken the trouble to support you were repeatedly accused of dishonesty, lying, and conspiracy to rob you of your children when the reality was that both of you were lying – in fact they were simply seeking to give your children stability.'

It was well over two years since I'd first met Gina and her children on that Christmas Day, and I was relieved beyond words that it was finally all over. The whole thing left me broken and shell-shocked. The good news was that those poor children had been rescued from an abusive family, and had hopefully gone to a happier and more loving home. I just hoped that they'd all stayed together. However traumatic the ordeal had been for me, it had been much worse for them, and it emphasized to me the importance of always speaking out if you think a child might be in danger. Maybe I'd been a bit naive that time, but I'd certainly do it again if I had to.

CHAPTER 29:

THE LANDLADY

'd discussed with my agents, Cole Kitchenn, the idea of doing some more theatre. I'd recently toured with *Calendar Girls* and did a spate of TV roles, but I was yearning to do something a bit more creative. My agent suggested I meet the director David Thacker, who had a brilliant reputation for his work at the Octagon Theatre, Bolton. He went on to cast me in my first ever Shakespearian role: the nurse in *Romeo and Juliet*, in February 2011. After that I played former magician's assistant Sheila Grundy, wife of the famous steeplejack and mechanical engineer Fred Dibnah, in *The Demolition Man*, also directed by Thacker. I found it incredibly rewarding working with David because I learnt so much from him. He wanted to make Shakespeare more accessible to everyone and he taught me not to be afraid of it. He told me to learn the part so well that I could say it backwards. He also encouraged me to question every line that I said, so I understood its meaning perfectly. Working with him really changed the way I viewed myself as an actress. My next role, however, was to be one of the biggest of my career so far and, as it turned out, quite a controversial casting decision.

My agent had told me that there was a part coming up in *Coronation Street* and that I fitted the mould. I'd worked with the show's producer, Phil Collinson, twice before, and we'd since become friends, and the first interview was with him and the show's executive producer, Kieran Roberts. The meeting went well and

I was asked back to do a read-through to camera in a northern accent, but then I didn't hear anything for ages. Meanwhile, the casting director came to see me in *The Demolition Man*, in which I spoke with a thick northern accent. Eventually I was asked back one more time to do a screen test at the famous Granada Studios. That day I got into a black taxi from Bolton where I was performing and said to the driver, 'Can you please take me to *Coronation Street*?' And the next thing I knew he was trying to put it into his sat-nav.

'No, I mean Granada Studios. The TV show. *Coronation Street*.'

To say I was pretty nervous that day is an understatement, and I'd tortured myself about what to wear. The coveted role was as the Rovers Return landlady: should I go brassy? Smart? What sort of shoes would she wear? All I'd been told was that she wasn't going to be the anything like the Rovers landladies of the past. By the time I got to the studio I was shaking. Not only had they been seeing people for the role all day, leaving me until last, but I was expected to perform in front of Tony Warren – the man who had created the series back in 1960 – plus four or five other very important people. My screen test involved two big scenes, which I'd had to learn. In one of them – with Chris Gascoyne, who plays Peter Barlow, and Jane Danson, who plays Leanne – I delivered the news to Leanne that I was the mother who had abandoned her thirty-odd years ago. It was quite emotional stuff for a screen test, in fact I even cried, but when it was over I had a pretty good feeling about it. I also did screen tests with John Michie, who'd already been cast, and Michelle Keegan. Still, there was a seemingly endlessly long gap after that with no news, but I was told that the decision had gone right to the very top: to ITV's director, Peter Fincham. It was a nerve-wracking few weeks, but in the end I got the news that I'd been dying to hear. The part was mine.

Being in *Coronation Street* was never going to be straightforward for me because of the constant commuting between London and Manchester. I knew that I might not be able to get back every day, but I don't think I realized just how difficult it was going to be. Still, I had no intention of making Manchester my permanent home.

Maia was in the midst of her GCSEs at the time, which is tough on any teenager, but she goes to an exceptionally academic school, and she's extremely motivated as far as her studies go. That's every parent's dream as far as I'm concerned, so although I wanted the job, I decided that the least disruption that she had the better. Moving wasn't an option. It was bad enough that on the night that I got the call telling me that I'd landed the role, she cried tears of unhappiness while I was crying tears of joy. Despite promising her that I'd be home as much as I could and assuring her that Manchester was only two hours away on a train, she was convinced that we would never see each other. We both knew that whatever happened, our lives were going to change completely. I had to do it, though. I needed this job and to earn money to keep us both, and of course it was a role in a landmark show that I'd watched since I was a child. Yes, it was another soap, like *EastEnders*, but to me it was a TV institution, as well as being a great drama.

The funny thing was, I had a meeting with the producers of *Waterloo Road* just after I got the part of Stella. They more or less offered me a part, too, but a part in *Corrie* was just too good to turn down. Besides, I'd worked in Cyprus and Portugal and on a remote Scottish isle, so geography had never been a good enough reason to turn down a great job. I told myself that if they wanted me, I'd do it for three years and I'd make sure I was able to take a few weeks off when Maia was sitting her exams. It wasn't easy for either of us. I've heard people say that children need their parents more when they're younger, but I think teenage girls need their mums when they're going through adolescence. Once I accepted the role I was determined to make good on my promise to get back to London as often as I could.

John Michie played my husband Karl, and the two of us had worked together in the 1980s on a short-lived ITV soap called *Albion Market*. Once I was on board we did some screen tests with a few different actresses until Catherine Tyldesley was cast as our daughter, Eva. Before our first appearance on the cobbles there was a big trailer heralding our characters' arrival, which seemed to be on every five minutes, and I was slightly worried it might be setting us up for a fall. It showed the Price/Munroe clan – Stella, Karl and Eva – stepping out of a car and striding down the street, while windows cracked and glasses exploded all around the horrified regulars in the Rovers Return. Then, the three of us opened the pub doors and stood in the doorway looking menacing. It was all done to a blistering rock guitar solo, and looked more like something off *The Sopranos* than *Corrie*. After such a fanfare, the public were going to be expecting us to really make our mark the minute we plonked our suitcases down and shut the Rovers door behind us. I suppose it was quite flattering, really, because they rarely did such big teaser campaigns when new characters came into the soap, but I thought that the trailer made me look like a real femme fatale who was going to cause mayhem the minute she set her stilettos on the famous cobbles. No pressure, then!

My first scenes were no less nerve-wracking. I was behind the bar in the Rovers, which is tiny in real life, and thrust in front of all the show's famous regulars, including Roy and Hayley and Ken and Deirdre.

'Smashing to meet you, Roy. That's a proper jumper, that!'

'Smashing to meet you, Deirdre. Ooh, lovely top!'

Stella was on a charm offensive right from the word go, but the filming schedule terrified the life out of me. We shot five days a week, but during that week you might be filming for twenty different episodes with four different directors on loads of different scenes. When I looked on the wall at the shooting schedule for my first week I was utterly petrified because it all looked so confusing.

'There's no way I can understand what's going on by looking at that,' I told anyone who'd listen. 'I think I'm going to need some help here.'

In the end I had to have someone with me who showed me exactly what was what and how it all worked. Simon Gregson showed me around the pub and Antony Cotton showed me how to pull pints. It actually felt like I really was going for a bar job. As time went on I realized that although it seemed like a mad system it somehow worked, but for those first few weeks I was a bit like a rabbit caught in the headlights of a great big unstoppable truck. Some days I'd be all ready to head off home thinking that I'd finished for the day.

'Oh no, Michelle, you're due on another lot now,' someone would pipe up.

'Am I? Oh!'

I was still doing *The Demolition Man* in Bolton during my first week of filming on *Corrie*, and I was supposed to be out of there by 5.30 each day, but although it had all been cleared with the show's hierarchy, the news hadn't filtered down to the scheduling team or the crew. On my second day on the job I was down to film a scene in the Rovers at 7.30 at night.

'But I've got to leave at five,' I told one of the assistant directors. 'I'm on stage at half seven; I can't be pulling pints in the Rovers.'

'Oh. Oh, OK,' he said, slightly perplexed by the news.

In the end we had to drop the scenes from the schedule and I felt terrible. I'd only been there five minutes. Would everyone think I was behaving like a diva already?

I just had to push through it. I thought I could be superwoman: working all day on the set of *Corrie*, dashing off to do the play in the evening, and then learning lines late into the night. It was insane. I was petrified of the sheer volume of work I had to do and the enormous amount of lines I had to learn. There was scene after scene and I seemed to be in all of them. In many ways I was counting my lucky stars, but when you're the landlady of the Rovers Return you're virtually ever-present because the pub is the heart of the show. And although it's an incredible role to have bestowed on you, it's also very daunting. They are some pretty big shoes to fill. I don't think I stopped for the first two years. In fact, even when I went into hospital for a small operation, I was back in the next day, rushing off to lie down every five minutes because I was still in agony. I've always had a dedicated work ethic and I was pleased to see that most of the actors on the *Street* were equally committed. It's weird because in my personal life chaos tends to reign and I usually find myself tearing around in a cloud of disorganization, but as far as work goes, I like to be on time and on form. It's something I learned right back at the beginning of my career, because if you weren't up to scratch in those days, you were out.

John Michie was a lot more relaxed about tackling the northern accent than I was. I wanted to do my best and get it right because I thought it was just the sort of thing that people would focus on, and boy was I right. It was six or seven weeks before my first episode went to air, which meant that I'd been working on the show for quite some time, yet still had no idea what the public's reaction was going to be to the Rovers Return's new landlady, Stella Price. I didn't even dare watch my first episode, which aired on 16 June 2011. Apart from the fact that I was nervous, I really don't like watching myself on screen – I never have. The first clue I had that all might not be hunkydory was when I received a text from a concerned friend on the morning after the episode had aired.

'Don't take any notice of them, Michelle. Ignore them.'

What? Ignore who? What was going on? It was like when you get a less than flattering review in the press that you haven't yet seen, and then someone tells you that the reviewer was talking rubbish and it was all wrong.

'What review? What did it say?'

'Oh, nothing, nothing, it doesn't matter.'

'No, you have to tell me now. What did it say?'

This was in the days before I was on Twitter, but plenty of other people were and pretty soon the jungle drums were beating. The lowdown was that my northern accent was absolutely laughable and many people were saying that I shouldn't have been cast at all. I should have known it was on the cards. There'd been some doubtful mutterings and finger-waving in some circles about me being cast, even before I'd appeared on screen. Oh no, no, no – Cindy Beale can't be in *Coronation Street*. That just won't do. Some people wanted me to fail before I'd even started, and talk of my supposedly dodgy accent was just the ammunition they needed. Suddenly, the internet was rife with the story of how terrible I sounded and the press had a field day with it, too.

Phil Collinson phoned me, as did Kieran Roberts.

'Are you all right, Michelle?' Phil sounded concerned.

'Yeah, I'm fine,' I sighed.

But I wasn't. As more episodes went to air, the stories picked up speed and the laughing seemed to get louder. I sat down on my own in a room and watched some of them, just to try and work out what all the fuss was about. I didn't get it. I'd worked hard with a great dialect coach called Mark and was continuing to do so, and as critical of myself as I often am I really didn't think I sounded bad at all. My opinion didn't matter, though; it was the public that counted, and as far as the media went, everyone seemed to be having fun with the story. I couldn't seem to avoid it. I turned on the radio one morning to hear someone chuckling about it on a phone-in.

'Have you heard Michelle Collins' Manchester accent in Corrie? It's a joke, isn't it?'

Then I heard it was trending on Twitter and that people were arguing about it on all the social networking sites. I was the talk of the town for all the wrong reasons.

I had no idea how to deal with it. I'd never really suffered any tough criticism about my performances and this couldn't have been more public. I was deeply upset by the whole thing but I didn't want to show it, so I began to disengage from everything and everyone. I surrounded myself in my own little bubble, especially at work. I found myself walking around looking straight ahead and not making eye contact with anyone. Even when somebody did speak to me, I remained distant. Perhaps it was a strange way to behave, but it was the only way I could get through the day. Most of the other cast members didn't say very much, but looking back that was probably because they didn't want to make it any worse. Lovely Chris Gascoyne called to ask if I was OK, and also Jane Danson, who plays Leanne Tilsley, née Battersby, came over to talk to me one day.

'Oh, don't worry,' she said. 'Everyone hated the Battersbys when we first arrived but they got used to us in the end. It'll be the same with you.'

I nodded and smiled, but at the time I thought she was just saying it to make me feel better. I felt bruised and exposed. The thought that I might be failing at something that I was trying so hard at was eating me up. It started to affect my whole personality. If you had asked anyone else in the *Corrie* cast what I was like in that first few weeks they'd probably have said something like, 'Oh, she's a bit uptight, that one.' I just wanted to put my head down and be as good as I could because that was all that mattered to me. The trouble was that with all the travelling up and down from London, trying to be a mum to Maia, the packed shooting schedule, and every other minute of the day either learning lines or working furiously with my dialect coach, I was pretty much done in. God only knows how much Virgin Trains have made out of me. I'm sure I wasn't a lot of fun to be around, and I didn't have much time for socializing either. Still, the stories and the bitchy comments continued.

'Why couldn't they give it to a northern actress?' was the other thing I heard. 'I'm a local actress, I could have done it.'

Give me a break, I thought. Surely you don't give someone an acting job just because they live two bus stops away? I was worn down and angry by then, and on some days I was ready to throw in the towel. Then I'd sit down and mull it all over and I'd think, no. They're not going to beat me. No way! If anything, it made me work even harder because I was determined not to go under.

A couple of weeks after my first appearance, Phil Collinson approached me saying that he was going to appear on *This Morning* to defend the fact that he'd cast me, and he asked me if I'd go on with him. He was angry after an article in one of the tabloids had suggested that he'd only given me the job because we were friends, accompanied by a picture of the two of us at a Terrence Higgins Trust event. He was also unhappy about the accusations that the show had too many gay characters on it, which all seemed a bit silly to me. Phil felt extremely protective of the programme, and me, and by this time all the talk of me getting into *Corrie* through some secret door was starting to get to him as well. It felt like a witch-hunt, with the world and its mother having their say about my appointment to the show. Phil and I sat on the couch at *This Morning* with Phillip Schofield and Jenni Falconer, and to be honest I found it quite weird having to sit there and defend myself against all these unseen critics. At one point, Jenni suggested that some of her northern friends didn't think my accent was very good and asked would I consider dropping it, like David Tennant had with the southern accent in *Doctor Who*. Phil pointed out to her that David had never changed his accent whilst playing the Doctor, and argued that neither should I. He said that the producers of *Corrie* were very happy with my performance and that Stella Price was there to stay ... and she was staying northern. People just had to get used to the new family and give the characters time to settle. There had also been a story in *The News of the World* the previous weekend about a huge ratings slump, which turned out to be completely wrong. *This Morning* did their own investigating, and Phillip Schofield told us that the ratings had actually gone up since I'd joined and the show had performed notably better than in the same period the previous year, which made me feel a hell of a lot better. I think Phil Collinson was a great producer for *Corrie* and he really cared about the show. He took the accusation of favouritism as a personal slight. To suggest he would give an actor an important role just because they happened to be a mate was quite demeaning.

You can't just sneak in through the back door to a job like that, and the idea that people thought I had was mortifying.

Like most things that blow up all of a sudden, after a few weeks the talk started to die down. More and more people were coming up to me on the streets of Manchester and telling me that I was OK – and so was my accent.

'They should leave you alone; I think you're great,' one lovely woman said to me.

In the old days we would have said that all those news stories were 'tomorrow's chip paper', but they don't wrap chips in newspapers these days, and with the power and constancy of the internet, nothing ever really goes away. It's all still lurking there just waiting to be Googled. Still, I was over the moon that things were settling down. Looking back, I think that the whole accent thing was a lot of fuss about nothing. ITV had blasted such a big fanfare about my arrival that a lot of people were waiting to pounce on the first thing they could. I'm an actress and I'd played a northern character more than once before without any problems. The whole thing was just a testament to how big *Coronation Street* is.

CHAPTER 30:

THE TWEET

If I've ever suffered any discrimination in the entertainment industry, it's more likely because I've sometimes been labelled 'just a soap actress' rather than having anything to do with my age. Now I'm in my fifties I think I'm over that difficult period that many actresses find themselves in when they're in their late thirties and early forties: too old to play the girlfriend but not quite old enough to play the mum. Of course, that's a bit of a generalization, but you catch my drift. It's a bit of a 'no woman's land'. In show business a lot of people tend to fight against their maturity rather than embracing it, and I feel a bit sad when I see women who've had really conspicuous nips and tucks just to stay in the game. I've got nothing against a bit of touching up; I think that's everyone's prerogative. I just don't see the point of doing something that everyone can blatantly see. They still look the same age, but with the added hindrance of visible surgery, and the chances of you getting the role of a down-to-earth mother, wife or businesswoman are lessened.

This kind of thought or opinion needs to be well thought out and expressed with extreme caution, though, as I found out to my cost when I made an off-the-cuff comment on Twitter in the spring of 2013. When you work as an actor on *Corrie* you're actively encouraged to 'tweet' but I'm not the best with social networking and it took me a while to get the hang of what it was all about. Maia is always pulling me up about how bad my spelling is when I post something on Twitter, but half of that is because I'm doing it on my phone, usually while I'm in the middle of concentrating on something else, and I never check anything back. It's even worse when I don't have my glasses on. One night I was having a conversation with a friend and we were talking about how people looked and about various actors and actresses who'd been 'enhanced' or had some kind of surgery. It was the type of casual chat that any couple of girls might have over a cup of tea or a glass of wine. Meanwhile, while we were gossiping away, *EastEnders* was on in the background, and I tweeted a random thought without thinking. Trust me, this is never a good idea.

'Why do actresses have ridiculous lip jobs done?' I mused, after seeing evidence of it on that evening's episode of the soap. 'Watched Easties tonight. Was shocked! Big lips just seem to take over the screen. Too distracting!' The comment was clearly prompted by what I'd seen on *EastEnders*, but it was really a general comment about actresses who choose to have really obvious lip enhancement, and it wasn't directed at anyone in particular. Some people assumed that I was having a go at one particular actress in the show, and then began firing nasty messages at me, accusing me of bullying. I was quite taken aback. I'd never mentioned anyone by name, and the last thing I'd consider myself to be is a bully. I was a bit of a novice at Twitter, however, and I just hadn't realized the power of it, especially being in the public eye. If I'd sat there and considered the connotations of what I was saying before I posted the comment, I wouldn't have done it. It was too late, though. Suddenly it seemed like everyone had something to say.

When I got up the next morning my tweet had gone viral. A friend of mine sent me a text:

'What's going on? Have you seen *Digital Spy*?'

'Oh God! What have I done now?' I replied.

When I went online, the story about my tweeting and the subsequent backlash was everywhere. I was hurt and embarrassed. I consider myself a feminist and I would never condone a personal attack on a woman because of her looks. I do, however, have genuine concerns about the amount of very young actresses I've seen using cosmetic surgery to enhance their physical appearance, some before they're even in their twenties. And that was my point. Badly put, perhaps, but certainly not vicious or bullying. Still, the torrent of hate tweets and abuse continued to the point where I became very upset. I felt like I had to defend myself, but I just didn't know what to say. Anything I said would just be adding fuel to the fire. At first I began answering the messages.

'I don't tolerate bullying. If I've offended I'm sorry. But people shouldn't make assumptions.'

'No bitching please! An observation that's all. Strange now who's doing the bullying! No more tweeting for me!'

Engaging with people who are up for a fight on the internet gets you nowhere, however, and in the end I just gave up. I felt terrible. People were going to think I was a bitch whatever I said, and I hated the thought of it. Maia also has a Twitter account, and she was furious with what had been going on. Eventually, she got hold of my phone and sent a series of tweets from my account.

'Hi. It's Maia here, Michelle's daughter. I would just personally like to ask anyone who is thinking of writing malicious, hurtful or any other synonyms of "nasty" comments in the form of tweets to my mum they can direct them to me. Feel free to send anything thing you want, the ruder the more entertaining. Michelle is a single mother who works from 7am to 7pm everyday and the tweets are actually making her quite upset and she really doesn't need them at the moment.'

I was very proud of my daughter for jumping to my defence, but I think she was more impressed that her comments made it into an article in *The Guardian* about celebrities having protective family members.

Still, I kept my Twitter head well and truly down for a while after that. As I said in one of my tweets that night, 'Inane comments only from now on.' No more commenting on topical issues for me.

Despite the fact that Twitter was originally seen as a great way for people in the public eye to connect with their fans and followers,

I sometimes think it's backfired somewhat. A lot of celebrities are afraid to express an honest opinion because there's always a group of people ready and willing to bombard you with unpleasant messages just because they don't agree ... or just because they can. I certainly won't make that mistake again.

CHAPTER 31:

UP IN FLAMES . . . AGAIN

've said this before, but being accepted as a *Corrie* regular was how I imagined being accepted into the royal family might feel. It took me a long time to win people over and to get my confidence up. As time went on, I slowly started to creep out of my shell and enjoy it a bit more. I was getting used to the fact that *Coronation Street* was a huge beast of a show; a juggernaut that stopped for no one. No actor or character was as important as the show itself, and once you were off and running you just had to put your head down and hold on tight. The cast is huge: I think there were over sixty people when I started. The good news was that being in the Rovers meant that I came into contact with them quite quickly, because everybody ends up in there at some point during the week. That made getting to know people a lot easier. John Michie and I got on well, and along with Catherine we soon became a credible family within the tapestry of the show. As I got to know my fellow actors better I began to see what a tight unit they were – very much like a family. For the first few weeks I'd felt like I was out there on my own, but then I'd see some of the cast rally around with genuine concern when one of their fellow actors was having problems or going through a romantic break-up. It was a supportive environment, and a case of 'what happens within the walls of *Corrie* stays within the walls of *Corrie*'. They were all quite open, and, on the whole, very down-to-earth. I began to make friends: Barbara Knox, who plays Rita, Jane Danson and Chris

Gascoyne, Alison King, David Neilson, and also Malcolm Hebden (Norris) who's hilarious. People like Anne Kirkbride and Helen Worth – Deirdre and Gail – were great and had so much experience to share. Helen and I have become great friends and I loved the scenes we had together as warring mothers-in-law Stella and Gail. I have such a lot of respect for those long-serving cast members and I miss them all. I also had the support of Sue Johnston, who played my mum, Gloria. I'd met Sue on a few occasions before we worked together and had always admired her. She's a fantastic actress and she became like a real mum to me, as well as being a friend and confidante. My scenes with her were some of the most enjoyable, especially all the bits we did behind the bar in the pub, with my daughters, Leanne and Eva. The four of us were a force to be reckoned with and there was a real matriarchal feel about it, which is something that British soaps have always done so well.

Being the landlady of Britain's most famous boozer was a double-edged sword, however, because so much of the action takes place there that I always seemed to be first in on a Monday morning and last out on a Friday. Even when I didn't have any lines myself, I often found myself in the backdrop of someone else's scene because it was taking place in the pub. Actors on the show say that the most nerve-wracking part of the job is doing scenes in the Rovers. They've actually got a name for it, 'the Rovers fear'. It's because you're usually part of a big ensemble when you shoot a scene in the pub. You might only have one line in amongst everyone else's, but if you forget it or muck it up, the entire assembled cast have to start again. I was in the pub the whole time and my feet were constantly killing me because I was forever in high heels. I'm not complaining, though. Tough as it was, I was handed the most fantastic storylines during those first two years and I loved doing them. Stella was run over by a car, bankrupted by her husband, cheated on, and then almost burned to death. I even won an award at the *Inside Soap* awards. Not for 'best actress' or 'sexiest female', mind you. No, my award was for the 'unluckiest character in soap'.

Filming the huge fire at the Rovers Return was one of those

moments, like the tram crash in the live fiftieth anniversary episode, that felt very special, and I was very excited that Stella was going to be at the centre of the story. The reason it looked so realistic was because it *was* realistic, and as exciting as it was, I certainly wouldn't have wanted to do it every day. In fact, after all my encounters with fire over the years, I could hardly believe that I'd been stuck in a burning building for one of my biggest storylines. When the director, Tony Prescott, pulled me aside and asked me if I was 'OK with fire', I replied, 'How long have you got?'

All the interior stuff was shot in a big warehouse on duplicate sets, and the special effects team were fantastic. We also had a great stunt man called Richard, who we knew and trusted. Despite that, there were some serious flames happening in extremely close proximity to me and burning timber falling all around us. In fact, there were a couple of moments when I thought my pyjama top was singeing. I felt like I was filming an adventure movie like *The Towering Inferno*, which I'd watched as a child, but although I felt a little anxious at times, I knew we were being well looked after. After all, there was a gorgeous team of firemen on hand, just in case.

Stella was trapped in the fire for ages, but was ultimately rescued and carried down a ladder by Paul the fireman, played by Tony Hirst. This in itself brought a new and unnerving problem to light: I wasn't wearing any knickers. Well, Stella had just got out of the bath and was in her pyjamas ready for bed, so she wouldn't be wearing knickers, would she? So as Tony threw me over his shoulder and carried me down the ladder in one of the most dramatic scenes of my career, all I could think was 'Christ, I hope my pyjama bottoms don't ride down or everyone will see my bum. And what if I break wind on the way down in front of the whole cast?' Things were no better for them. They all had to stand out in the freezing cold with no lines for four nights in a row, gasping every so often. Tony, meanwhile, was a brilliant fireman and took the whole thing very seriously. The poor man ended up doing his back in and was in agony for quite some time after.

We spent four or five days and nights filming outside on the street and then another week filming in the warehouse. Every night of the shoot, Jackie, one of the wonderful team of make-up ladies, sprayed my hair and face with fake soot. After three nights I couldn't even get the stuff out when I washed it, and standing there in my rotten old pyjamas with filthy hair and a black face, I looked like someone who'd been homeless for a very long time. For the next couple of days I quite enjoyed going into work with no make-up, looking like someone from Fagin's gang. It was much easier to get ready for work. The thing I loved about the fire episodes was that everyone really went for it, and I had some challenging and dramatic scenes. It was at times like that when I realized that I was working on a really good quality drama and not what some people consider 'just a soap'. We had a great director and a script that we could all get our teeth into. The scene where Stella was knocked over by a drunken Carla Connor wasn't quite as much fun, although it still looked pretty good. It was dark and rainy and the director wanted a shot of Stella lying motionless in a puddle at four o'clock in the morning. The stuntwoman, who'd been more than happy to dive in front of a car and roll over a bonnet, didn't look too impressed.

'I'm not lying in that,' she said. 'I'm not lying in a puddle. I don't get paid to lie in puddles.'

'Oh all right, I'll lie in the puddle then,' I said.

Another terrific scene was when I had to have a cat-fight with Shobna Gulati, who played Sunita Alahan. Stella discovered that Sunita was having an affair with her husband, Karl, and consequently dragged Sunita out of her house by the hair. It was proper classic *Corrie*: a good old scrap between two women on the cobbles. Poor Shobna got slapped so many times doing that scene; I did feel sorry for her. We had some talented directors on the show, and I sometimes think soap directors are underrated, because although the amount of good work they have to produce each week is incredible, it's often taken for granted. I've heard plenty of people say things like, 'Oh, I love *Coronation Street*, it's my guilty pleasure!' And I always think, why does the pleasure have to be a guilty one? It's a brilliantly written, well-executed drama. Watching celebrities run around in the jungle or sit in a house for two weeks is what I'd call a guilty pleasure. I do like hearing feedback from the public, though. People often talk to me when I'm travelling up to Manchester on the train, and I'm always happy to say hello. Not too long ago, a lawyer came up and told me how much she enjoyed watching the show.

'I love Stella,' she said. 'She's such a woman of today.'

It's comments like that that make all the hard work worthwhile.

One of my favourite moments working on *Corrie* was when the Labour leader, Ed Miliband, came to visit the set after the 2012 Labour Party conference in Manchester. As well as me, there were quite a few ardent Labour supporters in the cast, including John Michie, Ian Puleston-Davies who plays Owen and David Neilson, who plays Roy Cropper. On the last night of the conference there was a big dinner, which John compered, and *Coronation Street* had a table at the event. The next thing I heard was that Paul Cottingham had called the show and said Ed wanted to come for a visit. Everyone was really excited when he walked into the Rovers Return, and Ed genuinely seemed thrilled to be there. First he came and chatted to Michelle Keegan, Catherine Tyldesley and me, who were all behind the Rovers bar. I'd met him a couple of times before, but I was quite chuffed when he gave me a friendly kiss on the cheek. Having just delivered an hour-long word-perfect speech at the conference, there he was asking us how we managed to remember our lines five days a week. After posing for a few photos with us he headed out onto the cobbles to meet Eileen Derbyshire and Malcolm Hebden – Emily and Norris – while they were doing a bit of filming. Hats off to Granada TV for making it happen. They're quite strict on that kind of press call and they wouldn't do it for everyone. I was very proud that day. Not only was I the landlady but also I was standing in the Rovers having my picture taken with the leader of the Labour Party, and perhaps the next Prime Minister. The best part about it was that he looked like he was really enjoying himself, because it doesn't matter who you are, everyone gets excited when they walk into the Rovers for the first time. Derek Jacobi is a huge *Corrie* fan, and he and his partner visited the set once; in fact, they loved it so much that they asked if they could sit in the pub and be extras in the upcoming scene. This was something they probably lived to regret because it turned out to be one of those days when nobody could remember their bloody lines, and the scene just went on forever. I think they thought they'd just be sitting there for about five or ten minutes but it was well over an hour before they were able to get out of there.

'I'm really sorry,' I said to Derek on the umpteenth take. 'It's not always like this.'

'Oh it's OK, darling, don't worry, it's fine,' Derek boomed. 'We're loving it!'

In April 2013, when Phil Collinson's time as producer was up, the new man at the helm, Stuart Blackburn, called me in to see him.

'I love what you're doing as Stella,' he said, 'and it's great how it's all working with you and the girls in the Rovers.'

I'd only recently signed my contract to do another year on the cobbles, but there was a shock waiting for me just around the next corner. A few weeks later I was told that Stella Price was being moved out of the Rovers and that former cast member Liz McDonald was on her way back. It was a bit of a blow, to be honest. In fact, I'm not sure I would have signed up for another year if I'd known it was about to happen. I'd joined the cast as the Rovers Return landlady and that's what Stella was to me. I wasn't sure how it was going to work if she wasn't running the pub, and I can't pretend I wasn't disappointed. Friends in the cast told me it was nothing personal and that when a new producer comes in they always like to shake things up and change them around. I knew they were right and that it was probably nothing personal, but once my screen mum, Sue Johnston, announced she was leaving, I considered the possibility that it might be time for me to go as well. In some ways, not being in the Rovers was a bit of a relief because my workload went down dramatically and I was able to spend so much more time in London with Maia, but when you've always been at the pivotal heart of the show and then suddenly you're not doing very much, it's tough. Once Stella's murdering husband Karl had been locked up and the Price family had moved out of the pub, my fears were realized. Stella just seemed to be hovering around without purpose, popping in here and there with the odd wise word for her daughters. That wasn't enough for me, especially when it meant being away from my family. I need to be challenged as an actor, and like I'd always said when I was working on *EastEnders*, if ever I ended up just pouring cups of tea then I wouldn't want to do it anymore.

Things change, and when you're working on a long-running soap you have to accept that they survive on new blood coming in with fresh ideas and energy. So despite the fact that I was a bit miffed when it all happened, there's no room for long-term self-pity when things don't go the way you hoped they might. You can't take anything personally. I'm walking away from *Corrie* with no malice or bad feeling, just happy memories of working on a great show. I'd always said I wanted to do the show for three years, and in the end that's how long my run will have lasted. Now I feel like I want a job with a beginning, a middle, and an end, and I need space to be a full-time mum again. I was just happy they didn't decide to kill me off. It's funny, though: after all that time working on the show, I'd never plucked up the courage to hang out in the green room. I'm not really sure why but just the thought of it made me nervous. In that room I was a little kid in the classroom that wanted to hide quietly at the back instead of answering all the teacher's questions up at the front. It's not like there was anyone I disliked intensely or wanted to avoid, but it harked back to those first few weeks on the show, which were rough for me. Perhaps it was a bit like being traumatized by a bad childhood experience that never leaves you. I don't know. While I was working on the show I spent all my down time in the dressing room, and that was fine.

One of the strangest days working on *Coronation Street* was on the last day of filming at the old Granada studios before the production moved to Media City on the banks of the Manchester Ship Canal. Fittingly, Stella was in the final scene in the 'old' Rovers along with the resident landlady, Liz McDonald, and a few other cast members. The show's set in its various incantations has been at the old site for over fifty years, with so many iconic characters passing through. Yes, the studios were a bit shabby around the edges, but they had so much character. You could almost feel the ghosts of the old *Corrie* characters wafting around the place. Everyone from the actors to the crew to the make-up people felt very strange indeed in those final hours on the old set.

I only worked at the new studio for about a month before I left, and I did find it a little bit weird. It won't affect the show, I'm sure. As far as *Coronation Street* goes, nothing or no one is bigger than the show itself, not even the building it's in. I'm proud to have been a part of it, and I'd like to think I created a character that the audience will remember because I loved playing her. It hasn't always gone exactly the way I would have wanted, but that's the nature of being on a show like *Coronation Street*. You have to take the rough with the smooth, because the experience can bring such great rewards. I mean, it can't be bad, can it? Even Sir Ian McKellen has been in it!

CHAPTER 32:

THIS IS ME NOW

During 2013, Mum's health wasn't all that good. She fell over in the street getting out of a car while she was visiting her sister in south-east London, and she had to be taken to hospital. I was on holiday in France at the time and I had to come back as quickly as I could, but luckily Vicki was on hand to rush straight up to the hospital as soon as she heard. Lewisham Hospital was great, and by the time she left all the nurses were in love with her, calling her their baby. I put a post up on my Facebook page to let people know that Mum was poorly and the amount of people who commented or messaged me to send their good wishes was incredible. She was overwhelmed when I read them all out to her, but most of my friends adore my mum so I wasn't surprised.

Once she was out of the woods I decided that she might need an extra bit of love and affection. Dogs have always been a big part of my life, and I've had quite a few over the years. There was Dudley, who ran away to the Arsenal stadium, Jemima Angel, who was sadly killed by a car, and Jingle, a beautiful white Samoyed who I adored. These days I have Humphrey, a beautiful little pug/Shih Tzu cross who loves being carried around in a basket. As dogs had brought so much happiness to me, I decided to get Mum one from a rescue charity called All Dogs Matter in Highgate. It's a wonderful charity that the actor Peter Egan introduced me to. He's truly passionate about animals and devotes most of his time to animal causes, even travelling to Afghanistan to help rescue dogs there. Pets can be such a calming influence in the crazy lives we lead these days, and Mum adores her new dog. He's a toy Yorkie called Nano and he's completely changed her life. Still, worrying about my mum like that has made me evaluate what's important in life, and where I'm going. I'm fifty-one now and I feel like I've spent the last thirty years running around being as busy as I can and worrying about what was going to happen next. It's because I've always been so scared of failing and I've never wanted to let the grass grow under my feet. I've always imagined that if I sat still for too long, I might be missing something. In recent years I haven't travelled as much as I used to, and I haven't seen as much of my friends as I'd like. I think I've earned a bit of downtime now: a bit of time for myself, and to be with Maia before she flies the nest and goes off to university.

These days I love the fact that I'm not so famous that I can't walk down the street, get on the tube, or go to the local pub and have a drink with whoever is sitting next to me. I think that to be a believable actress I have to lead a normal life, because most of the time I'm portraying ordinary everyday women. You need to keep your feet on the ground as much as possible, and my family and the same friends that I've kept for many years are the people that help me to do that. Simon Frost is like the brother that I never had, as well as being a friend and confidant to Mum. Once an actor, he now works as a mentor and life coach for all sorts of people. He's more of a lifesaver for me, helping me with all the ins and outs of my day-to-day life for the past ten years, particularly while I was working flat-out on *Coronation Street*. He pays the bills, does my banking, organizes my diary, and sorts out anything else I need help with. If there's anyone in life that I can trust implicitly, it's him. He's one of the many good friends that I'm extremely lucky to have in my life and I love him dearly. In the entertainment industry you tend to meet a group of people on a particular job, and then you spend a huge amount of time with them for the duration of that play, film or television series. You get to know them very quickly in a very short space of time and it can be quite intense – 'Oh darling, of *course* we'll stay in touch!'

Over the years I suppose I've made many friends on the projects I've worked on, but these days I tend to do that less. Now I have a family and a group of people that I've had around me for years, I guess I don't need to go around collecting lots of new friends. I hardly have time to see the ones I've got, let alone cultivating a heap of new relationships everywhere I go. That's something I intend to rectify now that I'm going to be back in London full-time.

That being said, I made friends working on *Coronation Street*, and once it had moved to its new home in Media City, I finally started sitting in the green room and it felt great. Was it because I was leaving, or had I learned to accept my part in the show's history? After all, someone in the cast did once tell me that it takes three years to fit in there. Still, it's great to leave the *Street* feeling positive and happy, and who knows what's in store for Stella Price now she's heading off to New York to start a new life. Perhaps she'll come back one day, a bit more wicked and wild – at least she can never die in childbirth off screen like poor misunderstood Cindy did. As an actress I've loved so many of the parts I've played over the years, but very few actors have done the double and crossed over from Walford to Weatherfield with such wonderful, iconic roles. That's something I'm especially proud of.

I'm hoping that Maia will be just as lucky as I have been as far as friends go, because to me it's one of the most important things in life. Nowadays some people, particularly teenagers, seem to see life through a screen on a social networking site, whether on a phone or a computer, rather than going out and mixing with real people, and that concerns me. I spoke to a teacher recently who told me that the seventeen-year-olds she taught were the worst she's ever seen for being glued to their phones the entire time. On top of that, I read a survey that said that nearly half of all women would rather give up sex for a month than go without their smartphone. My family and friends have been there for me through thick and thin, and some very tough times, and no Facebook message or tweet can compete with that.

These days I'm less likely to be found falling out of illegal drinking bars in Soho, and more likely to be walking Humphrey on the beach in Norfolk with my friend Rebecca, chilling out with Caroline and my godson Jake in Monaco, having dinner in Rome with my old party pal Bunmi, who lives there with her two kids (who I'm also godmother to) or simply sipping coffee with Maia in our local Italian café. Mind you, I've still got my memberships to Shoreditch House and the Groucho Club. I'm far more rooted now than I've ever been, despite the fact that for the last few years I've had three homes: my house in London, my dressing room at *Corrie*, and my rented house in Manchester, which I shared with my two housemates, Jay and Scott. Jay works in the costume department on *Corrie*, and Scott – a good friend for fifteen years – is a make-up artist. We called our house in Manchester the *Big Brother* house and I miss it. My friends all laugh at me, because whenever I turn up anywhere I'm dragging a suitcase behind me, invariably heading to one of these three places. It's funny really, when I'm away from London it's not so much the house I miss; it's the people and the animals. I'd be quite happy living out of a suitcase as long as I have my family and friends around me. I enjoy people and I need to have people around.

When I was younger I had my fingers burned talking about relationships in the press. I singed them quite badly doing that article about my relationship with Fabrizio, and have again a few times since. You've only got to pick up a copy of *Hello* or *OK!* to see a celebrity couple grinning at the camera and telling us all how happy and how much in love they are – I've done it myself. Then the next thing you know, the romance is over, there are stories of infidelity or a big bust-up and everyone feels like a bit of an idiot. That's why I don't really like talking about my relationships nowadays. Apart from not wanting to jinx anything by waxing lyrical about it, I've also got a teenage daughter to protect. Now she's old enough to understand, I don't particularly want stories about my love life all over the newspapers. The thought of Maia reading them makes me uncomfortable. It's funny; someone said to me just the other day, 'I never hear any gossip or bad things about you, Michelle.'

I was a bit put out at first. Did that mean I'd become uninteresting or dull after all these years?

'I've had my bad girl moments in the past, and some I'm not that proud of,' I said.

'And I might be older and wiser now, but I'll never be boring.'

I do have a man in my life, though, Michael, who at thirty is twenty-one years my junior. Everybody knows about the age gap now and my friends and family just accept it. I did get lots of 'Mrs Robinson' comments when we started out, but I don't let it bother me too much. Words like 'cougar' and 'predatory' make me laugh when they're applied to a woman who's dating a younger man. Why is it so much more accepted for an older man to date a much younger woman? It's all 'yeah, go on, get in there mate!' I suppose that's just one of life's little injustices which I'll have to ignore. Michael and I were introduced by my niece, Charlotte, and we've been together for about eighteen months. He has been a great support during my time working on *Coronation Street*, which has at times been fairly stressful with all the to-ing and fro-ing from Manchester. On Valentine's Day 2014, we headed off to New York to stay with my friend Debbie and see Ian McKellen's new play, and had a wonderful time. Michael is handsome, smart, and a very important part of my life.

Fabrizio now lives in Australia, where his ex-wife and twins live, but in October 2013 he went over to Italy to visit his father and invited Maia and me to come over and spend some time with him. My strong-willed daughter wasn't all that keen at first, being a typical teenager, but once we were there she absolutely loved meeting her extended family. I think it's so important for her to know her roots and who and where she came from, and with Fabrizio living so far away it's not always been easy to keep that connection. One of Fabrizio's twin sons came over with his dad, and with Maia being an only child it was wonderful to see her getting along with her half-brother, who she hadn't seen for a few years. She also got to see her grandfather for the first time in years along with her auntie Iris – Fabrizio's sister – and her cousin Marco. After a short visit to her grandfather's house, we went to a beautiful hotel in Torno, which is on Lake Como. The hotel was stunning, built into rocks with the most beautiful views of the lakes. It was a fantastic family reunion and I feel like it opened so much up for her. It felt like the beginning of a new chapter rather than the end of an old one.

I suppose that's why Christmas 2013 was so special. On the big day, Maia, Michael and I spent the day with Paul Young and his wife, my dear friend Stacey, at their family home. I first met Paul outside Caledonian Road tube station when I was in Mari Wilson's band and he was in a band called the Q-Tips – we've been friends ever since, although these days it's Stacey I see more of and she is one of my closest friends. Maia and their three children get on like a house on fire, and Paul is a fantastic chef, whipping us up the most wonderful Christmas lunch two years running now. Then, after spending some time with my Mum and Sid plus my aunt Jenny and a few other friends, I headed off to a beautiful house in Bagnone, Tuscany for New Year with fourteen of my closest friends. Bunmi and Sharon both came with their daughters, Maia's auntie Iris and cousin Marco were there, Dr Mark and his husband Andrew ... and of course Maia and Michael were there amongst all my nearest and dearest. We went for long walks, cooked, watched movies – *Dreamgirls* and *All About Eve* – and lounged around in pyjamas and onesies with our feet up. It was Italian bliss. On New Year's Eve, we had dinner at a lovely restaurant, then went back to the house and danced around the kitchen to our iPods until four in the morning. I highly recommend it. Having all the kids there with us was what made it so perfect, because spending time with Maia is the thing that means the most to me now. Gone are the days when I was a carefree young actress going out to wild parties on New Year's Eve: things have changed. I haven't felt this happy and settled for a long time, and rather than being terrified of the unknown as I have in the past, I'm still ambitious and looking forward to new challenges with optimism and excitement. This is me now. Although I'd like to think that there was still a little flicker of that wide-eyed north London girl in there ... somewhere.

INDEX

247